MOSTLY HAPPY

MOSTLY HAPPY

A Stay-at-Home Mom's Journey through Divorce

E L I F   E K I N

iUniverse, Inc.
Bloomington

MOSTLY HAPPY
A Stay-at-Home Mom's Journey through Divorce

iUniverse books may be ordered through booksellers or by contacting:

iUniverse
1663 Liberty Drive
Bloomington, IN 47403
www.iuniverse.com
1-800-Authors (1-800-288-4677)

ISBN: 978-1-4697-8316-1 (sc)
ISBN: 978-1-4697-8743-5 (hc)
ISBN: 978-1-4697-8317-8 (ebk)

Printed in the United States of America

iUniverse rev. date: 03/21/2012

I must be myself. I cannot break myself any longer for you, or you. If you can love me for what I am, we shall be the happier. If you cannot, I will still seek to deserve that you should. I will not hide my tastes or aversions. I will so trust that that is deep is hold, that I will do strongly before the sun and moon whatever only rejoices me, and the heart appoints. If you are noble, I will love you; if you are not, I will not hurt you and myself by hypocritical attentions. If you are true, but not in the same truth with me, cleave to your companions; I will seek my own. I do this not selfishly, but humbly and truly. It is alike your interest, and mine, and all men's however long we have dwelt in lies, to live in truth. Does this sound harsh today? You will soon love what is dictated by your nature as well as mine, and, if we follow the truth, it will bring us out safe at last.

—Ralph Waldo Emerson, *Self Reliance*

CONTENTS

ONE

OUT OF AIR

*You realize you are drowning in your own life:
the life you watered, nurtured, and tended must be
abandoned for you to grow.*

MAY 13, 2010

It has been a week since I got the telephone number. It is funny how a little Post-It note can scare you. I folded it up and stuck it in my wallet. If I call that number, life as I know it will change. It is the number for a divorce lawyer.

It is inevitable that I will call, but actually starting the process is frightening. Calling that number feels akin to removing the safety from a grenade. As much as I plan and talk to people about the future, no one knows how much damage this emotional grenade will cause.

I recently joined a crafty-mama-type forum, and most of the other moms are stay-at-home moms as well. I thought I would ask their opinions or ask whether anyone had done it. It is quite intimidating for a stay-at-home mom to entertain the idea of divorce. I haven't found anyone who has done it. It makes me feel a bit isolated. Will I have to work full-time, or will I be able to work part-time for a bit? Will I be able to stay in our home, or will I have to move? There are so many questions. My daughter has been home with me; how will this transition affect her?

For many years, friends and family have seen how beaten down I've been by this marriage and have told me to just divorce him and move back to Rhode Island. My answer for years was always the same: I am mostly happy. Not many people can say that they are 80 percent happy. Mina and I have a happy life and lots of friends. Things get stressful on the weekends, mostly Saturdays. But for now, until Mina goes to school, this works for us because we hardly interact with or see Hakan.

"Mostly happy" turned quickly last fall into "completely unhappy" when Hakan decided that he needed to move back home—*now,* he announced. The constant declarations of moving and the constant badgering question "Are you going to come?" created such anxiety in my soul. I felt like a trapped rabbit. How was I going to get out of this situation? One day when Hakan got into Mina's face and asked whether she was coming with him, that little sprite pulled herself up to her full height, looked him straight in the eye, and said, "*This* is my home!" as she slammed her books on the floor in front of him. "*You* can go and take Sofia [the cat] with you since you love her!"

Can a mom be proud and appalled at the same time? I was so proud that she stood up to him but appalled that a little girl of barely three years old had to be in this situation.

I needed help. I called a therapist.

MAY 15, 2010

It has been a difficult few days. We had a small argument on Monday, and that seems to be the catalyst for Mina's change in sleep pattern. She will not let me leave the room after she falls asleep. She seems to need extra comfort this week. In small steps, I seem to be preparing for the possibility, whenever it may happen. Mom and I are working hard to get Mina to nap on her own. If she has to go to preschool or day care, she will need to know how to do this. I am filled with so much resentment that I have to think about all of this. I didn't sign up for this when I said "I do."

I still haven't called the number, but Mom did pick me up a book that I should read before meeting with a lawyer. It is called *125 Questions to Ask Your Lawyer*. Am I finding excuses not to call? While Mom is here, I should get through it, mark my questions, and hide the book. I have my therapy session on Tuesday, and I really hope it isn't canceled. I really need to go over some things.

Emre, my brother-in-law, contacted me last week, concerned for his brother. "Elif," he said, "I have been Skyping with Hakan, and he seems really depressed, more so than usual. When I spoke to my parents about this, they were evasive, and I feel like they are hiding something from me. I love my brother, and I don't know how to help him. Please tell me what is going on."

I took some time before I wrote back. This was the first time that someone was honestly looking at the situation and realistically trying to find a solution.

"As much as I know that you want to help Hakan," I said, "please think carefully on what you are asking me to tell you. Once you know all the ins and outs of our problems, there is no *un*-knowing it. There is no delete button to return to blind ignorance. I will tell you everything, but take some time to think about it."

I was so surprised that it took him only two days to say, "Yes, I want to know!"

Well, he didn't know what he was getting into. I told him everything: problems with his mom, problems with Hakan, everything. We have had a very good correspondence. He has been understanding in many ways and not defensive or pushy.

"I can see how all this has been difficult for you, Elif. When I go home, I am going to sit down with my mom and discuss this with her. It is unacceptable for her to send you such rude letters, and I will make her promise to never send you such letters again. Please kiss Mina for me!"

I love that my brother-in-law is willing to stand up for me in front of his mom, but why couldn't my husband do that years ago?

It has been really frustrating that everyone seems to have selective memory and cling to revisionist history. Hakan and I got into a small confrontation the other night regarding Mina's sleep. He thinks that I prevented him and Mina from bonding because I didn't pump enough milk for bottles. Regardless of whether or not I pumped, there are other ways to cuddle and bond with your child. Bottle-feeding or not bottle-feeding should not prohibit other ways of bonding. I was up all that night, going back in time, trying to remember the whole pumping issue. I remember that it used to take me *hours* to fill just a tiny amount. Being home alone, it was difficult to find the time to pump that long while taking care of an infant in conjunction with other domestic duties. Also, because not much would pump out, my milk ducts would clog, and I would get engorged. It was painful. The combination of many factors led to the decision not to pump anymore. Besides, around ten months, I started giving Mina Odwalla's soy Vanilla Al'Mondo protein milk. Hakan could have fed her that or her smashed baby food anytime, but he chose not to. He was always too tired from work to hold her or take care of her when he got home. I usually had her in the bouncer in the kitchen or on my back. Of course, he remembers none of this.

I am concerned about finances after the divorce as well as custody. I can fill in all the online calculators I want about child support and alimony, but they still don't tell me what I will need to do to supplement. Am I crazy risking all of this? I run the risk of him leaving the country to go back home, and I will have nothing. I have a hip condition called avascular necrosis. Basically, at some point, I will need a hip replacement. What happens if he skips the country, and I have no health insurance? I have finally come to peace with the possibility of selling the house and moving back with my parents for a while. It would be sad, but the house is not worth the aggravation if I can't afford it. If I am going to uproot Mina, I will bring her home to my parents' house, where she can feel secure. I did check online, and I can relocate back home. My friends and family were afraid that I would be stuck here because of his job and that I wouldn't be able to leave. All I need to do is give sixty days' notice and provide a plane ticket for him to come and visit Mina. I think I can handle that.

I have been working really hard at sewing and posting my goods on Etsy. I really would like to have a steady income by fall. I want to be able to stay at home with Mina as much as possible so it is not such a drastic change for her. I am still holding to my word to last through the year. It gives everyone a chance to change, and it also gives me a chance to get my sewing business going. If things go the way I think they are going to go, then this time next year, we will be in the middle of hell.

I had a dream the other night. Mina and I made our trip to Turkey in April. I thought it would be nice to surprise my mother-in-law on her birthday. I saw Mina with a big bouquet of flowers ringing the door to their apartment. We stayed there for a week or so to get over the jet lag, and then Mina and I took a trip to Egypt—just Mama and Mina. People would probably wonder why I am thinking of my mother-in-law at a time like this, but I want his family to know that I am just divorcing *him*, not his family. They are all more than welcome in my home at any time for as long as they want. We have worked out our problems on our own, and we enjoy each other. It meant a lot to me last year that my mother-in-law stood up for me in front of him. She stood by my side and told him to back off.

It is pretty obvious that Hakan is having a hard time with Mom being here so long. Mina speaks English all the time, and she doesn't want to talk to his family on the Ojo video phone or through Skype. She screams. It is the same way when his family is here; then she doesn't want to talk to my family. Mina just focuses on the person visiting, and that is it. She understands that they are only here for a limited amount of time, and she is going to soak up every last drop. I don't say a word when his family is here, but he is pretty uncomfortable when the shoe is on the other foot.

I take refuge in my garden and use the soil to ground me. It is cathartic for me to get all my hurt, anger, and frustration out on the weeds. Sometimes I place a mental picture on the head of a dandelion and pull the weed killer trigger. Phew! I feel better now!

Time to get ready for the weekend. Always a challenge when he is home for an extended period of time.

MAY 16, 2010

I feel like I am living a lie. Hakan and his family seem to think that I am committed to making this marriage work, but I am not so sure that is the best thing for me and Mina. He was in Amsterdam for a conference last month for over a week. It was amazing how *light* I felt. Mina and I were so *free* to do what we wanted to do. We could dance at 6:30 in the morning and bake cookies at 8:00! We were just happy. There was no anticipation of an argument or any stress. I realized that I can handle taking care of Mina on my own pretty easily. I know that after a divorce, things are not that easy when you factor in emotions and finances. But there would be some peace of mind.

One day when I was reading the forum on the Sewing Mamas website, I saw that someone had posted a question about how to cut the food bill. One person responded with a very succinct answer: "I divorced my 300 lb husband." I chuckled because that seemed to be the answer to my happiness dilemma: "Divorce my depressed husband."

As I move forward with my therapy and toward some sort of resolution, I am sometimes filled with so much guilt. For me to be happy, many others will probably be very unhappy. I am not one to cause pain to another person, and this has been very difficult for me to come to grips with. My therapist says that should not really play a part in my decision because they can choose to deal with their feelings constructively or not. It is not my fault if they choose to wallow in self-pity. I do not really think that it will be such a shock to everyone since I have been begging for help from people for three years. No one wanted to believe that the problems run so deep.

I do not want a divorce to keep him from Mina. I just want him out of my every day. I want to feel alive again. I want to feel free again. I want to feel that it is okay to be me again. It hasn't been okay for me to be me for a very long time. It has always been conformity to his family's philosophies in order to keep tensions in check and everything stable. I am tired of juggling everyone's egos. I need to sit down and just *be*.

This house has been a comfort to me. It is so calming and grounding for me to take my cup of tea outside, sit on the steps, close my eyes, and just *feel*: feel the breeze, feel the warm sun, hear the birds and squirrels, and just know that the universe has so much more to offer me. When I go back into the house, I just don't feel that my life is my own or that

Mina's life has choices because they are all tied up with his obsession with moving home to Turkey. It feels like a corset tightening around me, and I can't breathe. I don't want Mina to live this anymore. She is so much better at standing up for herself than I am, and it makes me so sad that she is learning such hard lessons at such an early age. I want so much more for her.

It is just not right when a child does not feel safe with her own father. I almost cried when she said that she was afraid Baba would leave her in the darkness and not be able to protect her from the monsters and alligators that hid behind the trees.

Hakan is trying to become father of the year *now*, but she really doesn't trust him. He wants to be involved with putting her to sleep, but where was he when I really needed him three years ago? Now, after only two sessions, his therapist wants to meet me. He hasn't begun to work out any issues, and he has probably been spinning the truth, selectively, and I will have to set it straight. My soul is too tired to do this right now. He is probably just talking about how I won't move back home with him and not even delving into the history of how I came to that decision. Why do I have to justify? Why do I have to go in there and defend myself—again?

I spent more than two weeks with his aunt and uncle when they came to visit, and they kept trying to change my mind—give it time, they said. I have had ten years to think, talk, and argue about our problems. How much more time do I need? Now Mina is approaching school, and I need to put her first.

It is amazing how much stronger a woman can become when she has a child. In order to protect your child, you can do some amazing things. Should I have left a long time ago? Maybe, but I was so beaten down that I didn't know who I was. I lived for him and his dream, and I lost myself along the way. My family and friends have sat me down over the past few years and tried to shake me out of it with mini-interventions. I finally feel like I have turned the corner and I feel . . . taller, somehow. I really feel that I have a lot of support in whatever I choose to do. There is a clan of family and friends and online supporters behind me, and I feel them surround and protect me.

Do I want to move back with my parents? I don't know. I see pictures in my head of my life, and sometimes I see Mina and me living near the ocean. It feels okay.

May 17, 2010

I feel ignored. Hakan has so much bottled up inside, anger and resentment toward me, that he can't have a normal basic conversation. We drive in silence to his office. I can feel that he is controlling himself because what he *wants* to talk about, he knows he can't. I try to make light conversation about weather, work, stupid stuff, but I get nothing. I just do not understand how his family thinks that this should be okay. If he wants to make things work, why doesn't he want to talk to me? Why is he so rude to my mom? He is not making a good impression on her this visit.

The past week has been difficult with regard to putting Mina to sleep. He has been out in the living room alone with Mom, yet he makes no attempt to acknowledge her either. He sticks his earphones in his ears and watches his Turkish comedies on his laptop. Then we planned a nice grilled fish dinner out on the deck last night. Mom got some nice hummus and crackers and opened some beers. Instead of participating in a nice evening, having some drinks, and enjoying the weather as a family, he was on his iPhone checking his e-mail and Facebook until the fish was ready. How is this okay? If I ever did anything like that while his family was around, I would hear about how rude I was for days. He really gets upset at the closeness between Mina and my mom.

It is funny how normal things can make you suspicious. He was pretty much absent the whole day yesterday. He chose to go to work around 1:30 p.m. for a couple of hours and took his laptop. Here I am thinking, *Is he really going to work, or is he going to the office to talk in private to his family on Skype?* I do not like thinking things like that. That is not who I am! I actually logged into Skype to see and then immediately closed it. I am not going to stoop to the sneaky level. I am better than that.

May 20, 2010

Mom left yesterday, and it is almost too quiet here. I had my therapy appointment on the 19th, and it went well. She says that I need to think about having a proactive approach to these arguments instead of just waiting for them to happen. I have been feeling like an argument is looming and waiting for the infamous shoe to drop. It creates a lot of anxiety when he comes home because I do not know what exactly will bring it out. I feel that being proactive is akin to pulling off a Band-Aid. It stings for only a second, and then it is over. At the moment, I am staring at that Band-Aid wondering what sort of wound I would open up if I just ripped it off.

I spent Mina's nap reading the divorce prep book that Mom got me, and it is very helpful. I do feel more prepared and feel that I can regain control over my life. I think I am going to break down the tasks weekly so it is not too overwhelming for me. First thing, I need to write a marriage biography, objectively, not emotionally, something like an outline. That shouldn't be too difficult to do. Then I need to team up with a friend, collect documents, and make copies. Third, I will need to touch base with my family's accountant and see if he can get together copies of all of our tax returns. It is so helpful and empowering to have a to-do list. It is really daunting to think of beginning the process, but this book has made the process less scary. I have been reading questions and stories of previous clients. Their stories have helped me think of other ways to compromise. I am not looking for vengeance or to sock him with unreasonable constraints. I just don't want to be married anymore. I just do not feel that I can grow into who I am supposed to be with him.

All day, after reading the book, I was thinking about two different endings: staying in Utah and this house versus moving to Rhode Island and starting fresh. Both have advantages and disadvantages.

Utah: Staying in Utah, in this house, would be the most stable for Mina at this point, and Hakan would have easy access to his daughter. This house and this neighborhood are everything that I have ever dreamed of. It is a family-oriented street, walking distance to a little neighborhood shopping, and walking distance to one of the best public schools, and I have been able to farm out our yard to grow our own food. I have created a life here in Utah. However, if I ever wanted to move back to Rhode Island, this would be the time—before Mina gets to school and begins making strong friendships.

Rhode Island: I have been thinking more and more about cutting my losses and moving back to Rhode Island, taking just what we love and need and moving back home. He can have the house, the furniture, and things and do what he wants with them. Mina and I could start fresh. We could buy new stuff that is more "us" and take our time finding our way. I wouldn't have him around all the time, but on the flip side, he may get custody for the whole summer and all her vacations. A story I read in the divorce book made me think of this. It referred to a stay-at-home mom who moved back to family, but the father got the children for two months in the summer, every vacation, and every other Christmas. Utah may have different laws. I read that the relocating parent only needed to give sixty days' notice and provide a plane ticket for the other parent's visit. I am concerned about the idea of two months of custody. If Mina does not feel safe with him in her own house, how will she feel if she has to spend an extended period of time living with him? I need to think of her mental state. The other consideration is international travel. With his family living abroad, how do we work out all that travel? I am willing to take her abroad for a month's stay with his family, and I am also willing to stay all together in his family's house. I just need to be in control of the passport! I want to make sure that my child comes home to *me* at the end of the visit. Too many kids of international parents get abducted and hidden. I need to take great care that this does not happen.

Maybe one solution is to stay in Utah until Mina is ready for kindergarten and move to Rhode Island then. He has mentioned that he does not want to stay in Utah forever. Maybe the time would help him find a job on the East Coast, and the distance would not be as great.

My brain is tired from thinking of all these possibilities. My therapist thinks that it is great that I can logically think out all these things, but the one variable is emotion. We equated my logic with bowling pins and emotions with the bowling ball. I can line up all these scenarios, but that big bowling ball of emotions can come barreling down the alley and knock everything to kingdom come! I have the unfair advantage of emotionally preparing for this divorce. He does not. I have a feeling he will become very nasty about the whole thing and not want to compromise one bit. His family is scrambling right now because they can see where I am headed, and they are trying to fix the relationship. His brother, Emre, is going back home this weekend to talk with his parents about our issues and hear his side of our problems. I wrote to Emre this morning, "Thank you for really taking the time to listen to me, and I really appreciate your open-mindedness. I am aware that your family will start to spin the truth and blame me for most of it. I cannot control what others believe or do not believe. I can only tell my truth, what I have lived and experienced. Each person has their own truth to tell. I think we should all respect these truths and try to come to some sort of understanding and acceptance. My relationship with your mom has improved because we both recognized our issues and dealt with them. Because we both were trying to make amends, we were able to grow."

Hakan just doesn't remember anything, so he doesn't think he has done anything wrong or hurtful. With that in mind, I don't feel heard or validated. I feel crazy. If so many people hadn't witnessed or heard firsthand, I might just think that my memory was cuckoo!

He must be talking with his brother because he brought up the fact that I don't think he wants to take or did not (in the past) take an interest in Mina. He just does not remember. Can I fault him for that? He said that he really has no idea where I am coming up with this stuff.

I am feeling a bit suffocated. Hakan is really trying to push Turkish and the Turkish culture on Mina and me. "Elif, it would be so nice to come home, be able to speak all together in Turkish and hear Mina listening to the Turkish kids' music CD my mom sent instead of always Angelina Ballerina, Angelina Ballerina, Angelina Ballerina!" Turning to Mina, he said, "Mina, why don't you want to listen to the Turkish music that Babanne [Turkish for "grandmother"] sent you? It would make her feel so sad that you don't like it!"

After taking a calming breath, I said, "I am not the type of person to push something on someone and make them 'like' it. You cannot do that to a child because they will soon resist everything associated with what you're pushing—Turkish, the culture, and ultimately, the family. She is already starting to do that with the video phone. Besides, her ballet CD is just ballet classical music. It has Angelina explaining the ballet in English—that's it. Most parents would love it if their child wanted to listen to classical music all day every day!"

If there is one thing that really bugs the crap out of me, it is the rolling of his eyes when I stand up to him.

"If I don't push these Turkish things, then I don't get what I want," he replied defensively.

Has he not learned that pushing me tends to have the opposite effect? I felt my chest tighten and the wall around me grow taller. I told myself and others that I would try to keep to the one-year decision deadline, but I think it needs to happen sooner, much sooner. I cannot live like this, and I will not have Mina pushed and badgered all the time to like this or that.

I have written to Gaia to help me photocopy documents next week and will have my marriage biography done by then. I will have my father contact our accountant to make copies of all our tax returns. Maybe he could send them to someone here in Utah instead of my house.

I need to not be so attached to this house. I need to be willing to let go of paradise here for something better. I remember when I worked at the museum with the African collection. I loved, loved, *loved* my job. I got let go, and I was devastated. I didn't understand why. Sometimes, when something bad happens, you don't understand why immediately. It takes time for the future to present itself. I understand now that I couldn't grow anymore at the museum, and I needed to move on. There were other life experiences to have and more important people to meet. Now I am grateful for the adversity and the knowledge. I have to think that this house—loving this house and neighborhood—is the same thing. Sometimes you need to let something beautiful go in order to be able to receive something more nourishing.

It is interesting that once my mind makes a mental break with the old, something new comes along. Mina and I decided to go to the slide park this morning, and we met another family. Come to find out, the mom is a painter and has a house that she is going to try to convert into a moms' community center. She and I will get together, and I may be able to teach kids' classes there or work with this mom on creating fun parties for kids. Bam! There it is, around the corner—opportunity.

MAY 21, 2010

I was up most of the night last night thinking. I feel that I need to start this process sooner rather than later, and I feel this sense of urgency. It scares the shit out of me. How did I allow myself to get into this sort of situation? How did I lose such control over my life and, now, the life of my child? I was up all night thinking of different scenarios, custody and living arrangements, when and how to tell him, and then it was time to get up.

Let's see if I can get it all down on paper and look at it:

If I told him while we were in Turkey, we would have someone to look after Mina while we had the conversation. We would each have family around us to give us comfort. There really is never a good time to be the bearer of bad news. If I stayed in Utah, he could come and read to Mina each night before bed and see her on the weekends. By staying close, I would only have to go to Turkey maybe every other year. I really would like Mina to experience things other than Turkey. I remember as a child resenting the fact that we could never go anywhere else. I do not want her to feel that way. I want to have the option of taking Mina and spending a month at the beach in Rhode Island or taking her to different country. His parents could come whenever they wanted and stay no more than a month. If they came, then he would have to add some more alimony during that time to cover food expenses. I have been looking into telecommuting jobs so that I can supplement the alimony and child support. I would like to be able to stay at home as much as possible with Mina until she goes to school. Maybe this is naive of me to think about, but why can't it be a possibility? I can teach my child well, and why can't that money be invested in my teaching Mina rather than sent to a preschool? It is the same money going out of pocket. When Mina hits kindergarten, then the child support can be reduced.

If I was to move to Rhode Island, then the trip to Turkey would probably have to be every year to correspond with his trip. That would be time toward visitations. Oh, it is all so confusing.

I spoke with Mom yesterday and asked her to start writing depositions and letters regarding what she personally witnessed and experienced—same for my friends—and to get them notarized. I also asked her to speak with the accountant, and she will have all the taxes waiting at their house ready for me. Since so much is available online, I don't think there is much financial stuff that I need to copy—mortgage, retirement, his AMEX card statements. It is just so overwhelming that it is hard to begin. I need to stay focused and positive. That has always been my asset and has brought a lot of good into my life. I need to remember that.

Physically, this whole situation makes me feel cold. I am not a person who gets cold easily, but I noticed that I shiver and get really chilly when I talk about it with someone, and it's happening now, while I am writing about it. It is seventy degrees in this house, and I am sitting at the laptop, shivering. I have goose bumps up and down my arms, and my feet are ice. I do not really know how to interpret this. What is my body trying to tell me?

MAY 26, 2010

Most days, I feel pretty good and pretty strong. Today, I feel like I am being hit with bricks from every direction, and all I want to do is sit down and cry. My chest feels so heavy and it is only 3: 00 p.m. I am really off-balance these days. Hakan has been trying really hard to build a relationship with Mina, and it is screwing with my schedule. I feel really obsessive-compulsive when I say that, but predictability helps me deal with the day's events. He has been leaving later and coming home earlier to see Mina. She is not eating breakfast well or dinner. After our dinner, it is off to the slide park to bond more, and that screws with the nighttime schedule. I just feel *off*.

I was really irritated that he began a new computer game just as I was cooking her eggs. Of course, she would not want to eat when there was the opportunity to play on the computer. That led to a tantrum later and very aggressive behavior that I had to curtail. Finally, he was on his way to work around 10:00 a.m., and I could settle into our day: coffee, bookstore, lunch, nap.

I find going to the bookstore to be a little oasis away from the turmoil, and today that rug got pulled out from under my feet. I didn't see it coming. With Abby and Megan not working at the bookstore that day, Carol, another bookseller, took the opportunity to inform me that they have been uncomfortable with our visits to the bookstore for months. Nothing personal, she said, but that bookstore was grounding for me. Mina and I could just escape into new and different books for an hour and then go home. I feel terrible for making them uncomfortable, and now we will be able to go only on story-time days.

A new routine is needed in so many ways, but can things come one at a time, please?

We made it home and did lunch, but the universe still conspired against me. Lawnmowers, weed whackers, trucks, dogs barking—it all disrupted the quiet time, and Mina could not nap. Now that she wasn't getting erasers for rewards anymore, she didn't want to go to sleep alone. She screamed, she yelled, she cried, she hit, she threw things. She *did not nap*. It took all my self-control not to break down into tears too. Finally, she calmed down and wanted to try going to bed again after an hour of not getting her way. At long last, I have some quiet. I want to be able to have that tantrum and throw things and break down. I just feel that if I let go, I won't be able to stop. I am so tired of all this, and I haven't even begun the battle yet. How am I ever going to make it through? It is times like these when I doubt how strong I am. I want my mom. I need my mom, and I wish to God she didn't live so far away.

I remember when I was a kid and didn't want to go to school. I would sit down on the floor next to my father and put my head on his knee. I would beg him to let me stay home and not make me go back to school. I thought that my parents were so magical; they could make all my wishes come true and all my problems disappear. Obviously, I read a lot of fairy tales. Somehow, if we lived closer, maybe I wouldn't hurt so much and would feel loved more because there would be someone close by who could put their arms around me and hold me while I cried. Sometimes, I just want to cry and cry and release it all until I am dried up like a raisin.

How am I going to do this? When do I get to the point where I say, "I do not wish to be married to you anymore"?

We had a long talk last Friday night: beginning at Noodles, continuing on to Whole Foods, at the ice cream parlor, in the car, and at home for another hour. It began with Mina following me to get a to-go container.

Hakan commented, "Mina needs to go to preschool so that she can get used to people other than you, her mom. She is just glued to you and won't stay with anyone alone if you are not there, and this is not normal. Most other kids who go to day care or preschool are able to separate from their moms. You and Mina are like one person, inseparable from each other! This is not a normal relationship."

"Hakan, I don't accept that as a valid reason. She is quite social and does very well staying with people she trusts. I can leave her with Daisy and Sofia anytime, and she doesn't even blink an eye when I leave. When I come to pick her up, she tells me to leave and come back later because she is having too much fun with them. She is just not comfortable with you."

He shifted uncomfortably in his chair, and we moved on to shopping, yet the conversation continued as he tried to justify and clarify his position.

"What do you mean, she is not comfortable with me? I have been there for her and have taken care of her."

Really? I thought. "Um . . . when? Hakan, since she was six months old, she would scream if you tried to pick her up and scramble away to either my lap or your brother's lap if we were in Turkey. Even now, when we were at Red Butte Garden with your parents, you tried to pick her up, and she screamed. She became a big wiggly noodle and ran to your mom, after which you sighed heavily, frustrated, and stormed away. When have you taken her anywhere? In four years, you have taken her in the car, alone, out of the house, *once*!

"You sank deep into your depression and left me alone to take care of her and you. You have more of a relationship with the cat than with me! How is it that you and the cat get 'alone time' after you get out of the shower, but when I try and hug you, you just refuse me and walk away? I have loved you for years, and you don't want to see me. You couldn't change me, so you ignored me."

He just stood there, blinking and gaping at me at the deli counter at Whole Foods, speechless. Yet, I was not done. The dam had broken, and I couldn't seem to stop the gush of repressed feelings and thoughts.

"You keep telling me that your heart froze to me in 2001 when you were so depressed and I didn't say then, 'Okay, Hakan, screw Utah. You are sad; let's move back to Turkey.' Maybe I didn't say it then, but I said it in 2003. You had just been promoted that year, and I saved and saved all the extra money. During that year, I saved $25,000. It was not enough. 'Why isn't it $50,000?' you asked me. One night, we were on our way home from eating sushi. It was spring and rainy. You were so despondent, so sad. When we stopped at the light at 1300 South and 1300 East, I said to you, 'Okay, Hakan, let's go back. We saved up some money. Look at tickets to move back.' Do you remember what you said? 'It's not time yet.'

"I may not have said what you wanted to hear in the time frame you wanted, but I *did* say it."

As I was talking, I could really see him taking it all in, and there was some awareness behind his eyes; they softened. Because I could see the person I had fallen in love with opening up again, I relaxed into revealing how much he had intentionally/unintentionally wounded me with words over the years.

"I loved you, and I begged and begged you to love me. Two years ago, I sat on the couch while you sat across the room, and in tears, I asked you if you still loved me. You didn't comfort me. You didn't look at me. You looked straight ahead and said, 'I don't have to love you; I just have to love my child.' According to you, I am uninteresting and boring; you say you have nothing to talk about with me; nothing that I do interests you and is worth hearing about. Can you see how hurtful those words can be?"

This was just the catalyst to talk about past, present, and future. By the time we got home, I was tired—physically, emotionally, and spiritually.

We were home and sitting together, as a family, on the floor, with Mina by the coffee table, and he looked up at me with tears in his eyes. He got it.

"I finally understand how much I have hurt you, and I never intended to hurt you. I was so consumed by how I thought my life was going to unfold and how the reality of my life wasn't anything close to my dreams."

"Yeah, but you did, and some hurts are really hard to come back from. Years of begging to be loved and begging for help with no answer changes a person's heart and soul." I think he finally got the severity of the situation.

Mina is finally sleeping, and I feel a lot better for writing all of this out. Today is done; it was not fun. Tomorrow is another day; one by one, I throw those bricks away.

May 29, 2010

It is Saturday, and it is sunny. Mina and Hakan are both resting, and I am watching the trees blow in the breeze. Over the past few days, he and I have talked a lot about preschools, and I took the proactive approach and sent him links. He liked the Fine Arts Preschool and called to see about openings in the fall. They do have openings, and it might be a nice environment for Mina: an arts-based curriculum and only three days a week for a few hours.

Of course, the weekend comes, and moodiness abounds. He asked Mina if she would be interested in going to a dance school, and she immediately asked if it was the school that Nana had found for her. I wasn't going to tell him that Mom had found the link because he would be upset and feel bad. Well, I was right. He got all snippy and defensive, and that made for a *lovely* evening. Sigh. Really, why does it matter who found the link if this is a good fit for Mina? It is all this competition—Turkish versus English, Turkey versus America, him versus me—that drives me crazy. He wants her to love him and his family so much more than mine. He wants equality in everything, but he has been absent from this family for over three years! Yes, he has been great at bonding with Mina in the last week. She has responded well to his attention and greets him at the door with a hug and kiss. Why can't he be happy with the steps that he has taken and see the results? His expectations are so high, and sometimes I am at a loss as to how to respond.

We came back home from dinner at Daisy's house, and Mina picked flowers for me. He said, "What? None for Baba?" Mina told him that she picked him some a few days ago. I knew I should say something, but I couldn't find the words.

He is resentful of her love for Angelina Ballerina and not a Turkish character. He resents her love of ballet music. Who cares what she loves right now? It will change. Why push her to love something else if she doesn't want to? I struggle with this stuff internally because I do not know how to voice it. I am trying very hard to use words and verbiage that are not inflammatory. At the moment, she and I just ignore him when he says stuff like that, but that is not a solution.

We were on the Ojo video phone for a few hours this morning, and his father seemed really tired and thoughtful. Emre leaves to go back to Portugal tomorrow. I am sure he has had multiple conversations with them about our e-mails back and forth, and they are probably feeling a bit alone with both sons gone. It makes a parent become introspective and retrospective, I am sure. I took a step back and watched the morning progress, and at one point, there was Skype on the laptop and the Ojo both watching Mina as she performed her ballet. How is this a normal existence for a child? On the flip side, having his parents on the Ojo all day on Saturday helps pass the time with Hakan. It is escapism on my part.

I know, in my gut, that I will be okay once the divorce process has started. I am really having a hard time wrapping my head around commencing the process. Everyone seems to be concerned with my being able to get Mina out of Turkey this summer if we go. I don't feel that fear anymore and asked my mom to stop stirring up the paranoia again. I dealt with that in therapy, and it is done. I don't want to revisit the fears. I do not know why I feel this great need to go this year. I do not feel that I need to prove anything to anyone or even to myself. I want to be there to represent myself and allow questions to be asked and answered or asked and not answered. In some ways, it provides me with some closure. It is hard to explain. I have worked so hard to forge a relationship with this family over the past ten years. I respect the feelings that they will be going through. I want them to know that I will listen to what they have to say. I may or may not respond, but at least I will let them be heard. Sometimes that is all people need: the opportunity to be heard. My therapist says that she sees me going before a firing squad and wonders why I feel the need to make such a sacrifice. Maybe I am being naive. I think this is a do-or-die summer for the continuance of a close relationship with his family. If they love me and respect me the way they say they do, then we can have open and honest conversations. If they close their minds and their hearts to me, then our relationships can progress no further, and I will know how to proceed. Am I crazy? Maybe. Maybe I have too much faith . . . is that such a bad thing?

MAY 31, 2010

It is really interesting how the mind works, how it remembers, how it shapes the memories with color, sound, and smell, and also how it can pull abstract visuals from films and apply them. I have a tendency to slip into an alert but meditative state when doing something repetitive. My mind slips sideways. It happens most often when I am putting Mina to sleep. One day, a phrase entered my mind: "My mind slips sideways when it is in the 'in-between.'" Slowly, I have come to understand and embrace the little film clips that come when my mind is silent. I think it is my subconscious trying to show me what I can do, what I am capable of, what sort of possible future there is, and so on. Sometimes, I feel like I am peeping in on myself in an alternate reality. Everything seems so real and palpable, and the love I feel from the others in the sequence just fills my entire being so much that I hate it when that "life-clip" ends. I know that it is out there, but taking that first step toward it is frightening. I was driving home yesterday from Costco. As I was driving, a clip from an Indiana Jones movie (I think it was *The Last Crusade*) popped into my head. It was the scene where Indiana Jones is at the top of a cavern and needs to get across to the other side. Being a man of science, he knows he cannot leap across. Taking a deep breath, he hears his father's voice in his head: "You must believe, boy." And with that, he puts his hand over his heart, closes his eyes, and steps out onto a camouflaged walkway to the other side. He had to *believe*, have faith in himself, and take the first step.

It is so fitting to my mental state right now. Why can't I believe? I have all these positive things going for me, so why can I *not* believe that everything will be all right and step out of my shell? If I had just me to think about, it would be easy—well, easier. There is Mina to consider. The dichotomy is that I didn't feel strong enough to leave before her. Now that I am stronger, I am having difficulty leaving because of her.

Every time I feel like I am getting ahead, I look down the road, and there is still so much that I have to do. I feel really good about getting my Etsy store up and running and getting it up on Facebook, but now there is promoting and getting on Flickr and blogging about it and team building—and I am exhausted thinking about it. Then I go and make more jam.

If I want to rip away this last icky Band-Aid and tell Hakan that I want a divorce, then it has to be in the next six weeks. It gives me heart palpitations just thinking about it. How can I promote and get my sales going, get my finances in order, do a budget, see a lawyer, continue with my therapist, go with him to his therapist, and get ready for a trip to Turkey? Just when I feel like I want to dive in, we are headed to Disney World in three days. In reality, four days in Disney is not going to make or break my schedule because I wouldn't be able to do much with him home on the weekend anyway. It is just another thing to get ready for.

He asked me the other day if he should RSVP to his student's wedding this September in Zion National Park. Of course, I told him yes, but all I could think was "where will *we* be in these proceedings then?" It all goes back to living two lives, and it is draining. I guess living one life honestly is probably not as difficult as living two lives like this.

Maybe when we get back, I should write a checklist, a daily to-do list, and have reminders sent to myself via e-mail—plan each day instead of aimlessly falling into it. Note to self: Monday, June 7, plan life . . . after a cup of coffee!

June 1, 2010

I feel like I am molting like a butterfly and that I am being forced to release many of the securities that I have grown accustomed to. Yet another loss today. I feel like I have lost my best friend, Samantha. This is someone who has gone through this, survived, and persevered, and now, I feel she is abandoning me when I need her most. She sent me this message:

> I need you to know that I value you your friendship. The
> past two years have been particularly hard for me. I have done
> my best to give you my ear, keep the majority of my opinions

to myself, and be a good friend. I know that at times I have failed at all three.

What you are facing is a hard road, one I have traveled from a very different place. I am confident you will persevere. I need you to know your judgment that my road was "easier" is hurtful. There is nothing easy about being left by someone you love, when you don't know why. I had no family support or financial means, but I have survived. You will survive and thrive as well.

Over the past two years I have been so busy being *so* angry and trying to prove to everyone that I would survive that I don't think I've ever let myself really be sad about all of this pain. I am sad now. In fact I am grieving in a deep and very painful way. I have insulated myself to handle the pain.

My life is still changing, and I am hopeful things will look up soon.

I felt that you deserved to know that this is where I am.

Samantha

I guess everyone travels this road alone, but somehow I always thought that she would be by my side. I apologized if I had hurt her in any way and told her to take whatever space she needed. I am not going to call again. I have enough on my plate at this point. Damn it, damn it, damn it! I want to burst out in expletives and throw and break things, but at the moment my little ballerina is twirling to her music in front of me. I have to bite my lip and count to ten to stop the tears from coming so she won't see me.

I also received a nasty note from my mother-in-law, and I think I have been naive to think that they would ever see my side of things. They will coddle and protect Hakan no matter how he has behaved.

Have I been blind to all of these things? How can I believe and hope when people whom I had grown to trust are not who I thought they were? I guess it is back to the divorce book I go for help and comfort. Maybe if I hug the book, it will hug me back and reassure me that I will be okay.

On a good and productive note, I was able to get my Facebook page up and running and sent off to people. I also got the blog started and a domain name. It's a step, and I really need to focus on the steps forward and not the steps backward.

June 8, 2010

There is something very comforting about a zucchini bread baking in the oven. It just fills the house with yummy goodness, and you can almost imagine your mom stepping out of the kitchen. My life seems like a surreal roller coaster ride these days. I start out feeling pretty good, and then I slide.

I am feeling pressure from so directions to wrap up this problem as quickly as possible, and it makes me feel like hyperventilating. Am I really being naive thinking that I can hold off this decision until after the trip to Turkey? I am trying to do right by everyone, and I care about these people. I want them to be able to have one last vacation all together. My parents are concerned that there may be too much stress for me over there and that I may not be able to leave Turkey with Mina at all. I am trying with all my might not to get sucked into their paranoia. I have had this discussion with my therapist, and I feel okay with going there. I don't like how easily I begin to doubt myself. I also don't like how I actually give consideration to spam e-mails about instant money. It makes me feel desperate.

I understand my parents' concern for Mina and my well-being, but quickening the pace of this makes me ill. It is making me feel unmotivated to do much of anything actually. I think I am still tired from Disney. Disney was a nice escape from normality. There is nothing there that can remind me of anything at home. I checked my troubles at the gate and picked them up (safe and sound, unfortunately) upon departure. I was hoping (why am I still hoping?) that I would feel differently about this situation after a family vacation that was not in Turkey. I am thirty-seven, and this was my first vacation. Hakan just had all these expectations of how he *thought* we should react at a certain moment or respond to the trip to Disney. We can never measure up to his imagined expectations, and I am left telling him to leave Mina be. We got in around 8:30 at night. Mina was so tired and so, so hungry. He sat next to her on the couch, and turning to her, he said, "Mina, I am sad that you didn't say, 'Thank you, Baba, for taking me to Disney.'"

"Hakan! She is *three* years old, for God's sake! Her giddy anticipation over seeing Pooh and friends should have been your thank-you. Please do not make her feel bad so that *you* can feel better. It is not okay."

It just reaffirmed the fact that I need to get her out of this environment, but how?

I have made multiple therapy appointments for the coming weeks, starting tomorrow, with my new therapist. I should trust that the universe has a plan when change happens. I was able to make an appointment with the therapist I had originally wanted last year. I guess some things *do* work out in their own time. I took a chance that Daisy would be around to watch Mina and made an appointment for tomorrow. I can always count on Daisy, and there she was, as always. It is such a relief to me that I have at least three friends that I can count on to be there and help me through this. I have to catch myself when I want to call Samantha and ask a question. I feel like I am mourning so many things that if I actually let myself let go, I will become an empty shell—yes, yes, I know, ready to fill up with good stuff, but that shell doesn't fill up right away.

While I was ordering Mina's soy milk from Amazon, I ordered myself a new Reiki book and the companion teaching guide. Supposedly, it has tips on how to set up a practice and gather clients. My idea is to transform Hakan's office into a healing room. There is so much more I want to do with my life, and I just don't feel like I can be the person I am supposed to be while married to him. Is that selfish of me to want such things? Does wanting more from life make me selfish? I want Mina to have a strong example of a life well lived, not a life of sacrifice and suffering. I feel like an anomaly: a stay-at-home mom venturing forth with grandiose ideas of "what could be."

JUNE 16, 2010

It has been a while since I have been able to sit and write. After returning from Disney, I had to jump right into preparations for the Friday workshop at the bookstore. Lately, I have been feeling like Alice looking through the looking glass. As time goes by, I can see myself on the other side of all of this. It is almost as if I could reach my hand through the mirror and just about touch the new me. As much as he has tried, his nastiness still comes out and strengthens my belief that I cannot stay with him. Last week was such a busy, crazy week. I relished a cold beer after a tough day. The workshop itself was pretty intense, and as we drove to a restaurant for dinner, I thought in advance about ordering a glass of wine. I knew I would get some comment because Hakan usually doesn't like to order drinks because they are too expensive, but screw it, I decided; I wanted a glass of wine and was prepared to deal with whatever comment he could fling. Well, fling he did. I ordered the wine, and he said, "Well, you are slowly becoming an alcoholic, between the three beers this week and a glass of wine now." When he feels slighted or ignored by me or Mina, he just lashes out with nastiness. It is not right, and Mina should not have to feel bad because she wants to do something else other than read or play with him.

Samantha called and apologized for what she said. She said that she had talked about a lot of what had happened with her therapist and said that it isn't my fault that things happened to her the way they did. We had a good, honest conversation about how we both feel, and I flat-out told her that I felt abandoned by her at a time when I really needed her.

Gaia is back, and I am hoping to photocopy some financials with her. I think that I probably need to copy only Hakan's Amex card statements and the 401(k) stuff. Everything else, I can print off of the Internet. Maybe I can have my tax returns sent to her house. If I can get a binder of information together by mid-July, I will feel I have accomplished something.

I have really been hustling to get onto various Etsy teams so I can get more exposure. I feel really good about the last few and feel that I am in a good place. I reactivated my Flickr account and will start working on that—so much busy work to get started! Once it is all done, it will be easier to maintain. I just want some regular business by fall. So many others can make a living by doing this; why not me?

June 25, 2010

I am coming up on the self-imposed deadline for calling the lawyer. Sigh. I wish I could just *jump* over the ickies and land on the other side. I told myself that I wanted to call the lawyer in July and make an appointment before I go to Turkey. I want to have some knowledge before going over because I have a feeling my aunt and uncle will be asking about the process. Mostly, I am feeling pretty strong these days. I have met and like my new therapist. She understands the bicultural issues, and that is such a relief. I have been trying to take a proactive approach to dealing with life these days because I am going to have to do it at sometime—might as well start now!

I started with my vacation to see my aunt and uncle this summer in Turkey. Usually, visiting my family is fit in around Hakan's family's plans. This year is different: not only is it later in the summer, but we also have Emre, Hakan's brother, to consider. He flies in from Portugal on August 6. I was getting tired of everyone planning our trip without even consulting me as to what I would like to see happen. So I took the bull by the horns, wrote to his brother and my mother-in-law, and proposed a plan of action. It was well received, and I feel pretty victorious. Finally, after ten years, I stood up for myself and for what I wanted.

Each day, I sit and consider my options and my future. I question every little thing and try to play out every little scenario. Then breakfast or dinner comes, and Hakan and I eat in silence, with nothing to really say to each other. Usually on the weekends, we have the Ojo on the table with us, and we talk to his family. That is actually a relief to me sometimes because it breaks the silence. We have grown so far apart that I don't know how to bring it all back together. As much as he is trying, the lack of laughter or conversation fortifies my resolve that I do not want to live my life like this. Is it so much to ask to have a *real* conversation at mealtimes? Am I being selfish by thinking that? It just seems too empty and hollow to live like this.

When I tried to explain that to Hakan's aunt while she was here, she just shrugged it off and said that *all* marriages are like that. "Elif, my angel girl, love comes and goes, and you just have to deal with it. Marriages have their ups and downs, love and loveless times. This is the way of life. It is up to us, women, to persevere for the sake of the children."

I don't want that kind of life. I do not want Mina to learn that that kind of life is okay.

I have been working on the technology end of Etsy, and I have blogged and set up my EtsyKids page. Under the advisement of many EtsyMoms, I will retake many of my product photos and bribe Mina to pose for me. We haven't negotiated a reward yet. I am thinking chocolate chips, but we will see what *she* has in mind.

My mom keeps telling me how nervous she is this year with my trip to Turkey. She wishes that I wouldn't go. She said that she could play sick so that I would have to go and tend to her and not be able to go to Turkey. I want to go; I need to just go and relax. It is the first year that I am not anxious about the trip. I need Mina to be occupied, so that I can work on Etsy stuff, think, and write.

At the moment, I am taking advantage of some quiet time. It is Friday, so I do not need to cook. The house was picked up and cleaned yesterday. Mina is taking a bath, so I probably should save this for now before she turns into a pink raisin!

June 30, 2010

We had a humdinger of an argument on Saturday! Friday night, I went out to get some last-minute groceries and pizza for dinner. When I got home, locking the car went right out of my head. Well, we got burgled . . . again! The first time, Hakan left the car unlocked, and the thieves took his sunglasses. This time, it was my fault, and they completely cleaned us out, even taking the registration and other car papers. Hakan realized it when he went to get his sunglasses before going on a hike with Sam. They left, and Mina and I went out for breakfast to get a balloon animal.

When he got back, he just looked at me, and I knew he was furious at me for not thinking systematically, like him, and calling the registry, the police, and so on. He kept telling me that it was common sense and that everyone would think to do those things, and *why*, he asked in frustration, do I not get upset by anything? First, it is unfortunate that we got burgled, but it is not the end of the world. Should I dwell on it all day and ruin a beautiful day thinking about it? We were arguing quite forcefully, and I flat-out told him that he made me feel like an idiot and stupid by the way he expressed things. Mina was screaming at us to stop talking so loudly. I took her outside and explained to her that we both think differently, and sometimes that creates problems. I apologized for being loud but said that I felt I needed to stand up for myself. I didn't want someone to make me feel bad about myself, and sometimes defending yourself can get loud.

I am tired of pretending that there is a marriage. We do not really have a conversation. We still eat in silence and watch TV in silence, and then I go to bed. We both are aware of the summer plans to go to my aunt's house but have not actually talked to *each other* about it. It is really weird. There is no affection except for the habitual off-to-work kiss goodbye and the good-night kiss.

Yes, I still haven't called the lawyer, and I said that I would this week. It makes me feel all twisty and icky inside to have to do this. How did this relationship come to this? How did I get here? I am not a hurtful person, but I feel like I am surreptitiously doing something that will hurt a lot of people. I am still having a hard time with this guilt. I keep having to remind myself that I didn't start this road all on my own. Circumstances brought us to this point.

On the flip side of normalcy, I am feeling a bit giddy about this investment through Gaia. I was up all night doing math in my head. The payout should be eight times what I put in. If I keep reinvesting the money, it will keep compounding, and the numbers become staggering when they are written down on paper. Gaia came over this afternoon, and we worked it out, and all she could say was "wow!" This time next year, I could have complete financial freedom and then some! It is an awesome and freeing feeling.

JULY 1, 2010

These days I can't seem to sleep very well. My brain keeps churning until about 1:00 a.m., and then Little Miss Sunshine has me up around 5:45 a.m. Last night was no exception. I keep going through scenarios in my mind about how to tell Hakan what I am feeling and what I want. I keep going back to telling him and his family in Turkey. It is the only thing that makes sense to me. In last night's scenario, I had written both Hakan and his parents a letter while Emre took Mina outside to play. Then Mina and I spent the night at Hakan's aunt Canan's house. I understand now why many women write "Dear John" letters. It is easier to write it and rewrite it than to say it.

I think I will try to draft the letters before my next therapy session on July 14 and have my therapist go over them. In the letters, I seemed to hit on all the feelings and emotions that they would be going through. It seemed that if I identified and *named* these emotions, their explosiveness was somewhat deflated.

As I was lying there last night, I went through our daily conversations: "Good morning." "Have a good day!" "Hi, dinner's on." "Would you like to watch something on TV?" "Good night." We each talk to Mina, but we do not converse with each other. It was no different yesterday. When I came out from putting Mina to sleep, he was sitting in his chair with his laptop. I tried to talk about how the caterpillars were forming their cocoons; I didn't get a response. Then we began watching a show about the universe, and a commercial for a different show came up. I mentioned that my parents have been watching that show—no response. There is nothing. He has nothing that he can talk with me about. How is this working for him? When we are alone in a room together, the level of tension kicks up a notch. Each of us puts on our protective shield, just in case.

Physically, I am getting a bit more tired because of lack of sleep, and I am starting to develop a rash on my tummy, just around the sternum. I start to itch just about Mina's bedtime. I sometimes wonder if anticipation of the "after she is asleep" time that is making its appearance as an itchy rash.

July 7, 2010

I just can't keep my mind still these days, and I am still not sleeping much. I am scared of what I feel is the best thing to do for myself and for Mina. That's it in a nutshell—I am scared. Yep, still scared after all of this therapy and journaling.

In my heart of hearts, I do feel that telling Hakan and his family while we are there is the right and honest way to handle things. It seems to bring out the paranoia in people when I say that, but if I changed the country and city to, say, the United States and Boston, would the reaction be different? Most are afraid that I will not be able to get myself or Mina out of the country and that his family will try to hide her. My gut is not agreeing with that.

As I lie in bed at night, I envision writing letters to both Hakan and his parents, explaining things. In my "dream-scape," I have Emre take Mina outside to play, I give the letters, and then Emre takes Mina and me to the aunt's house for the night. We reconvene the following day in late afternoon to talk it out, after all the initial emotional explosions have settled a bit. I really do not know any other way to do this that is respectful for everyone and their feelings. Hakan will have his family to comfort him, and I can tell his family face-to-face how I came to the decision. Now, it is on to the actual letter-writing. I want them written before I meet with my therapist on the 21st. I want to read them to her and see how better I can word things. I am trying very hard not to use inflammatory language or blame. That is a hard thing to do when there is a lot of resentment at the root of this whole problem.

Maybe if I start drafting the letters here, it won't seem so official.

Dear Hakan,

I want to tell you how proud I am at how you are developing your relationship with Mina. You have taken the time over the past few months to really get to know each other and learn how to play with each other. It makes her very happy.

I also want to say that I appreciate the steps you have taken to get well by going to therapy and starting on some antidepressants. I know that it was a difficult step for you to make, and I am really proud that you are continuing through the process.

You have listened to many of the things that I have had to say and have tried to repair the our relationship. For that I am grateful.

I still remember the first day we met, at Grappa. Your green shirt caught the sunlight as it bounced off the water, and I knew then that you were the one. We were so in love. I felt so loved when you would actually *leave* your parents and family alone in your house and come and stay with me in mine. Our faces just lit up the room wherever we went.

Somehow, over the last ten years, that light has gone out. I remember remarking a few years ago that your face didn't light up anymore when I walked in the room, and then I asked you if you still loved me. The lack of answer and the silence broke my heart. As I sat crying on the couch, I wondered what I had done that was so wrong that you had stopped loving me and comforting me.

I have tried for so long to make you happy. I really wanted to reach and exceed your expectations for me, but I always seemed to fail. I tried to learn Turkish, deal with interfamily issues, comfort you, and take care of everything that could possibly upset you. In that process, I lost who I was, and my self-worth was completely tied up in longing for your love and approval.

We started off together on one road, hand in hand, together. Along the way, that road seemed to slowly divide, and now it seems that we are going down completely different roads. The only bridges that cross between the two are Mina and the house. There seems to be nothing else that bridges that gap.

I cannot be the person you wish me to be or vice versa. We have grown into two completely different people to each other and from our original selves so many years ago. We sit in silence when we eat. We don't have anything to talk about.

I cannot pretend anymore that this marriage is working, and I do not think it is fair to any of us to continue this way. Mina is completely aware that we have problems, and I will not have her learning that this is the kind of marriage to strive for. When I heard from Mom that Mina had called her on the Ojo at two years old and said, "Shh! Nana, Baba made Mama cry last night . . . I have to go; they are coming!" that broke my heart.

My own father was distant and put my mom and me down for most of my life, and I guess I just sort of accepted that that was the way it was supposed to be, and look where I am . . . in the same place my mom was. I do not want Mina to learn this. We can coexist in the same house as usual, but this is not living.

This is difficult for me to say, and I have been struggling with this for a long time, but I can't be married to you anymore, and I think we need to begin looking at alternate arrangements. I know this is very hurtful to you and your family, but I am telling this to you while you have your family around to comfort you. I also care about your family and respect your family, which is why I felt that it was the right thing to do in person.

Mina and I are spending the night at Canan's house, and I will explain things to her there. Tomorrow, we can all come together and talk this through once the initial shock and emotions have settled a little bit.

I do care about you, but I cannot stay in this relationship anymore.

Elif

July 8, 2010

I have had long talks with Samantha and Sofia about stuff over the past few days, and I have all sorts of things to think about. It is good to talk it out with friends. It is interesting to hear the different perspectives. Samantha's major points were "protect yourself" with an exit plan, see a lawyer, know your rights, and so on. Sofia is worried that I am still thinking more about others' well-being than my own.

After I tell him, then what—do I put on my emotional body armor and stay in Turkey the rest of the trip, or do I return a week early? I told Sofia that I wished I could fast-forward through these next two months. I feel like I am at the portion of a rented movie where the FBI warning comes up and tells you not to bootleg, and you can't fast-forward through that screen. You just sit there, saying to yourself, "Come on, come on, come on . . . pass this screen so the movie can start!" Just replace the word "movie" with "my life," and that is where I am these days.

I keep thinking about *after*. I can't be sure whether he will choose to stay in the house for the full three months or find an apartment. I do not know how much frustration he will fling at me and Mina. I do not want him to keep blaming me in front of Mina. I have been very conscious about not bad-mouthing him to Mina. I had heard from divorced friends that a divorce would about take at least three months to complete, from beginning to end. I was up two nights ago thinking, well, if I filed for divorce before leaving for Turkey, then three months would be up at the end of October. That just feels really devious to me and so hurtful. How can I do that to someone? Sofia came up with a great, and obvious, idea. If things become really hurtful, I can just tell him that Mina and I will spend the rest of the three-month period at my mom's house. Maybe just threatening it would make him stop.

On another front, Mina is beginning to realize that her Turkish is different and she cannot communicate as well in it. I see a lot of me in her right now. She is getting self-conscious about speaking it because she doesn't want to say something wrong. Last weekend, we were scheduled to meet Hakan's new Turkish friends in Park City for dinner. Mina and I were out in the back giving her babies a bath in the tub. She looked at me and said that she didn't want to go to dinner with the Turkish people. I asked her why, and she said, "Because I don't like Turkish people." Oh, *boy*! I am glad Hakan wasn't around to hear *that* statement! Her spirit seemed to close in, and she ducked her head in and played with her babies. I told her that we didn't even know them yet to form an opinion and that the only difference between us was the language; I asked whether that was making her nervous. She looked at me sideways and nodded. I asked her if she was feeling shy and nervous about the language, and she nodded. I reassured her that I was just as shy and nervous as she was.

After five weeks in Turkey, she will have much better Turkish. That is one of the main reasons for my going this year. I am trying hard to help her absorb and retain as much Turkish as possible before the shit hits the fan. Sofia asked me yesterday why I was going because it seems that I am thinking more about the emotional well-being of Hakan and his family and not taking care of myself. As much as I am going to be the bad guy, I need to have closure for myself and know that I did everything I could possibly do to make this blow as soft as possible. They may never recognize what I tried to do, but that doesn't matter to me. I am only accountable to myself, and I need to be able to look myself in the mirror each day. In the long run, the time dealing with such animosity is a millisecond compared to the rest of my life. Time passes, maybe not as quickly as one would like when in the thick of it, but time will pass, and then it will be time to come home. I am going to enlist Emre as a mediator. He seems to really listen and understand where I am coming from. I am going to ask him to implore that his family and Hakan not play the blame game with Mina. If they begin to do that, I will get a ticket and return home early. I think that I have become strong enough to withstand battle at this point. I may be stepping into the firing range, but I have a sense of who I am and who I want to be now, and that will protect me. Truth and honesty are the best shields you can find. "I am rubber, and you are glue! All your insults bounce off me and back to you!"

July 13, 2010

I began this journey toward an ultimate gift to myself, emancipation. It has been a long road to get there, but I feel so much better and stronger for the journey. The time to verbalize my truth is coming quickly and will happen very soon. It is interesting that when your being is ready for the truth to come out, the truth shows itself little by little subconsciously.

Over the past few months, I have been giving to myself and to others to regain myself. I got lost in a marriage. I lost myself in my husband's dreams and goals with total disregard for myself and my feelings. I have grown up a lot in the last six months, and yesterday, I heard Madonna's song "The Power of Good-Bye."

The song resonated with me and reflected how I was feeling at that moment:

Your heart is not open, so I must go
The spell has been broken . . . I loved you so
Freedom comes when you learn to let go
Creation comes when you learn to say no

I posted that video on Facebook, and boy, did it cause a ripple effect! In the end, however, I felt stronger about it. My mom wrote me and asked me if I was okay because her neighbor had seen it and was concerned. Hakan came home, very nervous, and asked if he had offended me. I was not ready to verbalize my life decision at that point, but I think the video has been a little hint to people of what is to come. I cannot grow into myself married to him, and I know that now. The greatest gift I can give to myself this trip to Turkey is to be honest with everyone and tell everyone that the marriage is not working for me. I need to tell everyone, face-to-face, because I need to know that I did everything I could to soften the blow. It may not be the way others would do it, but I need to be able to look myself in the mirror and face Mina. It is so scary to be at this junction, but I feel at peace with the whole thing.

July 15, 2010

Okay, maybe I didn't *call* the lawyer, but I e-mailed her. Does that count? It's a step, right? Cold calling is tough for me.

Anyway, I met with Gaia yesterday, and she said that the payout for the investment would be about $8,000 and that Liselot will hold it and reinvest it. I am not going to touch it and will let the money just grow. Gaia told Liselot, "This is Elif's ticket to freedom."

As I become stronger, I realize what is not okay. I know others have been trying to tell me and show me, but I was not ready to see. I cannot be *me* in this marriage. Every time some expression of "me" pops up somewhere, I get an irritated look or an exasperated sigh. For example, last weekend we had twelve Turkish people over for a cookout. It had been a long time since I'd had so many people over for a party, and I wanted it to be fun! I love cooking, and I love cooking for a lot of people. I spent the morning on the Ojo cooking with Hakan's mom and got a lot of stuff done. I looked around the shelves and pantry to see what ingredients I had to make other stuff. I didn't exhaust myself or go out and spend a ton of extra money; I had fun in the kitchen. Hakan kept passing through the kitchen and would sigh.

"Why do you always do this? You always do too much, make too much! Everyone would be happy with just potato salad and meatballs!"

"Hakan, if you are concerned about the money, I have just been pulling stuff from the cabinets and freezer for supplies. I haven't really spent anything extra to do this party."

"You just do, do, do, and it makes people uncomfortable! No one expects all this. No one else does stuff like this! Why do you have to be different?"

It brings me to joy to cook for others! The things I made were not difficult, and everyone loved them. I had almost nothing left by the time everyone went home. I felt vindicated in what I did. But this is just an example of how I feel like I have to stifle my "me" impulse.

Yesterday, I made a lunch for Gaia. She doesn't eat regularly, and I had some extra luncheon meat. I made her a sandwich and a little snack box, but I felt I had to hide them so that Hakan wouldn't see and ask. I hate having to hide myself and who I am. You shouldn't have to hide your true self from your life partner. I want to be free to be who I am. I want to be able to grow into a better person from where I am right now.

When Gaia left me at the bookstore, I asked her if I seemed stronger to her at all because I felt stronger in myself. She said that I seemed at peace. Daisy is here for me as well. Since she works with Hakan, I have tried to limit the divorce conversation with her. I don't want to put her in an awkward position. She told me that she supports my telling everyone in Turkey and that she feels assured no one will be endangered with so much family around. She also offered her house as a haven if Mina and I need a place to stay.

The other night, I visualized myself going into battle as I told him and his family the news. In my visualization, I could see my friends surrounding me and becoming almost body armor. It was an interesting picture. Samantha and Sofia were leg armor, Gaia had her arms stretched wide open in front of my chest, and Daisy—because she is so tall—was behind me, arms open, head over mine like a shield. If I can hold this image in my mind's eye when I sit down and hand off the letters, I think I will fell loved even in a room of animosity.

July 16, 2010

I have worked on a budget today. I printed out bank info from the web and went through it today. If the lawyer asks for a total of $3,500 a month (maintenance + child support), that should be more than enough. I used an online calculator for child support, and that total was about $900. That is only $2,600 in alimony or maintenance. Considering Hakan brings in a decent salary, he will still have more than enough for himself and for savings. I took the twelve-month average from last year and came up with these monthly expenses:

Mortgage/insurance	$1,967.00
Electric	$55.00
Cell	$90.00
Water	$52.00
Quest phone (phone, Internet, cable)	$130.00
Questar gas	$60.00
Amica	$85.00 (car insurance)
Groceries	$500.00 (for me and Mina)
Hip juice + vitamins	$200 ($150 goji juice + $50 vitamins)
Gas for car	$60.00
Total	$3,199.00

July 20, 2010

Yesterday morning over my morning coffee, Samantha and I e-mailed back and forth for a while about the impending trip and what to do after I tell everyone. That is so hard to decide now. Most everyone I talk to advises me to get out of there as soon as possible and leave early. I am not so sure. I am feeling really calm about the whole thing these days. I am just starting to sleep better, and my swollen glands have started to diminish. I feel like I am entering into the eye of the storm with this trip to Turkey. The beginning will be easy and calm, but the winds will raise a loud voice and whirl around me after I say everything I need to say. Is it delusional of me to want to give this family the benefit of the doubt? I am not hoping that they will side with me against their son or nephew, but I am hoping that, after a period of high emotions, there will be sadness and understanding. I really want to believe that I truly have developed a relationship with this family that will surpass this divorce. I feel that if I go in there with a return ticket in hand, emotions will turn against me for not trusting in them. If I can keep our passports and money close at hand, I can go if the situation becomes difficult and stay with friends until the trip is over. The week would be spent mostly with his family because Hakan will be at a conference. What I do will hinge completely on the amount of animosity they deal out. I am used to a goodly amount of animosity the last week anyway because we are leaving. I am used to his mom being moody. It is just the level of moodiness that I can't predict right now.

Do I really want to spend seventeen hours in an enclosed plane with him all the way home? Not really. However, we do not usually talk or even sit next to each other on the ride anyway, and I am usually tending to Mina. The first week back will be tough, but work and getting Mina into school will make the time pass, and then it will be time to go home to Rhode Island.

I am tired of trying to think of all the possible end-result scenarios. I cannot control them, and trying to control the outcome is making me sick. If I have learned anything through all this, it is that I cannot control how others react; I can only control myself. I feel like I have passed through the door of acceptance, and I have just a few more to go. People always say, "As one door closes, another one opens"; whether it is to something good or bad, it is an experience to help you grow.

It has been interesting to see how our lives have slowly started to separate even now. Hakan's new Turkish friends have him invited to many things. The other day, he went to Lagoon the whole day, and then he was off to one of their houses the following night when I put Mina to sleep. Since he can communicate with them better, he must feel so much more free to be himself than he feels when he is with me. And you know, that is okay. I have even noticed that I have begun to eat differently than I used to. Before, I would cook a meal that he would like, and I would eat it. Now I seem to cook just for him and make a salad for myself. I seem to slowly, unconsciously be taking control over my life again.

Today's project is to write the letter to his parents. I guess I cannot put that off any longer since my therapy session is tomorrow.

Dear Mom and Dad,

I love you. When we first met all those years ago, we were each walking down our own roads with our own ideas of life. As the years went by, the distance between us diminished, and now, through a lot of hard work and understanding, we walk down the same road together. I am really proud of how we were able to work hard and work through our differences. I have grown to love and care for you as much as my own parents and look forward to our weekends together on Ojo. We have learned how to communicate with each other better, and we understand each other so much better.

I know that you have tried to help me and to help Hakan with our problems, and I am so grateful. I am grateful that you took the time to listen to me and what I had to say. Hakan and I have been going to therapy, individually, for the past few months. He has grown as a father, and that makes me happy. It is important for a child to have a strong, loving relationship with her father. However, I do not feel that our problems are resolving themselves. We are different people from when we got married so many years ago, and we have been walking down separate roads for a long time now. I have tried hard over the years to meet his expectations and to make him happy, and I cannot do it any longer. I know that this is difficult for you to hear, but I cannot remain married to your son anymore. I am telling you this in person because I love and respect you. I am not trying to ruin a vacation, but am trying to provide support for Hakan during this difficult time.

I also want you to know that you will never lose me as a daughter. I have grown to love and care for you and enjoy your visits. I hope that you remember that you are welcome to stay with me anytime and for as long as you choose.

Love,
Elif

July 23, 2010

It has been an interesting few days. The more I do to prepare for what's coming, the more I seem to accept and move on. It is a process, and I must pass through all the doors to get to the other side. It is interesting—the more I seem to move on, the more Hakan is trying to get closer; it is like he senses something but can't quite put his finger on it. He calls to say hello around lunchtime, leaves Post-It notes thanking me for a nice dinner, and so on. I guess the energy in the air is shifting, and he can feel it too.

I took Mina to the therapist's office Wednesday because I really needed the therapist to read the letters I had written to Hakan and his parents. She read them and thought they were beautiful. She said that the amount of thought and caring is apparent throughout, that she has a good feeling about the outcome. She said that I was a very brave woman for doing it the way that I am doing it and that it takes a lot of courage.

On the way home, we stopped at Shopko to get a hole punch and binder dividers. Samantha laughed when I told her I was making a binder with all my info it. I *love* to organize and make binders, and it surprised me that I didn't have a hole punch! Maybe I wore the old one out with so much binder-making.

Anyway, I am trying to consolidate all my information into one place: marriage biography, finances, journal, e-mail correspondence spanning ten years, tax returns, and anything else I can find to go in. I have been surprised that e-mails last so long online. I was able to go into my e-mail accounts and find appropriate e-mails all the way back to 2000! I think it will help to show that this has been ongoing for a while. I have put them in chronological order, but the lawyer will have to get an independent Turkish translator to translate the Turkish letters.

I also found early correspondence between Hakan and me. It is so sad to look back on those messages now. I loved him so much. There was a lot of love at one point, and it saddens me to see where we are now and how we came to this point. I read our e-mails from when he was doing his six weeks of military service in Turkey, in October 2000. I remember buying up a ton of greeting cards, one for each day, and writing a little note in each. Each day that he was over there, he could open one and feel me near him. I also made him a little motivational love journal to take with him. I remember using CompUSA's color printer to copy all the images that I would eventually glue into the journal. I wasn't supposed to use the printers for personal use, so I would have Samantha as a lookout sometimes! I remember that while he was gone, I would sleep with his stinky t-shirt, so that it would feel like he was still there with me. Love is like a flower; it just withers and dries up if not attended to properly. It is like that potted plant that you have in the corner that you see every day and about which you keep saying to yourself, *I will water that the next time I come into the room.* However, "next time" never comes, and when you finally wake up and notice, the plant has dried up and can't be saved, no matter how much love and attention you shower upon it.

Hakan came home yesterday and said that his mom had asked us to remember to bring my wedding band back to Turkey to get it sized smaller. That just feels weird, but I have to do it or conveniently forget.

July 24, 2010

It was a good morning. It was the first time I have done something for *me* on a Saturday. Mina and I were up early with errands, and we headed down to the farmer's market not to shop, but just to walk around. We had such a nice time together. I had wanted to do this for a long time but felt uncomfortable leaving him and not calling his family on Ojo. Just another piece of myself that I let slip away. Mina and I walked hand in hand, got a nice smoothie and some chocolate chip pumpkin bread, and sat on a patch of grass. We sat and watched life go by.

I got home, put Mina to sleep, and saw Hakan for about a half hour before he left to go climbing with Sam. It is really hard for me to sit here and talk to him about future stuff: getting back into climbing together, Sam's wedding, planning anything. It makes me feel uncomfortable because my soul is lying to him.

I finished up the binder as much as I could. I printed out the last few e-mails that I found the other night, added the finances, printed out the letters, and put them in envelopes. For three and a half weeks, I am going to have to pretend everything is fine. Can't anyone see on my face that it is not fine? I feel like it is blinking like a neon sign across my forehead!

I can't wait to get to Turkey and be able to sit and read. I think I will begin with *The Happiness Project*. I figure it will help keep me centered and strong.

I just need it done. I am tired of comparisons between Mina and the other Turkish children. Hakan came back from the Turkish get-together last night and said that the other Turkish children are up until 11:00 p.m. and seem fine with it, that I am too controlling over Mina's early bedtime.

I asked Mina the other day if she was excited to be going to Turkey, and I got a downward nod of the head. The answer was "no" followed by "I miss Nana." Yeah, I miss Nana too! When she says stuff like that, it is hard to keep from tearing up—like I am now as I write. She talks more about what she wants to do in Rhode Island this October than what she wants to do in Turkey. On the Ojo last Thursday, his parents asked her if she was counting the days, and she didn't look at them or answer them because she isn't, really! She is making plans with friends for when she comes back! It will be interesting to see how the dynamic plays out when we get there.

JULY 28, 2010

It has been an interesting couple of days. I feel like there is a big elephant in the room. Everyone seems to want to ask how things are but are almost, rightly so, afraid to voice anything. While we were on the plane, she didn't want anything to do with Hakan. She just wanted time with Mama and would refuse him if he wanted to sit and play. She would just tell him to go back to his e-mail. I got concerned when she started singing in the plane on the way to Turkey, "I don't have a Baba, I don't have a Baba." I thought I should ask her what she was singing, and she said that she was singing a song about a little girl who only had a Mama and didn't have a Baba. I asked her how the little girl felt about that, and she shrugged. "I don't know how she felt."

She is very good at standing up for herself if someone hurts her feelings, which I think is an important trait to have, one that I have lacked. I tried to prepare her as we were exiting baggage claim. I told her that everyone, her grandmother and aunt, would probably run up and kiss her. I didn't want her to feel overwhelmed after such a long day. Hakan's Aunt Canan ran up, but Hakan's mom was taking a video of us coming out. That must have pissed Mina off because she went up to his mom later that day and said, "Mama said you and Canan were going to run up and give me kiss. Canan ran; you did not!"

From what I understand, she had a very serious, angry look on her face. Hakan's mom was upset that Mina thought that maybe she didn't want to see her as much as Canan did. She tried to explain to Mina that she was taking a video and that she couldn't run, but that didn't mean she didn't want to see her as much as Canan.

This morning, Mina wanted me to take her to the slide park in the apartment complex. Hakan woke up soon after and asked if he could take her there, and at that time, she said she didn't want to go. I kept my mouth shut about the fact that she had just said that she *did* want to go. Then his mom woke up, and Mina went and asked *her* if she would take her to the slide park. Hakan laughed and said, "But you didn't want to go with me just a second ago."

Hakan's brother wrote to me today with concerns over a divorce. He is afraid that if we divorce, no one here will ever see Mina again, that I will not bring her here again. He expressed concern for his grandmother's health if we divorced and how devastated Hakan would be. At least he acknowledged that he was thinking selfishly.

Here is his e-mail, followed by my reply:

Date: Wed, 28 Jul 2010
Subject: Brainstorming

Hi Elif,

How are you? I hope you are doing well. Probably, you are sleeping all the time because of the jet lag.

I wish I could sleep this night as well. I had crazy thoughts and could not sleep.

Because of my laziness and/or my selfishness (I am questioning my career and looking for a new job when I find free time nowadays), I did not ask you about your relationship again, but this is my last chance to ask since you will go to Bozcaada & Ayvalik . . . and afterward, I will see Hakan, before I see you. Ohh, I should be there. I really love these places. I am looking for a new job all the time. I said I am selfish. Instead of questioning him and trying to help him, I am taking Hakan's time to edit my e-mails, which I am going to send to companies.

Tonight, I was scared to think what will happen if you divorce. I guess people have bad thoughts during nights. Anyway, again I was selfish, and I was afraid that I will not see Mina again—because if you divorce, you will not come to Turkey with Mina. I am living outside Turkey, but my family and girlfriend are in Turkey, so I will spend vacations in Turkey. How and when can I come to the US? If I come, what will I do if you are married to someone else? I cannot come . . . if I come, where do I stay? Then I thought of the effects on the grandmoms and had concerns about the effects of this situation on their health. I thought this, again because I am selfish. You know, I am very tightly connected to them. The one who really will be destructed in this situation is Hakan. He came as the third in my mind.

I just wanted to know, how is it going with Hakan? Is it better or worse? Because when I will be there, I will discuss this with my brother for sure. I did not talk about it in detail when I talked with my brother though Skype. And when I asked once, he answered that we can talk when we will be in Turkey. I said okay and never mentioned my conversation with you. When I was in Turkey at the end of May, I talked with parents, and Mom agreed that you had problems years before, and it is much better now. Now, it is time to talk with Hakan. I wanted to explain our conversations when I will talk with him. Maybe I will have to read your e-mail which you have sent to me and question him and make him face with the problems and situations he created, and maybe he will tell about his problems about you. Am I allowed to do this?

Emre

My reply:

I can understand how you can feel scared. I don't think I want you to actually read from my e-mail to you. I think you have a good idea of what is going on. If divorce happens, you should not be scared that we would not be back to Turkey. You should not be scared that we would not visit you wherever you are living. I am highly aware of everyone's attachment to Mina, and I will not keep her from anyone. If divorce happens, it would be divorce from Hakan, not the family. I have worked hard to develop a strong relationship with your family, and I am not going to throw that away. I need to think of what is best for Mina long-term. I do not expect anyone to understand me or my thinking; I am just asking you to be a voice for Mina. None of our problems should be presented to Mina. The competition between Turkey/Turkish and America/English needs to stop, regardless of whether we stay together or not. If divorce happens, I do not wish it to be put on Mina that Mommy broke up the family; Mommy is hurting everyone. Mina has already realized that there is a difference in our home from others and has started referring to Hakan as Daddy with other people instead of Baba. The relationship between Mina and Turkish, Turkey, and family is delicate. She is very protective of me, and any complaining about me will result in her resisting Turkish/ Turkey. If she is pushed too much, she will push back and refuse.

I have done a lot of thinking over the past few months and have sat and watched things that have been said and done. It is hard to describe. If I didn't have the experience with your mom, then I may not be as aware of the possible change that can occur. There was a definite shift in your mother's attitude, and it was quick and positive. My therapist is highly impressed with your mom—to be able to try that hard to change a character.

I am not seeing that change in Hakan with regard to me. He has become a great dad and has put a great deal of effort into forming a relationship with Mina, and Mina is happy. But it is still delicate. On the plane to Istanbul, she started singing, "I don't have a Baba, I don't have a Baba." I asked her what she was singing, and she said that she had made up a song about a girl who only had a Mama and not a Baba. She still doesn't trust at times that what he is doing is *real*. This morning, she asked me if I could take her to the slides. Hakan woke up a few minutes later, and he asked her if he could take her, and she said that she didn't want to go. Then Babanne woke up, and Mina took her to the window and asked if she could take her to the park.

Hakan still has high expectations of who he wants me to be and has a difficult time when I do not perform the way that he thinks I should. I have told him that when he does this, he makes me feel like an idiot and stupid. I should not have to control my inner self to be the person he would like me to be anyway. I should go; he already walked in, and I had to close the computer.

August 1, 2010

We have arrived at my aunt's house, and I am dealing with a lot of guilt. I am feeling so two-faced. His family has given us a nice trip on the island, and now my family is hosting them, not because they really want to, but because it will make life easier for me. I am feeling guilt from both ends.

My family took everyone out for a lovely dinner for Hakan's birthday and probably spent close to $300 on the whole affair. Today, they have planned an evening boat tour around the seaside. On one hand, it is nice to feel that they love me so much that they will do such stuff for others in order to make my stay easier, but on the other hand, it is such an expense considering the stressful familial circumstances.

I spoke to my other aunt, Zerrin, last night, and she will be coming down this week as well to the summer house after Hakan and his parents leave. My cousin Ekin is coming as well, and it feels like a gathering together to hear what is going on. I have a feeling we will be having longs talks while Mina is sleeping about my decision and my plans.

AUGUST 2, 2010

I finally feel that I have a moment to write. Everyone is napping, at least for the time being. I am feeling a bit nervous about telling *my* family about my plans. I want support, love, and understanding. I am afraid of judgment because they can be so harsh with their words. I am afraid that it will knock me off my path and place insecurities instead of instilling confidence. I do not know why I feel so nervous. My Aunt Binnaz has said that I should not stay in a marriage for the sake of a child. My Aunt Zerrin has been married and divorced three times. My cousin Ekin has been married and divorced and broke off an engagement recently. I do feel a gathering of familial energy brewing. My aunts rarely see each other, and my cousin rarely comes here. I feel they are all gathering to take care of me and listen to me. I hope I am right. It is interesting that I have such confidence that my mother-in-law will behave a certain way, but I am nervous about my own family.

I have been having fitful dreams as well. I had a dream the other night that I was meeting my friend Jen for coffee, and we heard a sound out the window. In a pond near us, we saw our friend Spogga's old iguana. He had grown to the size of an alligator and was rainbow-colored on his back and face. Then I was somehow in Turkey. In the dream, Mina was actually the child of Emre and his ex-girlfriend, Sedef. I was taking care of Mina after they broke up. In the dream, I saw Sedef, and she looked very old. In my dream, I had a vision of bars over her face, and it seemed like an ominous omen. I followed her down underground to a cistern, where she had tied herself up and was waiting for the water to come. Being without her child, having her child taken away, was too much for her. She was writing a letter to Mina and was leaving her a white pair of tennis shoes, thinking to herself that Mina still wasn't big enough to wear them. Then I woke up.

My fear of losing Mina is reaching my unconscious states, and it troubles me. I do not consciously fear that someone will take her away, but it seems my subconscious does. When I reflect on the dream, I always gravitate to the rainbow iguana. I have no idea what that means.

My agitation and anticipation grow with each day. If I stick to my schedule, I have twelve days left.

I have written to my cousin Esra, and she will be back from her holiday in Bodrum by July 20. She said to think a few more times before I drop the bomb on the family. I am glad that my Aunt Zerrin will be coming because she was once a lawyer (now retired) and can give me a better idea of the legalities I may need to face here. Do I need to make it official here as well? Do I need to immediately remove Mina's name from the T family "house" card recorded by the city?

He and his family leave tomorrow sometime, and I do not know when my aunt and uncle will have their first sit-down with me. My aunt and cousin are due to arrive on Wednesday, but when? I have released control over many things, but now I am feeling the urge to control the outcome again. I hope that over the next few days, I will be able to just let go and let events happen.

August 3, 2010

Well, we have had our first of many chats with my aunt, and it was difficult because she always converses like a school's headmistress, very direct and to the point. I started out by saying that I was scared of staying and scared of leaving.

"Well, my dear, you are contradicting yourself! What is it that you want?" she said.

I started to explain my reasoning and how he is always so angry.

"Well, you are always crying and full of self-pity! You have always been so! You will never get anywhere in life if you are always complaining and full of self-pity!"

Needless to say, I was not feeling so supported. She sees Hakan as well educated and a gentleman.

"Elif, dear, if it does not feel *right* for you to stay, then leave!" she very matter-of-factly stated.

Before all this, I spent about two hours dealing with a crying Mina, crying for her grandmother! It was really frustrating. She even wanted to stay in Turkey and live next to her. Well, I had a not-so-good-mommy moment and said, "You will have to choose between me and Babanne because I am not living in Turkey!" She went on and on, and I know she is a child and doesn't mean to hurt my feelings, but she did. She said that she never wanted to come to Ayvalik again or see my family—all she wanted was Babanne. She also told me that she felt safer in the water with Babanne than with me. At that, I started bawling my eyes out. That really hurt. Finally, she started calming down and wanted to go back to Utah *right now*! She missed her friends and her own house. I told her that wasn't possible now, but if she felt like that in Istanbul at any time, then maybe I could accommodate her.

I told her that we needed to be strong because we had a couple of difficult months ahead of us, and we would need to take care of each other. I told her that I loved her very much, and I hoped that she would understand one day what I am doing and why.

My other aunt and cousin arrive tomorrow morning, and I am sure we will chat again.

I had another not-so-great-mommy moment and started crying as I was reading to Mina when she woke up. Times like these make me miss my mom a lot. I had a bit of an emotional release and then took a shower to wash it off.

I have begun to read *The Happiness Project*. I figured that if I am going to be going through so much unhappiness, maybe I should get some clues beforehand on how to handle it. It has been really informative. I find that I am already doing many of the things that help you feel more energized and full of life, thereby leading to a happier existence.

August 6, 2010

At the moment, I have no idea what day it is. I have let go of a clock, a cell phone, and the frequent use of a computer. There are no clocks in our little house either. It is an interesting feeling to just float. The only way I know approximately what day it is is by counting the number of soy milk boxes on the counter. Approximately, we have four days left here. At the moment, my aunt's one-eyed, deaf cat Korsan (Turkish for "pirate") is sniffing my coffee and has stuck his whiskers in for a taste.

I have finished *The Happiness Project* and find that it has been helpful in dealing with everyone here on a daily basis. I have been using the "cut people slack" mantra and letting things go. When I feel personally assaulted or insulted by something someone has done or said, I have been taking a deep breath and looking at the other's personality and character. It has actually helped because it helps me to compartmentalize my responses.

I have to say it really irritated me when my mother-in-law decided to take it upon herself to teach Mina how to say good morning to everyone, and she felt the need to also *announce* it to everyone. I took a deep breath and said to myself, *Is it the worst thing that she could teach her?* I was not thrilled with the method; that's why I was annoyed. She, I guess, needs to feel like she has taught Mina something tangible and recognizable.

I have recently learned that she has written to my aunt—again!—about my and Hakan's problems! I am more dismayed than upset. The tone is not angry, but pleading. His family is holding the symbol of the wedding ring as a symbol of marriage status. My wearing it means things are getting better, but my forgetting to bring it worries them. That was not directly written, but that seems to be the feeling.

I feel like I have regained my footing after a few days of talking with my younger Aunt Zerrin and her daughter, Ekin. Ekin told me not to feel abandoned in Istanbul when I return there. She and her brother Yunus will be there, Esra will be there on the twentieth, and my Aunt Zerrin will come and help if I need her. They are going to make a list of telephone numbers for me to keep with me. Ekin said that if I feel uncomfortable in his family's house to call her, and she will get the keys for my Aunt Binnaz's Istanbul house. She agrees that it would be abrupt of me to go directly to my family's house and thinks first going to Hakan's aunt's house is a good transition. Neither my cousin nor my Aunt Zerrin feels that his family kidnapping Mina is a possibility and told me not to think about that aspect at all. They are more concerned about the whole family ganging up on me to change my mind.

My Aunt Zerrin says that I shouldn't be afraid of telling anyone because it is akin to pushing a button—once pushed, it is all over. She and I stayed up late last night drinking wine. It is helpful to have them around. It has been almost a decade probably since all of us have been together for this extended period of time. We have grown and forgotten and forgiven each other for wrongs from long ago.

Ekin leaves tonight after dinner and Zerrin tomorrow morning after breakfast. My Aunt Binnaz and uncle will accompany me to Izmir Monday and help me get on the plane. They have been generous and have recently deposited $2,500 into my account. Last night, I woke up with a little daydream. I thought I would take Mina to San Diego for Thanksgiving. I saw pictures in my head of us having turkey sandwiches on the beach on Thanksgiving Day. We would stay in a cute bed and breakfast and spend our days between the beach and the San Diego Zoo. At the time, I thought I would just splurge and do this for Mina and me, but now my family has provided the means. Maybe, if it is not so far, Sofia and her little boy, G, could join us for a couple of days over the weekend. Maybe if there is a good, cheap flight, I could fly Samantha and Ava out too. Anyway, daydreams, daydreams—the things that seem to keep me going one step at a time.

August 8, 2010

I was up most of the night thinking still about, well, everything. When it was just me talking about my and Hakan's problems, I guess it was easy to dismiss. When I (finally) decide to stop focusing on making Hakan happier and focus more on my becoming happier, suddenly everyone sits up and takes notice. It is threatening to them because they do not know how to deal with it; they always think with the collective family in mind and not about individual happiness. Energy is shifting, and they can see that I am trying to regain control over my life, and they seem to be scared by that. His mom lashes out by posting minor criticisms on Facebook, which I just ignore.

I had just closed the computer in the main house, made myself some tea, and gone out to sit in the garden and read when the phone rang. My aunt's maid said it was for me. Really? It was Hakan.

"I was just on Facebook," he said, "and saw what my mom posted on your wall. I found it rude and childish. I sat her down and yelled at her. She is not to be so petty and vindictive with things like that. I know that you tried to show these attributes of hers to me before, but I was unwilling to see and look directly at the situation. I just wanted to call you and tell you that my eyes are open, and I see it now. You will not have to deal with her moodiness anymore. I will take care of it. I have demanded that she remove her postings and refrain from such things in the future."

What is one supposed to *feel* when someone finally acknowledges a problem that has existed for years?

"Wow, thanks for doing that. I appreciate your new awareness, but if you were concerned that I was upset, I am not because these types of things usually happen when I come to Ayvalik."

I feel as if I should feel something more—affection? more gratitude? relief? But I just feel content that the slight was not "imagined." This shows that he is growing himself, and that is a good sign for his own health. Most of my thinking last night centered around the concept of core character. All of this goodwill and attention is fine, but as I reflect on the past months, our core characters are still quite different. Am I being too dismissive of the steps that he is taking? I *am* proud of his steps. He has come a long way from last year. It just doesn't seem to change my fundamental inner truth: I do not believe I can grow into who I am supposed to be with him. I feel like I need to ask if that is okay. Is it okay to need to just be done? If I take the analogy that Ekin used the other day—that it is all about pushing a button—then can't that same button start the ignition toward living again?

All I can hope for is that all of the work Hakan is doing on himself will help us to become collaborative divorced parents, rather than combative divorced parents. Again, I am probably being idealistic again and overly hopeful, but without hope where am I?

I have been soaking in all the relaxing time with Mina. We have been lying in bed in our own little house playing and tickling until eight or nine in the morning. Leaving early from our dinners out has given us the opportunity to walk through the streets on our own and have strawberry ice cream, just the two of us. Last night, she and I played in the slide park as we waited for my uncle's driver to pick us up. I rarely get moments to myself here, especially alone moments with her, just strolling around. It is really an empowering feeling to be able to stroll through these foreign streets and feel capable, language-wise, to get us what we need.

We fly out tomorrow evening. It has been nice to sit and recharge, enclosed within these garden walls.

AUGUST 9, 2010

I was up again, all night, last night. I really dislike down pillows, and I can't sleep well on them. I don't know if it is the pillow or my constant thoughts that keep me awake.

Last night was my last night here and the last time my family would have the opportunity to talk to me about things. I have to say, I am mad! Again, I am feeling dismissed. What is so special about Hakan that everyone rallies to his side? I don't bring up anything anymore—*they* do, and they ask why I feel this way or that way.

While we were enjoying a lovely view of the Aegean Sea, the sun set in the background in a fiery blaze, and this seemed to ignite my aunt and uncle as they began to really dig into the situation and tell me how they see it.

My aunt began, "Dear Elif, really, do you know what you are doing? Do you really believe that you have another chance to meet another man with all the qualities that Hakan possesses? He is good-looking. He has a great educational background, great résumé. He has a much better chance at finding a girl who will put up with these things than you will have as a single mom. The girls here in Turkey will chase after him. Who will want you, a single mom with a child? If you don't love him, then leave him. Just be honest with yourself and your future. You tell such amusing stories that maybe you should stop complaining so much and put that attention toward Hakan."

My uncle continued with these sentiments. "For years and years, we have heard through you and through your parents about your problems. You need to stop complaining and think of them and their health! Your indecision is making them ill and aging them. It is a bit selfish, I believe, to continuously complain and complain with no action. Either stay or go—just make a decision because we are tired of hearing your father so concerned for you. We feel your indecisiveness is adversely affecting his health. You can think of yourself, but think outside of your needs, to those of your father. You are causing your parents pain by prolonging this decision.

"In my opinion, it is too bad that Hakan did not have a cute assistant to chase him and have an affair with. Maybe that would have made you jealous and rethink things. I have a hard time believing some of the things that you tell us. It is . . . it is . . . like a film noir. Now really, aren't you exaggerating a bit on these matters?

"You say that you feel strong in many ways, but prolonged lack of decision makes you appear weak, thereby invalidating what you tell us."

If the fiery sunset had ignited my aunt and uncle's "honesty," it emblazed me. For the first time in my life, I challenged them. I poured myself yet another drink, looked my uncle straight in the eye, and asked, "Do you think I am lying? Do you think I would put myself and my *child* through all of this for pettiness and imagined or embellished transgressions? Look me in the eye and tell me that you think I am lying!"

The shock that I had countered them was apparent on their faces. Immediately, they began to backpedal and recant their previous musings. After years of never standing up for myself in such interactions with them, I felt I had finally grown up. Not only did I stand up for myself, but I held my ground.

August 11, 2010

We got out of the house today and went to the Body Worlds exhibit. Mina was so excited to go. We spent a lot of time in the baby section looking at all the little babies. She ran around so much looking at everything that she was conked out for a nap as soon as we got home. Emre was nice and thoughtful and offered to drop me at the little mall nearby while he met with his adviser. It was nice to just walk through the mall and spend some time in a bookstore. I was able to find some nice books for Mina and found *The Happiness Project* translated into Turkish. I picked one up for Hakan's mom and had it wrapped up.

Emre met up with me a little while later and bought me a nice iced coffee at Starbucks. We sat and talked together for over an hour about everything.

"Elif, I have to say that I am having a hard time internalizing all that we talk about, but I believe what you say and agree that if it is not healthy for Mina, just leave him. I know that he is my brother, but Mina's health and happiness are more important right now."

That was surprising to hear. It was nice to talk to someone who listened and didn't sit in judgment of what I said or immediately try to change what I was saying.

"You know, Emre, I have tried in so many ways to make this work, and I am empty inside and have nothing left of myself to give. Do you get what I am saying? I can't think anymore. I am tired of thinking. Thinking doesn't change the situation after so much time has passed."

There was silence at our table. All around us, Starbucks employees were busily calling out coffee orders, and people were excitedly meeting each other for their afternoon coffee and chocolate-covered *lokum*, Turkish delight candy. It was surreal in a way to see the Western influence of Starbucks comingling with the Eastern traditional candies and treats. Life didn't seem real in a way.

After taking the last sip of his iced coffee, he continued in quiet resignation to what will soon happen. "I can see that you are tired and that you have gone through a lot. I understand what has brought you to this point. Hakan's problems have really affected his parents too. They seem older and sadder. They finally realized how serious the problem was this year and sat him down to talk to him about your marital problems while you were in Ayvalik."

Again, we sat in silence as we both absorbed what we were going to have to deal with when our family began to understand the full severity of the situation. It was time to go and give Mina hugs, more to reassure myself than to comfort her.

Anyway, I feel good today. I feel *heard*. Tomorrow we are off to the covered bazaar and taking Mina with us. I think she will really enjoy it.

AUGUST 13, 2010

Well, I think I am at the halfway point of this vacation, and it is officially less than a week away from the time I will hand out (somehow!) the letters. I have to rethink my original plan. Originally, I was going to have Emre take Mina down to the slide park after she woke up from her nap. However, the heat is making that plan a dud. My next idea is to plan a day with Aunt Canan and Mina. I brought over a pattern for a baby doll bed and nightgown. We had thoughts of going to a fabric store to pick out material to make them. I think my new plan will be to have Mina come with us and pick out the material. That way, I will have Mina alone with Canan, which is what I had intended anyway. We can go do the work and then come back and stay at her house. I can leave the letters in a place they will find after I have left. Phew! Implementation will be tricky, but I am feeling a bit suffocated these days and need to rip the bandage off this wound.

It is overwhelming to go from no attention for years to the exact opposite now. There are flowers and arms around the shoulders and hugs and compliments and so on. But instead of feeling something warm toward him, I am feeling a bit suffocated. It is because I am not being honest and true with everyone.

I have been trying to take charge of my own happiness here and, as a result, make others happy. For example, this morning we were supposed to leave the house around 10:00 a.m. to meet Emre at Ortakoy (a place by the water where Mina could feed the birds). At 8:15 a.m., Hakan was still sleeping, as was his father. Instead of sitting and getting frustrated that my mother-in-law was just playing with Mina and we would not get out on time, I got up and began to make breakfast. I took charge of the morning by putting on tea and made a nice pursalane, pepper, and tomato omelet. I pitted olives and toasted pine nuts. It felt good to be cooking again. It helps clear the mind. It relaxed me, and they all really enjoyed the omelet. His mom commented on how much work I had put into the omelet by even toasting the pine nuts. We actually got out somewhat on time. While Mina and I waited downstairs, I noticed that one of the flowering bushes had gone to seed, so I passed the remaining time collecting seeds to bring home and plant.

As I have been writing this, I have set my plan in motion with Canan for going to the fabric store. I told her to pick a day—Wednesday or Thursday—to come pick us up and do the shopping, and then Mina and I would go back to her house to nap (I left the rest unsaid). She asked why Mina needed to come. I told her that it was important for Mina to be able to pick out the fabric for her baby's nightgown because we would be making Mina a matching nightgown too.

If we get all the materials this week, I can spend most of my (our) time over here sewing with Canan after the proverbial shit hits the fan.

I am signing off for a few days. We are headed two hours out of Istanbul to a little village for one night.

AUGUST 15, 2010

Two weeks from today, I can go home. Three days from today, the truth will be told.

We took a mini-trip to the Black Seaside this weekend. It was Hakan, me, Mina, Emre, and his girlfriend. It was extremely hot and humid, but we all had a nice time playing in the sand and in the water. There was a water conjunction where a freshwater river met the sea. Mina loved to play in the riverside because it was not so deep, and it was calm. The seaside was full of waves and water as warm as soup. These days, I feel really reflective at the beach. All I want to do is sit by the water's edge and feel the current come in and out. There is something very soothing about sand being pushed and pulled all around you.

Mina spent a lot of time looking for shells and rocks. Some of the really beautiful ones were those that had been broken, tumbled, and rolled about in the current. The inner sparkle or iridescence began to show through. Seems to be a good analogy right now. Sometimes, you feel a bit broken and feel out of control with the current around you, but in the end, if you move with the current and not against it, your inner spirit will shine forth more beautifully than before.

I am acutely aware of how devastated everyone will feel, and I have been doing a lot more around the house to show that I care *before* I tell everyone. I had Hakan and his brother stop on the way home to get some fresh homemade yogurt and some fresh honey for his parents. I had thought to have them stop and have the car washed, but maybe that would have been a bit too much over the top. When we got home, I did a lot of work in the kitchen unloading and loading the dishwasher, setting the table, getting dinner ready, and so on, so that his mom could have more time with Mina. I also told her that I was going to help her organize her kitchen cabinet. It was a jumble of half-used bags of pasta, rice, flour, and such. I made a diagram and a list of everything on each shelf, and one day we will go to IKEA and get containers. I told her that it is a hard job for one person to do alone, so we will do it together before I leave. I cleaned out all the duplicate bags and organized it a bit, so it will be easier when we have the containers. I also got onto the website and printed off some things that she needed and stapled our packet together. She was appreciative because it is overwhelming, and she liked the way all my stuff (in Utah) was easy to find. His father was grateful because they get moths in that cabinet all the time.

It makes me feel good that I am helping, but I feel like I am "guilt" giving. I do not know how receptive to me they will be once all this is said and done.

Hakan asked me what my plans were this week, and I told him that I wanted to go to the fabric store with Canan and Mina, but other than that, I have nothing planned. How can I explain that he and his family may not be up for doing things over the weekend?

August 17, 2010

I feel like I am starting to hyperventilate. I am trying to go with the flow, but dealing with Canan and her idea of plans is like going against the tide. She wants to do all *her* shopping for us this week because she will get extra points on her credit card, so that is why we are going to the bazaar on Thursday to get Mina's necklace. I really need to get this fabric errand done while Emre is here and before Hakan begins his conference. She keeps wanting to push it to Monday morning, and I keep pulling it back to Friday morning. We have so far settled on Friday afternoon after Mina's nap. Then she said we could do it Saturday. I keep telling her that I want to get all this running around done this week so I can concentrate on packing next week. If this doesn't materialize, then I need to come up with a different plan.

It doesn't help that my frustration level goes up when everyone seems to disregard Mina's meals. They just continue to play no matter where we are and don't think of feeding her. So whoever's house we are at, I end up in the kitchen searching for something to make for Mina because I do not know how long we will be there. It is 7:00 p.m., and she is just sitting and eating now. I have let go of most of my parental controls.

August 18, 2010

It is just about the last week, and tomorrow is the day. This week, we have gotten the kebab dinner out of the way, had a lovely family dinner at Canan's house, and will go out with Hakan's friends tonight. Telling him tomorrow will not ruin anyone's dinner plans. For that I am glad. Yes, as usual, I am thinking of other people. Do I need to? No, but I do.

Yesterday was an interesting day. We went to the private army beach with Hakan's Aunt Neslihan (his mother's younger sister). Nesli is different from the rest of the family, more like my family. She likes to see us but has her own life. She has a big Caravan trailer that she and her long-term boyfriend travel all around in. She, Hakan, and I sat and had a cup of Turkish coffee and began to talk about dreams (the sleeping kind).

She has a bit of a raspy laugh from smoking all those strong cigarettes. As she lit up again, she laughed, and the smoke billowed out of her mouth, moving over the sea. "Dreams? I try not to think of them; they usually foretell something bad."

We sat and compared dreams for a while, and then Hakan got up to go back to the beach.

"Um . . . Nesli, can I tell you about the dream I had in December? I remember trying to put on my engagement ring, and the diamond fell out of the setting, and I was left with two broken pieces that didn't fit together anymore. In my dream, I took the empty engagement ring setting, diamond, and wedding band to the original jeweler who made them ten years ago. He melted the wedding band down to make a bezel for the diamond, making it into a necklace, and put a ruby in the engagement ring setting."

She looked at me with a knowing look and said, "You don't think 'it' is fixable?"

Thus began our three-hour conversation about the last ten years of my life.

"Oh, you children! Why didn't you come to me years ago before it all went to hell? I just sat down with Hakan last week and told him that he has been silly, living his life in a dream world and living to please his parents! He has been living in the USA for over fifteen years and thinks he can assimilate back here in Turkey? That's crazy! He is more American now than Turk! You children! The life he dreams about is just that—a dream in his head, not based in reality."

As she spoke, the ash of her cigarette grew longer and longer. She recounted her conversation with Hakan, and it eerily echoed, almost verbatim, what I had been telling him for years. Waiting for the ash to fall just increased the anxiousness I felt during our conversation. It reminded me of when I was child following around my Turkish grandmother with an ashtray so that her long cigarette ash wouldn't sprinkle all over the meal she was cooking!

Mostly Nesli talked, and I listened. It seemed that she needed an ear to air her frustration with him, her own sister, and the way she and Hakan's father had monopolized our young lives.

Lighting up another cigarette and ordering two more coffees, she flung her short bleached-blonde hair back and continued. "I have sat my sister down so many times and said that they are suffocating a young marriage by always visiting Utah for so long, making you visit us here in Turkey for so long. What do you do when you come here? Nothing! You have tea at one aunt's house, then move on to coffee at another's. What kind of life is that for a young couple? That is for old people! You are young and should be able to get out and travel, not sit and hold your mom's hand because she missed you!

"Sometimes, I want to kidnap my sister and take her to a therapist! She needs help! Her whole life is wrapped about Hakan and Mina. She doesn't do anything except spend all day waiting to do Ojo with you and Mina for *hours*! You sit there in front of this . . . mechanical . . . thing . . . for the whole day. Of course your family life is a mess with Hakan because you have never been allowed to have time to get to know each other as a family! You are guilted into spending your weekend entertaining old people! It's not right, I say!"

She stopped for a moment to take a breath, looked me in the eye, and said, "Seriously, do you think this is a modern way of thinking? No!"

Then we started talking about me. I told her a lot of things about which she had no idea. She wished that I had come to her with all of this earlier. She listened to what I had to say, and I even told her that I had written Hakan and his parents letters informing them of my decision. She personally didn't think it was a good idea to tell everyone here. She said to give it another six months because she sees a healthier Hakan this year; she said that I should give it more time.

Today, Canan will pick me up, and we will be going back to the Covered Bazaar to pick up Mina's necklace. She has been very controlled about asking how things are. She has not once asked how the situation is between Hakan and me. It must be killing her not to ask.

My latest plan is to give the letters in person while Mina sleeps tomorrow. When Mina wakes up, we will go with Canan to get fabric, and I will suggest that Mina and I spend the night there so that he and his parents can grieve openly without having to worry about Mina seeing them.

The main problem I foresee is that they will think I am being irresponsible because I do not have a concrete work plan. Child support and alimony are very low here, so they will be coming from that frame of mind. I told Nesli that I had gone online and calculated numbers. We would be okay with the calculated amount. It is frustrating for them when I say that I am not worried and things will turn out well.

August 19, 2010

Shit! I have to do this today! The plan that I intentionally wanted has worked out, but now I am rethinking how to tell, yet again. Originally, I had wanted to leave the letters and leave with Canan to go to the fabric store. Now I am not so sure that is the best way to handle it. I have to suck it up and give them in person. Last night, Hakan and I went out to dinner with his oldest friend, Tugrul, and his wife, Arzum. I had thoughts of asking him to go somewhere for a drink after leaving them, but it was 11:30 p.m. by the time dinner was over, and I was tired (and a bit drunk from wine).

Today, while Mina is napping, I will take Hakan to a separate room and ask him to read the letter. Then I will take his mom to the living room and give her *her* letter. We can talk while Mina is sleeping, and I can ask them if it would be easier for them to grieve if we were not there for a little while. Hakan already has plans made for a boys' night with Tugrul, so he is all set. I will either stay here or go to Canan's house, depending on the reaction.

Tomorrow morning, we will meet my friend Gorkem for breakfast. He is the closest thing I have to a brother, and it will be good to see a smiling face. He is willing to come and pick me up if Hakan decides not to come to breakfast.

All this is making me a bit sick. I woke up this morning feeling icky! I have been coughing all morning, and my head feels like a truck is thundering through it.

I guess it's time to push that button, rip my life to pieces, and try to fit them together in a new way.

Before coming to Turkey, I wrote a letter to Hakan telling him that I did not want to be married to him anymore. Today was my self-imposed deadline to give it, and I did.

He read the letter, and we went outside and talked for about three hours. We had a very calm conversation and talked about a lot of things. I told him that I was very tired and needed to live again. These years have been hard, and I just want to be free. He took it pretty well, but the majority of the conversation circled around how much he has changed and how much he wants to change. I told him that I cared for him but was not in love with him anymore, that I appreciated all the work he has done to get healthy, and that I was proud of him. I had noticed all the tokens of affection and notes and appreciated the thought, but I felt that I should *feel* something from them that I do not.

He admitted many things:

1. His attachment to his family has greatly impacted our relationship, and he told his family so. He realized that he had always made decisions based on his mother's approval.
2. He learned only to be afraid of life from his father.
3. He realized that I would never be happy in Turkey.
4. He realized that he does not need to be perfect or have a picture-perfect life in order to be happy.
5. He realizes and sees how much words can hurt someone and stay long after the moment passes.
6. He realized that we stay too long with his family for visits and that their long visits are draining on me.

I am sure there is more, but at the moment I cannot remember. He has gone to a psychiatrist here twice and realizes that the therapist back in Salt Lake City is not as helpful as a real psychiatrist. He admitted that his pleas about suicide were just a call for attention.

"Please don't do this!" he said. "Please don't! You are not giving the new Hakan a chance. This feels rushed to me. Give me some more time to grow!"

"I have waited years and finally feel strong enough to do this. I just can't wait anymore. I told you in December 2009 that I was taking a year to get healthy, go to a therapist, and see how this relationship fares over the year. I began therapy in January. I can't help it if you started therapy a bit later in May. I realize I am further along in the process and have waited to see a serious change between us, but you chose not to go to therapy or take me seriously."

We were sitting in the kids' park on a bench, silently watching kids play in the playground.

"So who have you been talking to about this? More divorced friends? I think that you are being controlled and influenced too much by friends and family to get this done quickly."

"If I had listened to friends and family, this would have ended years ago. I am tired of trying and just want to start fresh and live again. I am finally not afraid of the fallout. Things will work themselves out. If I get bogged down with money and numbers and figures, then the money becomes more important than *me*. I do feel selfish thinking of just myself, but I needed to this time. To you, it must seem insensitive of me to keep to my decision after seeing how much you have changed. But I want to be free to be who I am inside. I am tired of hiding who I am inherently because of what you might say or the exasperated look you might give."

"Well, I went to a psychiatrist here in Istanbul twice, and she says that your close relationship with Mina is abnormal, that your adherence to each other has adversely affected our marriage."

I have to say, at that point, I got seriously defensive and was livid! "Did you give her any background or history as to why I was sleeping on the floor with Mina—because you kicked me out of the bedroom? Did you tell her that you wouldn't watch Mina at all unless I could guarantee that she would sleep the entire time I went shopping? Did you tell her that you are too tired when you come home from work to hold your child while I get dinner ready, and I have to wear her on my back in a sling in order to get all the work done? I never intended to take on sole role of raising Mina, but where was my help? You were not around, so I had to do everything. What exactly *did* you tell her?"

He had nothing to say to that and looked down at his feet.

"Please, give it a few more months. I see now the importance of us all being happy and that maybe we will not be together. First, happiness is important; second, staying together."

"I don't know how to answer you because I just don't feel the inclination to try anymore. I chose to tell you over here where you had more support. I didn't want you to feel alone."

"It must have been a difficult decision for you to tell me over here, and I greatly appreciate the thought, and you should not have had to put yourself in that position."

But I didn't know how he was going to react, so I thought I would have many safety nets around for him. I do not love him.

It's hard to stand my ground when someone has just woken up to his life, a bit too late. I feel like I am being harsh, but I am trying to be honest with myself and with him. He said that if we decided to do this, he would not make the process difficult. I am sure this is not the last of the conversations we will have.

He left to go out with his friend today, and I am going to rest. My throat hurts, and I am tired. I will take a Benedryl and go to bed with Mina probably.

That's about it, I guess.

AUGUST 23, 2010

I have been quiet for a few days because I have been getting over a cold. This whole thing has taken a lot out of me, and I just seemed to crash. Today, I feel much better. My cold is passing, and I am into the last week of the trip.

While we are here, we have had a lot to Turkish coffee. I keep turning my cup over and making a wish. Hakan's grandmother is really good at "reading the fortune." I have been curious as to how much my mood affects her readings. Interestingly enough, she is pretty accurate. Last week, before my talk with Hakan, she saw me face-to-face with someone "emptying myself out" in conversation. She saw that there was some uneasiness sitting inside me. That day, I gave Hakan the letter. Today, after the coffee, she looked up in surprise and said that I had "cleared" myself and had such a beautiful cup. My road went straight and then curved up, supported by three friends. Gee, I wonder who *they* could be?

I have written to my parents and told them everything, and they are on one level pleased that I have made a decision, but still they are traveling down the middle of the road. They do not want to influence me one way or the other. Hakan professes great change and a return to a more happier time and so on and so on. It is sort of anticlimactic for me. For years, I have been saying, you live in the future; you have never made Mina and me your family; your Turkish family means more; you value your mom's feelings over mine. He is now saying that I was right about everything.

It seems that most would see Hakan's behavior change as almost miraculous, and *wow*, I should give this another chance. I have really been sitting with this for a few days right now. There is no other way to describe how I feel except to say that it doesn't feel right to stay together. I wrote to my Reiki teacher, and she asked me how I felt in my tummy. Basically, what does your gut tell you? My gut tells me that *this* is the right time to do this, for everyone—me, Hakan, and most importantly, Mina.

He keeps pushing his case each chance he gets, and I let him talk, but I don't give any answers. For once in my life, I do not feel scared. That makes me feel strongly that this is the right decision for me, even if maybe not for someone else.

He asked me not to close the door to a future together. I replied, I am not closing a door, but choosing to go through a different one. He is in a state of denial at this point. He even suggested the other day that I should get my belly button re-pierced and that he and I should get matching tattoos. I just kind of stared at him. He said that I had always wanted another tattoo. Yes, that is true, but I don't go looking for a tattoo design; it finds me. Until then, I will wait.

It is hard to see someone wake up and see things. He is seeing things for the first time and is shocked. He looks at his parents and how they fight and bicker all the time. He finally sees how unhealthy that is for a child. He does not want to live a life like that. He would rather be apart and all of us happy than keep us together only to end up like them.

We are at Canan's house today. Canan worked overtime this weekend and finished the entire baby doll carrier, blanket, pillow, and cushion. Today we have been sewing the baby doll nightgown and hat with a matching set for Mina. Tomorrow, we are off to IKEA for the kitchen organizing project. Less than one week left at this point.

August 24, 2010

Well, yesterday was interesting. Hakan's father and I had a pretty heated argument. I was so upset that I felt like my whole body was trembling or convulsing. I tried to pick up my teacup and saucer, but because of my shaking, the teacup bounced sideways onto the saucer, spilling my tea all over the floor. I ran to my room, sat on my bed, and had a good cry. Tensions are high here as we get down to the last few days. Hakan's father was playing with Mina, and then Mina decided she didn't want to play anymore. His answer: "Well, I am never coming to play next time then!" It is a Turkish way of joking, and it is not okay with me.

Every time a child does not do what an adult wants, they make this kind of joke that makes the child feel guilty that she made the adult feel bad. Hakan does this, and she gets upset. When we were away at Kiyikoy, a waiter said something like this and got her upset. I asked his father to please not say phrases like that anymore. They make Mina upset, and I do not want her to get used to that verbiage. I wasn't mad or upset; I just asked quietly. He got all defensive and asked why I am always exploding at him. One thing led to another, and he started taking it to the extreme, saying that I go overboard with how much I think about Mina. Do I know more about parenting than he does? Do I think I know everything about being a parent? My pressure point rose, and I said that I have not gone overboard this year—in fact, the opposite. I said that I have *not* tried to control *anything* this year—nothing! I just asked him to not joke about withholding his love and attention if Mina chooses not to do something that he wants to do. It makes her feel bad, that's all.

After a good cry, I took a shower and washed it down the drain. We were off to IKEA to get containers for Hakan's mom's kitchen cupboard. The rest of the day went pretty normally, and I napped with Mina for a while. We took the Metro to my cousin Esra's house. Her son Kaan is just one year older than Mina. They played, and we talked. It is always good to see her because somehow we always end up laughing. When we were little and didn't understand each other, all we did was jump on the bed and laugh. We couldn't look at each other and not start giggling. We are still the same way. We talked about how most of the women in our family are divorced or in the process of divorcing. We joked that maybe it was inherited. My great-grandmother was married and divorced five times, and about 90 percent of the women who descended from her are divorced. Maybe this family fosters strong women who feel that they can have a good life with or without a man. Who knows? My grandmother stayed married, but they lived separate lives. My Aunt Binnaz is still married, but that is it. Ekin, Esra, Zerrin, Eser (Esra's sister), and now me—all are divorced or considering it.

After this, I am off to the kitchen. I am going to get out some energy by attacking some kitchen cabinets!

August 28, 2010

It has been a long few days, but we have only a short time left. This week drained me more than the previous four weeks. It was a full roller coaster, and I am feeling a bit wiped out. Thursday was another difficult day around here. His parents got Mina another two Barbies. I just got pissed and walked out of the toy store. I didn't say anything; I didn't say no. I just gave up and walked out. Every time I turn around, there is a new toy, a new gift, something. At this point, Mina had received 5 barbie dolls in a 5 week span of time. It is a bit excessive, in my opinion. They are completely unable to say no to a child. Everyone knew I was pissed, and I took a nap with Mina to calm down. Later, we went out to see the Galata Tower again, and Aunt Canan came with us. I have not been feeling particularly nice these days. She mentioned that Mina will straighten out in a few days after getting back. She believes this. I looked at her and said that was easy for her to say since she won't have to do the "straightening" out. I told her that everyone here just does what they want, gives what they want, without thinking of the effects it will have and/or whether Hakan and I will approve. They just do it anyway and turn a blind eye when I am being kicked, hit, and screamed at from the other room by Monster Mina, who doesn't want to stop playing. They think I am punishing her when I just sit on the floor and let her have her fit. This started *here*. Forty-five minutes later, she calms down and says she is ready for bed. She has actually bared her teeth at me and kicked me with both feet in the chest because she couldn't read another book with her grandmother (when it is 9:00 p.m.).

Canan just smiled at me and said, "Don't worry, don't worry, it will all fix itself. I truly believe this. What's the big deal? It's for a few weeks, and then you go away."

"You know, for years, I have always thought of your family and how they will be affected by X or Y. No one seems to think of my side, and maybe I won't think so much of this family's feelings anymore because it doesn't seem to make a bit of difference. There is no respect for me as Mina's mother. I get it now. I guess I have been hoping that people can change."

Friday, Hakan made a reservation for him, Mina, and me to stay on one of the Big Islands off the coast of Istanbul (Buyuk Ada). I knew that Mina would like it, and I knew it meant a lot to him. We had a nice day, and we talked a lot on the balcony after Mina went to sleep. It is hard for me to see someone hurting. I think it is finally settling in that this is probably not going to turn out the way he had hoped. He keeps saying that he has changed, and I see it, I do, but I still don't feel anything. I keep telling him that. I have refused his advances because it just doesn't feel right. I feel like I am lying to him if I reciprocate or indulge him. He doesn't know how he will survive being alone in Salt Lake City. He thinks that my walls can crumble just like that, with a little spark, if I let them, and our love will be like those in the movies: coming to the brink and back again stronger.

The three of us shared a bed last night, and it really affected him. It is the first and probably the last time he will sleep next to Mina. It was hard for me too. Is it better to have a memory to hold onto, or is it better not to know what it was like? He missed that part of her life. He has missed parts of my life, and it seems like he is waking up after a hundred-year sleep. In the morning, Mina found it funny that he wanted to cuddle with me because she has never seen that before. He held me and just didn't want to let me go because, I think, a part of him knew it was not going to be like this again. It makes me feel horrible to know that he is just holding on, memorizing, breathing everything of us in. It almost makes me want to give in, but I can't. I have come too far through the other door. He was crying on the balcony just before we left. Mina told his parents when we got back that Hakan was crying and crying, and they just knew.

He keeps pleading with me to give it a few more years and saying I could love the new Hakan. He is sorry that he hasn't grown up sooner. He realizes that he left me alone with his and his parents' problems because he wasn't grown-up enough to deal with them. He said that I went to the wrong people for help. How can I know to go to anyone else other than his parents? I did what I thought I could, and I can't give anymore. I just don't want to. On the other hand, I feel horrible, horrible, horrible when I cannot return a hug to someone. I know how it feels on the other side because I was there in his position for years. Now I am doing it to him. I will make it through, I know, but it is really making me ill, physically, to hurt someone this way.

TWO

OXYGEN MASK

*Should the cabin lose pressure, oxygen masks will drop from
the overhead area. Please place bag over your own mouth and
nose before assisting children.*

SEPTEMBER 7, 2010

It has been more than a week since I have had the energy to sit and write. Jet lag, tantrums, house stuff, and school shopping have tapped my motivation. The weather has cooled, and we had a great day, so here we are again.

I feel good and secure about who I am and where I am going, and I haven't felt that way in a long time. I have been doing things that I want to do and not feeling guilty about it. I left Mina to play with Hakan all afternoon this weekend and went outside to work in the garden. She was very clingy and wouldn't let him rest, and he had to endure (like all of us do) and play with his child until I was done. I have let her scream for over an hour while he has been sleeping and while he has been awake. I am not sugarcoating anything anymore with regard to her behavior and how this change happened. I have actually left her screaming in the house with him while I've made myself a cup of tea and sat on the steps.

I have called the lawyer and left a message for her to call me. I think he still believes that things are changeable. He keeps talking about babysitters and going to movies and out on the town. I am not in that dream anymore. I am working on new ones.

I have been able to have long talks with friends and parents, and I am finding a lot of support, which is helpful. My father keeps telling me to not start the "divorce process" until after I have gone to and come back from Rhode Island in October, and we have had an opportunity to chat. I can't wait that long. I feel like I made the decision a long time ago and have waited enough. I want this begun to move through it. I want to start the New Year fresh. I want a new year and a new beginning. It just seems right to me.

I feel like I keep saying that phrase over and over when I talk to people: it just feels *right* in my gut to do this now. I finally understand, and it took a long time, that I do not need to explain "why" anymore to anyone.

I had a therapy appointment scheduled for last Thursday, and I postponed it for a few reasons. Mina had been having a lot of tantrums, and I didn't want to leave her with just anyone for the first time. Amy and her daughter, Audrey, wanted to go play in the park, and I thought that was a more centered way to spend that particular Thursday afternoon.

I feel good about Mina starting preschool tomorrow. I think she will adapt more quickly than people think. We went on an adventure today with the bus. We took the bus from the dentist's office all the way to Barnes & Noble in Sugarhouse. We had a lovely time and stayed for story-time, and she made new friends. I brought her up, left her by the trains, and went to sit down way on the other side of the room, and she never once looked up for me or asked for me. She problem-solved with her new friend and played cooperatively. It was a pleasant two hours. I think this will be our new program for Tuesdays: yoga play, then story-time at Barnes.

I am thinking of the future and making long-term, fun plans. Mina and I sat in the backyard around twilight the other day and watched the quails fly down from the neighbor's garage to our tree and bed down for the night. We discussed how to develop the area behind the garage: a slide set or chickens. We have decided to clean out the area and put in chickens over the next couple of years. She thought it was a wonderful idea to be able to walk through her pink picket fence into a chicken coop.

I am also trying to put together an old-fashioned Halloween fall festival for our block. Everyone I have spoken to thinks it is a great idea and has gotten on board. I want to make it into an annual tradition. I am trying to bring back into my life the things that bring me joy and happiness. If I can't find it, I will make it.

As for Hakan, I do not feel so bad that he will be alone. He has a huge Turkish group around him and has become really good friends with one of them, Seyhan. I saw them joking around together the other day, and I knew that Seyhan would take care of Hakan.

I think Hakan would like a little more affection, but I just cannot give it to him. Again, I refer back to a movie, this time *Pretty Woman*. Richard Gere wants to kiss Julia Roberts, a *real* kiss. She says no because that is too personal. That is kind of where I am now. A peck on the lips is about all I have to give him; anything more is too much.

As we exited the plane last week, Mina was so tired and just wanted to go home. She held on tight to my hand. Hakan wanted to hold her other hand, and she refused. To me he said, "Well, if you held my hand as an example, she would do it too."

All I could do was shrug my shoulders. We still do not talk much and still watch TV in silence, and then I go to bed, so what has really changed?

SEPTEMBER 17, 2010

It seems that I get a chance only once a week these days to write. I don't know how to start. Starting school and getting into a routine has been difficult and overwhelming at times. In conjunction with that, I have realized that my mother-in-law has not really changed, and that has been disappointing to me. Last weekend, we spoke on the Ojo. Mina had asked to have her Cinderella Barbie sent from Turkey and did not understand that the mail does not come immediately. Mina went to lie down and think about that, and my mother-in-law said, "If only you had taken it when you left."

"Mom, I asked Mina multiple times what toys she was going to bring back, and she kept refusing me, saying, 'Mama, I have a little Cinderella at home. That's enough for me. If I brought these Barbies back to Utah, that would be kind of excessive, wouldn't it, Mama?' Hakan asked Mina, and she said the same thing."

Bristling with irritation, she replied, "Well, it is because Mina is afraid of you. She is afraid to go against your word—that is why she didn't want to take them."

I was so furious that I was shaking. Hakan had just woken up and was in Mina's room. I walked in and told him that his mom and I had exchanged words, and I had left her alone at the Ojo. I was done. I told him that she was insulting. I didn't need to call and get insulted in my own house. He agreed, and he went and shut off the Ojo. I couldn't even pour the cream in his coffee—my hands were still shaking.

I have decided that I will be polite and cordial, and that is about it. I will not call unless Mina wants it. I do not need to put myself in an uncomfortable situation anymore. Hakan said in Turkey that he would handle all the family problems now, so I do not feel obliged to smooth out waters. That's his job now. It is not an easy one, and he needs to deal with it.

Having seen all this, Mina has been unwilling to speak to them on the Ojo at all since then. Hakan has been upset about that, but he has not said anything because he knows how it started. His tension and sadness have been pushing Mina away because she does not want to be around him when he is like that. It just comes out in everything. While he reads a book, he is always commenting, "Where are all the fathers in these books? What? No father in this one either!" They keep battling back and forth about whether or not Mina will have a baby named Olivia. Mina is convinced that she has a baby in her tummy named Olivia, and we talk about her. He keeps telling her that there is no baby in her tummy and that she should not be preoccupied with having a baby. I keep telling him that the more he argues with Mina about this, the more she is going to do it. Who cares if she thinks she has a baby in her tummy? She is not planning her life around the baby. She has told me that she will go to school to be a doctor, have the baby, and leave her either with me or at day care. She is not modeling me. She just gets so hurt that he doesn't believe her. All I tell her is to listen to her heart. She has to be as big as me before Olivia can come out.

This week went well at preschool. She went in on her own with no problems. I left her at the curb, and her teacher showed her how to go in on her own. I felt pretty victorious. I had been saying all along that she would stay with anyone and anywhere as long as she felt comfortable. It is not that she needs to cling to me. That really became apparent yesterday. I had to go to a city council meeting about the open land space at the end of our street. Hakan came home, and Mina was going to stay with him but then would not. She started crying, holding me, refusing to let go, and telling me not to leave her here. Hakan actually said, "I don't get it—you will stay at school alone, no problem, but you won't stay with me?"

I feel like I haven't been to therapy in ages. When I rescheduled a few weeks ago, the fourth person I talked to forgot to mention that my appointment on September 13 would be somewhere else. So when Mina and I walked down there last Monday with the stroller, I got a bit of a surprise. The idea was to put Mina to sleep in the stroller and wheel her into the office. I figured she would sleep through half of it, and during the other half, she could talk to the therapist as well and start to feel comfortable with her. That way, later on when she was feeling confused, she would feel comfortable talking to the therapist about her feelings. However, when I actually *got* to the appointment, the receptionist informed me that the appointment was at another location. Frustrated, I had to cancel my session because there would be no way I could walk to the other location, way up on the University's campus. I had an appointment scheduled for this coming Thursday, but I had to change it because I couldn't find anyone to watch Mina at that time. Now that Mina is in school, I can schedule during those times.

This morning, I am headed to see the lawyer, hopefully. Hakan mentioned that he does not have a ride back from his meeting around 9:30 a.m. Figures—the same time as my lawyer appointment. I am going to head down on the pretense that he will find a ride. Really, the office is a five-minute drive from the meeting. *Someone* should be able to drop him off.

We are headed to Zion for a wedding this weekend, and I am ambivalent about going. I am feeling so overwhelmed here at home with so many things to do that driving all that way for such a short time makes me crazy. I am trying to breathe. I tell myself that Mina and I will go on an adventure and collect some nice leaves and twigs. Daisy will be there, so that will be nice.

SEPTEMBER 24, 2010

My weekly checking in with myself has begun!

I met with the lawyer last week, and I really like her. She is really down-to-earth and just plain ol' nice. She got my binder, found the biography helpful, and looked at the tax returns. We were able to get down to business.

She told me that as far as numbers go, child support is pretty cut-and-dry. You punch in numbers and get a figure. My figure is about $987/month, more than I had estimated—good.

She asked me if I was thinking about relocating back to Rhode Island. I was a bit confused and asked for clarification. "Before I file?" I asked.

Yes, she said, because if I moved back to Rhode Island—where I was married—and lived there for a certain amount of time before filing, then I would receive three times as much child support: approximately $2,700/month. As tempting as that is, I think that it would not be the healthiest thing to do for Mina: drag her out of school where she is comfortable, stay for a time, and then come home to World War III. I need to think strategically, not completely financially. If I am to get what I want from Hakan, then I need to walk this line very carefully. The whole situation would be very antagonistic and pretty difficult for Mina. I think it would add more stress and chaos to her life. I would not be getting more money total (between alimony and child support). It would just be allocated differently. I need to think of Mina's mental and overall well-being rather than the money.

As far as alimony, she said it is a crapshoot. It all depends on the judge. Some judges look back years at what you made and use that number to figure out alimony. I haven't worked full-time in about ten years. I have my master's in history, but no teaching certificate. She suggested that we "bulk" up front and ask for more money for a shorter amount of time, such as five years. After looking at the budget, she said that $2,600 was not an unreasonable amount to ask for. She also mentioned that we would easily be able to take over the house and the car.

The most difficult aspect is the relationship between father and daughter. She mentioned a counselor who would sit in the room with Hakan and Mina to try to get to the root of the problems. She explained the custody differences. Basically, it comes down to sole custody (me) or joint legal custody. She said that joint legal is really a formality. I would have to talk to him about schools, doctors, and other such important stuff and ask his opinion. However, I would be the deciding vote. If I did not agree with his answer, I could veto it and do what I want anyway. Holidays and visitation seem pretty straightforward. Summer is the tricky thing. Each parent can have up to four weeks' vacation time with the child. This is going to be the trickiest aspect of the whole thing, I think.

We went through the process, and if Hakan doesn't contest anything, the whole process—beginning to end—will last a month. I was surprised. Most things I had read online and what I had heard from others indicated that there would be a waiting time of about three months before everything was finalized. I felt so much more relaxed about the whole thing. Hakan had asked that I give "us" a couple of months to try before starting the process. Now I feel that I can give him that peace of mind and be able to work along my time-line as well. I can meet with the lawyer after coming back from Rhode Island and begin the divorce proceedings in November.

The relationship between Mina and Hakan is like a river—it ebbs and flows in different directions day by day. He takes great enjoyment from bugging her and pissing her off. I keep telling him to stop aggravating her, but he just says, "It's fun. I am an engineer. I like to take things to the nth degree." Yeah, but this is your daughter, and you are alienating her! And you wonder why she doesn't want to kiss you goodnight?

As he left for work today, he asked for a kiss, and she just ignored him. He seems to be feeling pushed aside, him and his family. He asked Mina if she will call her grandparents on the Ojo when they come back from vacation, and she said no. His mom and her mouth really messed up the equilibrium around here.

On a completely different note, the vegan dinner I made last week and froze for a Starbucks friend was met with rave reviews. All want to know when I am opening my own place. Linda, the Starbucks friend, and I were talking the other day on the phone, and she told me how all her guests have called her on different occasions to say how wonderful the food was. They all seem to remember my food from the Tea Grotto. Linda actually remembers seeing Mina and me walking to and from work in the mornings. We must have been a sight to see walking down the street: a little baby bundled up in multiple blankets in her stroller, grocery bags hanging off the handles and bulging from underneath, and me, maneuvering through snowbanks at 6:00 a.m.

I need to talk to Linda again about the subject of cooking. Maybe I don't have to find my own kitchen. Maybe the key is to cook in *others'* kitchens as a part-time personal chef. Linda's friends, who could be possible clients, are all vegan or vegetarian. I think I will bounce this idea off Linda. She likes good food but doesn't like to cook. Maybe I could go cook food for her in her own kitchen once a week for a few hours while Mina is at school. If I could get just a few people, that would be just the extra money I would need. I've checked into the personal chef business before, and the average hourly rate is about $25 per hour. If I cooked just ten hours a week, that would be $250/week. Anyway, it is a thought. I could prepare salads for them, get stuff ready to just put in the oven, make and freeze stuff, do whatever they need. It would be a way to make good food for people who appreciate it and not be a slave to a restaurant and its overhead.

I also was able to find a babysitter. She was in front of me all the time: Rachel from the bookstore. Mina loves to play with her, and she lives around the corner. I have been so anti-babysitter lately because I was feeling pushed by Hakan to find one so that we could go out to the movies together. Because I am really beyond the point of wanting to go out alone, I was really resistant to the concept. However, that is really silly in the long run because I will actually *need* someone to help me watch Mina when he is not around. Today, as we were leaving the bookstore, I asked Rachel if she babysat, and she does. I told her I would touch base with her next week about her schedule.

September 30, 2010

I am feeling kind of bullied today. I called Mom to add a few things to Mina's Rhode Island food list, and she told me that Hakan's uncle Mehmet (his mom's brother) and aunt had called my aunt and asked for a sit down "to discuss the children." One, I am not a child, and two, can't anyone in that family stop pushing their will on me and mine? Mehmet's wife, Guven, was once my aunt's student way back when. She was upset when she heard about our marital problems and called my aunt. My aunt called my father and asked what to do. My father had a conversation with her in which he strongly expressed that Hakan had never considered Mina and me his family, and that was one of the main roots of the problem. He told her that she better support me and Mina in the discussion, and from what I gather, she did.

I really feel like I am divorcing a village. Everyone has to have their say as to why I still need to put up with this for the sake of the "family." All I can do is just sit and sigh. I understand they are trying to hold onto this as much as they can, but can't they see that they are having a reverse effect and pushing me farther and farther away from them?

His parents are back from their time-share vacation, and I am curious as to how the weekend is going to play out. Mina took very little interest in talking with Aunt Canan this week and wanted to say goodbye after ten minutes. Canan was shocked and kept trying to push for more time, but little Mina just crossed her arms in front of her and turned her head away.

On a more pleasant note, I was able to have that chat with Linda about my part-time personal chef idea, and she thought it was marvelous. She thought the price was right, and she is going to pitch it to her friends. If I slowly book my mornings, I could make about $1,600/month. That would be a nice addition to alimony. I could work on Etsy stuff at home in the afternoons while Mina plays and cook in the mornings. I wrote about my idea on my 29 Gifts blog, and one lady gave me a good idea: cooking classes in the home. When I get to Rhode Island, I will sit down with my father and see if he can make me a website and format a client information sheet.

Even after writing all of this about his aunt and uncle, I still feel irritated. I was hoping to purge and feel better, but I can't seem to get it out of my head. It just makes me so grumpy.

OCTOBER 4, 2010

The circular image keeps making its appearance to me in a variety of ways these days. The words "full circle," "whole," and "cyclical" seem to drift in and out of my head. We had dinner at Ross and Kerry's house on Saturday night. They were our first friends when we moved here ten years ago. Hakan works with Ross, and their research has gone in different directions over the past few years. Ross decided to have a lot of people from work over for a barbeque. It was kind of strange for me to be there. I hadn't been in their house for almost three years. Mina hadn't started walking yet the last time we were there. We had all drifted apart after Mina due to baby stuff and also hip problems. Both Kerry and I developed hip problems and left climbing for awhile.

It was almost surreal to be at their house at the end of my relationship with Hakan. It felt kind of like closure in a weird and unexpected way. The end of the night brought big hugs from Ross and Kerry, and it seemed that they were really glad to see me and kind of sorry that they had let so much time pass between visits.

This morning, as I was driving to Jiffy Lube, I noticed that our old condo was up for rent again. How strange it would be to be back there again. Would Hakan return to something familiar or find something new? It was all too strange to think about.

This weekend was harvest time around here. The garden's life cycle is coming to a close, and I spent my time picking green beans, sunflowers, onions, and such. It makes me feel alive to be part of nature in this way. To see something start so small, like the tomato seed, and watch it grow makes me feel hopeful for the future. *Look how far that little seed has come in such a short time!* I tell myself, and then I feel like my ideas may not be so small anymore. Anything can grow with enough love and attention. But if you neglect yourself, or your garden, the weeds flourish and make you feel all itchy and twisty inside.

I was right when I told Hakan last December that I didn't know who I would be in a year. I am pretty proud of who I am and how far I have grown!

I finally got to the therapist today, and she said that she really respects me and told me that she respected the way I have tried to take the high road and do the most ethical thing in a tense situation. She said even though she knew I would be okay over in Turkey, she still feared the explosive potential. She admires the way that I keep forging ahead, opening doors, facing what's behind them, and moving past them. There just seems to be an unending set of doors, and sometimes that seems so daunting.

We talked about the aftermath and Mina. How do I help her through this? There is a place downtown, she said, that deals specifically with child play therapy, and they do a wonderful job. That's a comfort. All my ducks seem to be lining up, and I am ready for a rest in Rhode Island. Then, once we come back, I have to tell him—again—that I want a divorce. Will it be easier or harder the second time around?

OCTOBER 18, 2010

What a lovely morning: it's Mina's birthday! Our trip here is just about over, and it has been very restful. I tried not to do too much and canceled plans at times too.

The wedding I went to at the beginning of the trip was full of emotions for me. It was hard to go to a wedding, a beginning, when I am at the end, but it gave me hope for the future. Dee and Michael found each other again after twenty-five years. That is pretty amazing. The universe provides what you need at the time that is best if you are open to it. While I was at the wedding, I saw another friend—Sherri. She is another American married to a Turk, like me. They have been together for a long time, maybe a bit longer than Hakan and I. Cuneyt, over the years, started to drink more and get more verbally abusive. Sherri believes that her multiple sclerosis has developed from the stress of living with him. After two years of counseling, she has filed for a divorce. They have an eight-year-old boy, Kaan. I asked Sherri how things are, and she said that things are great. Since Cuneyt went into counseling, he has had *his* epiphany and completely changed his behavior and habits. She said now he is an angel to communicate with, but inside, she feels nothing. It was so nice and comforting to find that she feels as I do. It is so validating when there is someone else in the same situation, feeling—or not feeling—the same things. People can change their lives going forward, but they can't change their past.

I have had my talks with my father as he earlier requested. He just wanted to make sure that I was taking my time making the decisions, that I was going into them with my eyes wide open, and so on. I think he also wanted to say, in his own way, "I told you so." He said that he told me a few years ago that if I mentioned the word "divorce," everyone would scramble to fix things, but that people have to live their own lives and say things in their own time. I told him everything that I planned and put into motion while I was in Turkey this year and made a point of saying that I chose not to tell my Aunt Binnaz of my plan because I didn't feel so supported.

After having dinner with Samantha the other night in Providence, I came away with the feeling that she is still tangling up my situation with her own situation with Dwayne. In many ways, she is still associating my behavior and reactions with Dwayne's, not overtly, but it is there. It was really frustrating at times to be talking and not be able to just talk without the situation being somehow turned back on me. If I brought up a certain issue that still frustrates or irritates me, she would point out that it takes two people to create this problem and that Hakan didn't create all of this on his own. At times I felt that she needed me to say or list all the ways I had participated in the demise of my marriage; she felt that I had not acknowledged my role in all of this. Her "reality check" was very pessimistic. I felt that she was trying to draw my attention to how hard it might be when everything starts: life will never settle down, there are so many bumps that I will have to go over, and money will always be an issue. Sometimes it seems as if her anger, frustration, and resentment get directed my way when it seems that my divorce and aftermath may be easier in some aspects than hers was. I do not think that I should feel guilty if mine goes better.

I remember when I first found out about my hip, I was a bit jealous and resentful that 99 percent of the women I knew had delivered their babies with no problems. Why had this happened to me? Once I released my condition as something bad and embraced it, the pain diminished, and I have been able to be pain free for over three years. I chose to use it to grow rather than wither. Then it hit me—maybe many of Samantha's issues are almost matters of self-sabotage. Holding onto such anger and resentment blocks all the good that is waiting to come to her. Good wants to come to her, but something always seems to get in the way. I always seem to describe her life to someone else as three steps forward, five steps back.

On top of this, my father decided to have another discussion with me—about Mina. He thinks I need to be *more* strict in enforcing the behavioral issues: more consequences, harsher cause and effect. I feel like a push-me, pull-me doll. On one extreme, I have Hakan's parents saying I am too strict and need to relax, and then I have my father on the other side. I told him that I am doing the best I can do in most situations and that it is difficult to enforce things when Hakan undermines them because he feels I am too harsh on Mina. Also, I am just calming Mina down from all the indulgence in Turkey.

OCTOBER 23, 2010

Back home and ready for round two: scarecrow-making birthday party.

It has been a tough week, with lots of ups and downs. Mina had a really difficult time leaving and finally gets it that after we leave, we can't hug Nana. It was especially hard for me because I also want to hug Nana when we're apart. Mina would start crying, and then I would start, and then Mom. We were a red-eyed blubbering mess for most of Monday. Mina felt safe there and comfortable. Then we come home, and she is thrown back into school, and there is another separation, from Mama.

Going back to school was a difficult adjustment for Mina, and I had to spend all Friday with her at school so she could relax and remember how much fun it was to be there.

On top of all that, I am running around grocery shopping, getting things ready for this morning's party, and all I get are exasperated looks from Hakan. He just doesn't understand why we have to have another party for Mina; he asks, isn't *that* indulging her too? He hasn't directly said that I am spending too much money to do another party. His deep sighs when he sees the supplies say enough to me. It's interesting the things that he does and does not view as indulgences and the behaviors he will and will not allow. Anything that will reflect positively on him, his family, or

Turkey is indulged. At dinner the other night when Mina was running around and not eating at the table, he asked whether she had been spoiled in Rhode Island I responded, "She sat at the table and ate with us every night, so I am surprised that it is not continuing here."

He got pretty defensive and retorted back, "Well, I guess she only gets spoiled in Turkey, is that it?"

I really did not intend to start anything; I was just stating a fact. He is having a hard time seeing how close Mina became with my parents and how comfortable she was in their house. If she had been this emotional leaving Turkey, he would have gloated. She was not emotional when we left Turkey, however—in fact, she got ready early, put her socks on, and told everyone, "Let's *go!*"

She would rather talk with my mom than play with him when he comes home from work, and that must be difficult for him. She has been pulling back from him and not wanting him to hug or kiss her, and that must hurt him.

Miss Mischa, her teacher, and I had a long discussion yesterday about how to help Mina, and together we came up with a plan. Mischa feels that Mina is so verbal and has so many feelings inside that need to be expressed that maybe she should start a journal. To that, I suggested a big spiral-bound drawing pad. Then she suggested writing Mina's thoughts on the back of drawings, gluing leaves and such from walks, and creating a wonderful life journal. I think starting this type of thing now will help during and after the divorce to get her through. I also want to get a set of "feelings" rubber stamps so she can stamp how she feels on the page when she needs to.

I have been thinking a lot about how to make money after this is all over. It looks like the bank will be lowering the mortgage to 4.5 percent, and that will save about $300 a month. I also was finally able to read my books on teaching Reiki book. Another workshop idea was presented: teaching children Reiki. The author said that little kids love to have hot magic hands, and they love to "makes things better." I think that would blend nicely with a lot of the other children's workshop ideas I have.

Another idea came in a dream. I had dreams two nights in a row about trading penny stocks. When I first received e-mails about penny stocks, I disregarded them. Now, I am not so sure. I think, after two nights of dreams, it is worth looking into. I got onto two websites this morning: E-Trade and TD Ameritrade. I am leaning toward E-Trade because it has a longer free trial period and lower rates for fewer trades. I think I will give myself six months to trade and see what happens.

I can't remember if I wrote in here that I signed up with an online publisher for this book. I am going to try to finish up this specific journal and get it published sometime this spring. At the same time, 29 Gifts has posted a link for self-publishers as well. I take that as a positive sign that things are moving in the right direction.

October 26, 2010

Mina and I worked in the garden this morning before the snow came in. I wanted to harvest some tomatoes before they froze and toss the plants. Mina is having a hard time letting go of her cherry tomato plant "child"—"But Mama, I put lots of love into that plant! Don't throw it away!"

I think I will be learning how to harvest tomato seeds soon. I think that it will make her happy to have the seeds of her special tomato plant. It's an interesting thing, collecting seeds. It is very meditative for me. The careful separating of the seed from the pulp, the knowledge that life can grow again and nourish if the small seed is handled with care. It's a nice allegory to life in general. Everyone should cherish their life like a little seed: small but full of promise. We are going to make up little seed packets for Christmas presents for others to love and cherish.

I feel like a little seed sometimes. It is as if I am currently in the fall season of my life: pulling up the roots of the old, but saving the life-spark for regrowth in the spring. At the moment, I am that tomato plant uprooting myself, taking time to learn how to save the special aspects to foster later on.

This morning, as I was giving Mina her gummy bear vitamins, she offered me half her share: "Mama, you take it and be healthy. Then you won't have to go to the therapist anymore." What a little love. It breaks your heart and fills it up at the same time. Poor little thing can feel something brewing, and it is affecting school. She is so afraid to be left alone without someone who loves her there. Miss Tad says that it is almost like Mina came back from Rhode Island with a broken heart.

I met with Gaia yesterday morning at Starbucks, and it was so good to see her. She always has such a steady arm for me to lean on. We revisited our tea project, and I asked her to upload the labels that we have been working on for the last two years to www.greenerprinter.com. I want to try to complete something, anything. I feel like as much as I am pulling myself together, there are just as many strands dangling: the children's tea line, the documentary, Etsy, and the latest, the part-time personal chef idea. So many ideas, all incomplete.

There have been a few bright lights shining in my direction this week. As I mentioned the other day, the bank called Hakan while I was in Rhode Island and told him that they were going to reduce our interest from 5.7 percent to 4.5 percent, with no added cost to us. That will save us (and later, me) $300 a month. That is such a nice, unexpected, and most welcome gift. Also, I got an unexpected, personal phone call from the publishing house I contacted before leaving for Rhode Island. It was very positive, and Kyle thought that my idea was a good one in these hard times; he said that many could relate to what I am going through and that the book idea could be very marketable. The finishing timeline is good too, if it can be finished up in the first three months of 2011. That seems quite possible. I need to get the paperwork back to the bank and have that set up before contacting the lawyer again. My father spoke to our accountant and was able to get the PDF file of our 2009 taxes to send to the lawyer, and he wrote me a check for the $2,500 retainer fee.

My mind has also been preoccupied with the relationship, or lack of relationship now, with my mother-in-law. I am pleasant and say hello, but I do not engage or try anymore. I have tried so much over the last ten years and have had to forget all of her insults to me and my family. I had to forget that in 2006 she brought her own cleaning rags from Turkey to clean my kitchen upon arrival. Then, to further the insult, she told me that the brand-new towels from the store were not clean. If I wanted to learn how to clean, then I needed to ask her, her mother, or Hakan's aunt. No one in my family—not my mother, my Aunt Binnaz, or my Turkish grandmother—knew the best way; his family did. I had to forget how hurtful it was when she pushed Hakan to let her stay three months when Mina was born against my request of one month. Here I was with a bad hip, newly released from the hospital, and I was making *her* breakfast and doing *her* dishes. In the three months, she changed about five diapers and never helped with cleaning. If she helped with cooking, she cooked for Hakan: meat and beans, which I couldn't eat. One night, I even remember just having white rice for dinner. "Oh, I see that I have made everything with meat in it, but there is some fresh rice on the stove if you like," she said. Lovely. Maybe I am being childish, but I don't want to let the latest insult get brushed under the rug like always. I feel like I need to find a way to express how I am feeling with respect for her while also upholding my self-respect. If she wants a relationship with me, then *she* should be the one courting me back into the family. Yet there is just silence.

Tonight has been nice. Mina went to sleep really easy since she didn't nap, and Hakan went out for coffee with Seyhan. It is so peaceful really. I can sit here, write, and watch *Inspector Morse*. I think back on how he promised me that he could show me how much love he has for this family if I gave him a few more months. It really hit home on Saturday how empty that promise was. Mina's scarecrow-making party was that day, and guests were due to arrive at 11:00 a.m. I set a nice breakfast for all of us and put a pot of tea on. I tried to wake him up around 9:00 a.m. I thought that maybe, just maybe, he'd want to participate in this family party. I was really frustrated and disappointed when he rolled out of bed at 10:15 a.m. Mina and I had eaten our breakfast without him. We had waited for him long enough, again. He was upset when Marcia came early at 10:30 a.m. with Clare to help out. He was upset that I hadn't informed him that anyone was coming early; he was still in his pajamas. I had honestly thought, and told him so, that he would be up and dressed by 10:30 a.m. in case he was needed to set up the backyard for the party before people came. When I told him all that I had to do before people arrived, instead of offering help, he asked how I would be able to get everything done in such a short time. I guess it all comes back to narcissism. Is it his fault that he is the way that he is? Is it a product of nature or nurture?

OCTOBER 27, 2010

Boy, do I have a headache today, and I can't decide if it is from the weather (it snowed), lack of sleep, or frustration. I do feel a sense of relief after seeing Mina at school today. The last two hours went really well. I was able to sit in the lobby while she was in class. She took turns, participated, and hardly gave me a glance when changing studios. Miss Tad said she was very impressed! I need just one less thing to worry about these days!

I think I need to make myself another to-do list. Maybe that will help me feel less scattered. One thing that I did do today was sign up for a TD

Ameritrade account. I wanted to cross-reference the penny stock quotes from my e-mails with an actual trading company. I want to know if I can (somewhat) trust their stock suggestions. After checking out a few, I believe that I can. The promotional e-mail has inflated the percentage gain notably—it suggested a 500 percent gain, but the actual gain has been 160 percent. These penny stocks might just be the ticket for me to start with. Get an e-mail, go and buy, and so on. Now I just have to figure out how to get the money over to the TD Ameritrade account without drawing too much attention. I was hoping that I could use PayPal for it, but it doesn't look like I can. What I need to do is link my work checking account with TD Ameritrade. Time to hunt down the checkbook for all those routing and account numbers.

What I really want to do is sleep. I was up half the night worrying about Mina and school. She woke herself up with a nightmare about going to school: "Mama, I don't *want* to go to school!" Then she was up at 5:00 a.m., repeatedly poking me to get up and do shadow puppets on the ceiling with her nightlight. Today, I watched while her turtle shadow puppets blew me kisses. Not a bad way to start the day, I guess.

As for right now, I think I need a cup of coffee.

OCTOBER 28, 2010

I feel less scattered today. Mina woke up at 5:00 a.m. and went back to sleep, but I just got up around 5:30 anyway. I was able to enjoy a quiet morning cup of coffee and got a lot of videos uploaded of Mina's Halloween day at school. That allowed me time after Mina woke up to pick up the house. Mina and I went through her toys and reallocated some upstairs toys down to the playroom. The chaos was making me crazy. It is amazing how clearing your physical space can clear your emotional and spiritual space as well. I felt a lot lighter by 9:30 in the morning. By doing all the work in the morning, I had freed up our day to play. Hakan has a work dinner and will go directly to meet his Turkish friends at a basketball game today. We won't see him until tomorrow morning. We can just be "us" tonight, and that is also freeing.

We had a lovely walk up to the toy store and played, bought some candles, got a balloon, and walked home. Walking helps clear out all the yuckiness for me. I can just put Mina in the stroller and just walk . . . wherever. The toy store is just far enough to be a good walk and short enough that it doesn't make my hip ache too much.

As I was putting Mina down for her nap, my thoughts kept returning to my mother-in-law and writing that letter. I guess I will just have to write it out, just to release it. Here it goes:

Dear Mom,

I have taken a step back from our relationship after our last conversation. Your words, quickly spoken and uncensored, were very hurtful. I have tried for many years to forge a loving relationship with you and your family. I thought that I had succeeded. These past two years I have felt truly close to you and brought you all close to my heart. I released old grudges from previous insults and believed we were going forward in our relationship. It troubles me to think that maybe I was fooling myself into believing in something that was never really there.

My silence over the past few weeks has been twofold: (1) I do not want another one of your insults to be swept under the rug and forgotten, and (2) I am looking at myself and wondering if I deceived myself into believing you had changed.

In the past, any insulting word or action by you toward me or my family was pushed aside for Hakan's comfort. You expect someone to immediately apologize to you if you are insulted, but you never take responsibility for your own actions. If you know that you have hurt someone, you just sit there with *that* face, quiet, and turn away. Would it have hurt you to say you were sorry way back when in Park City in 2001 when you so determinedly wanted a Starbucks and almost caused my father to have a heart attack? No, you sat in the car, with your chin tight and toward the sky, staring out the window.

Your way is the only way, and you try to push your way onto others, regardless of whether it hurts someone.

I feel that I have done more than most daughters-in-law to make you and your family feel loved in my house and in my heart. After your recent comments, I feel that all my work has been in vain because you do not respect me. I have tried to be considerate of your feelings, but you seem disinterested in considering Mina. If you want to rebuild a relationship with me, I am open to it, but I do not believe that I am the one who needs to work hard at it anymore—you do.

I have been insulted and offended for the last time. I will not put myself in the position to be insulted again.

Elif

Now that I have written it, I am wondering if I will be able to translate these sentiments accurately. I guess I will sit on it and see how the spirit moves me. Maybe writing it out like this will lift the need from my shoulders.

Now I am off to fill out the paperwork for the lawyer and find that checkbook!

NOVEMBER 1, 2010

Great is the road I climb, but the garland offered by an easier effort is not worth the gathering.

—Sextus Propertius (50 BC-AD 16),
Roman Poet

This quote came in my e-mail this morning, and it was so on-target that I needed to include it. This road has been long, and I have tried to be as honest with myself and Hakan as possible, but this latest refinancing business has me feeling icky and manipulative. I am deliberately waiting to file until the refinancing is in. It is not as honest as I would like. Do I ease my conscience when I tell myself that I didn't go after refinancing? That it was a gift out of nowhere? Am I manipulating the system by buying Mina's Christmas presents *now* while I don't have to worry about money? Yes, in many ways I am. It is hard to justify such actions by saying, "I put in my dues for so many years that I feel owed some sort of restitution."

I can understand now why many people stay in and exist in less-than-ideal marriages. Inertia grounds you to the familiar, and it is easy to become complacent. Is the marriage horrible? No, but I have higher standards for myself now and for my child. I feel like I have changed glasses and see things more clearly. If he really, really felt the need to change things, he would have gotten up and helped with the neighborhood fall festival, for me as well as to be a part of it for Mina. He had asked what the schedule was for Sunday, and I told him the rundown of what needed to be done. It would have been nice if he'd gotten up and made an effort. These sorts of actions or lack thereof reinforce my decision. He has become pretty sad lately. I can pretty much read him at this point: he seems upset that Mina's relationship with his parents has changed, that Mina's Turkish has worsened a bit, and that she is defiant when asked to explain things in Turkish. She becomes defiant, and he pushes her to speak Turkish more—it becomes a vicious cycle. I stay out if because I believe that is *their* problem to work out. All these signs show me that Hakan is beginning to enter into his fall depression. Looking back, this behavior has started the same time each year for the last three years. Fantastic! And I am going to hit him with the worst news of his life at one of the worst times to do it.

It is our two-year anniversary in this house, and I just realized that I haven't even slept in "my" own bedroom. This seems like an obvious realization, but with everything rushing about in my head, this thought *just* occurred to me. Since Hakan asked me to sleep somewhere else in September 2008 because Mina's monitor light was too bright and disruptive, I have laid my head in many areas of the house, usually the guest room downstairs or Mina's floor upstairs. Gaia remarked the other day that I need my own space, and it is true. Maybe that is another obvious reason why I feel scattered and not so grounded all the time. Soon, I will fix that, soon.

I have, however, been able to ground myself and root myself in the fabric of this neighborhood. Mina and I, through treats and veggies, have become very close and comfortable with this block of neighbors. We organized a lovely fall festival, and everyone turned out. It was such a nice time. Mina was so excited and so willing to help set up. She took care of organizing the children's area while I set up the adult food section. Mina went back to our neighbor's yard and brought out the kids' chairs one by one, cleaned them off, and set them around the candy apple table. I am trying to create meaningful memories for her to hold onto and remember when things get tough. This festival will be an annual event and something for her to look forward to and plan.

I was hoping to take advantage of the publishing deal last week and sign on or before October 31, but preparing for the festival left me with not so much time to sit.

NOVEMBER 2, 2010

> Far away in the sunshine are my highest aspirations. I may not reach them, but I can look up and see the beauty, believe in them and try to follow where they lead.
>
> —Louisa May Alcott (1832-1888),
> American writer

I had a lovely morning yesterday breaking down the garden and having lunch with Heather. I think she feels kind of protective of me. I found out that her parents divorced when she was four, and they moved from Pennsylvania to Utah. Her mom was all alone out here with no family, and it was hard. Heather has been so wonderful in letting me know that she understands how hard it is to be going through this alone and that she is here to help however she can. It is such a comfort.

I brought up my concerns regarding our refinancing and filing afterward. She immediately said that I was protecting myself and my child. She said that I had been through enough over the years, that now I needed to start thinking of my *own* needs and how to protect them. She didn't find it manipulative; she saw it as just a mother bear protecting her cub and home.

It was a pretty pissy day in Hakan-world yesterday. He had to stay with Mina at school yesterday and was grumpy when he tried to drop her off, and she was aware of it. He had to spend three hours with her, and that is not easy for him. All he sees are the things that she does wrong there: she didn't participate; she made a girl cry; she didn't share. Yeah, and she is four. They are all figuring out social issues at this time. There is no reason to come home and make her feel bad about it all over again. Let's see how we can make it better for tomorrow. What did she do *right* or *well* in class? Let's lift her up with those attributes and sit down and quietly talk to her about the behaviors that need fixing.

Before he walked in the door yesterday, Mina was working at her desk and said, "Baba was pretty upset with me today because he had to stay. Shh! He is coming in—let's not talk about it anymore." Then she refused his kiss when he came in, grunted at him, and turned her shoulder toward him. Of course, he gets pissed at that and walks away. This everyday strain is too much for a little girl.

He must be getting e-mails from his mom about doing Ojo with them or with his grandmother. He sent an e-mail and asked if we could call his grandmother on Ojo yesterday because she missed Mina. By the time I got the e-mail and by the time Mina woke up from her nap, it was way too late. When he came home, he asked if we were able to call, and I said no. He became very defensive and asked if would be able to find some time tomorrow. I hate having to explain myself or why we were not able to do it. It makes me feel like I report to him. When he gets pissy about things, he wants a Mina-show. He wants her to sing to him this Turkish song about a little girl who lives along the banks of the Bosphorus. Our children are here to enjoy and play with, but in my opinion, they are not here to entertain us like a dog and pony show. They also do not perform on demand. When she didn't sing it the way he wanted, he said, "Oh well, give me a kiss good-night, pissy girl."

In response to that, I scolded him. "Don't call her names!" It is not okay with me for my child to be insulted or called a name because she did not perform to his standards.

As far as my new hobby, trading stocks, I have officially set up my own bank account with them and have transferred $100 from the money my aunt and uncle gave me this summer. The TD Ameritrade rep called me yesterday afternoon to see what my trading preferences were and what I was planning to do. I don't think he was prepared for my answer: I told him that I wanted to get my feet wet by trading penny stocks.

"Oh," he said. He was silent for a moment before he continued. "Well, have a good day and call us at TD Ameritrade anytime if you need help."

I had to chuckle to myself. He probably thinks I am a silly housewife playing around with her husband's money in the stock market.

NOVEMBER 3, 2010

It's official: I bought two stocks today! Yes, I trade in oil and gas, and my stock is up .01 percent with a net gain of blah, blah, blah. It will take a while to get the hang of this. Maybe I should order a "Stock Trading for Dummies" book. I thought I had ordered the penny stock suggestion from my e-mail, but I can't seem to find the stats on my page. I will figure out this stock trading thingamabob one of these days.

I actually took some time while Mina napped yesterday to go fill out the paperwork for the lawyer. I got it all filled out except for driver's license numbers and the retirement account info. Not too bad. I should call the lawyer before the week is out and make an appointment for next Wednesday or Friday—preferably Wednesday because of the kids' workshop at the bookstore on Friday. I am trying not to squeeze too many things into one day.

My parents and I talked about Christmas yesterday. This is the year they are supposed to fly out, but they are concerned about the possibly uncomfortable situation with Hakan this year. They are trying to be sensitive to his feelings and would feel bad having a good time out here when he is going through such heartache. They offered to fly Mina and me out instead. They are going to hold off buying tickets until we have figured out what is best and are not worried about the ticket price. When the time comes, they will pay whatever the price is to come here or to fly us there. The most important thing is everyone's comfort level.

In my opinion, the best scenario would be for Hakan to move in with Seyhan and Oniz during December. He will not want to be alone all at once and especially during the holiday season. He can take his clothes, climbing gear, and whatever he needs there. Taking his time to find a place and heal among friends would be the best for him.

After he moves out, I can have the thrift store come and take the bed and recliner out of the house, freeing up space for a new bed for me (and Mina) in my bedroom. Maybe by Christmas we will be sleeping in a bed, on a frame, and not on the floor. Getting Mina back into her own bed will be secondary to her feeling safe and secure at this point. Should she get back to her own bed, that will be fine, of course, but I am not going to make her feel abandoned after Hakan leaves.

So, here we go again—less than a week before I have to sit down and talk about divorce . . . again. First, we need to go to the bank and sign the new mortgage together, tomorrow. I know I haven't even begun the actual process of it, but I am so done at this point. Planning, thinking about, and executing all of this wears me down so much that I just fall asleep most nights with Mina around 8:00 p.m.

Yesterday, we grabbed Rachel and the girls to go vote with us and have ice cream. After finishing, we headed over to check on the chickens. Rachel asked if Mina and I would like to help take care of them this spring. I gave her an exuberant *yes*! Not only will it be fun and a great experience for us, but also it will give Mina something to look forward to and plan. She will be able to take a baby chick, name it, and raise it as her own. What a gift to give a four-year-old!

NOVEMBER 4, 2010

We signed the mortgage today and sent it out. It looks like we will be saving $282/month. We have also switched to a biweekly schedule (which is what I had wanted to do anyway) and have it set to come out of the savings account. November's payment will be skipped, and the new rate will go into effect on December 13.

Marcia took Mina and me out for a celebratory brunch at Eggs in the City, and then we were off to Wheeler Farm for a lovely respite.

Mina was all wound up and excited after a fun morning with Clare when we got back. After the girls napped, Mina and I were going to head back to see Marcia and Clare for afternoon coffee. Well, Mina was too excited to sleep. I didn't really force it because I wanted her to sleep easy tonight (which she did—asleep in fifteen minutes!).

While I was fixing dinner, Mina put on her "Queen of the Night" adaptation play from Mozart's *Magic Flute* for her babies. Hakan came home early to play with her, and she wanted none of it; she wanted to do her play. He wants her to do what *he* wants and wants it on cue. Most parents would love it if their child was putting on an opera for her stuffed animals and playing on her own. Well, that just started the evening off on the wrong foot because he mentioned to her that he didn't go to dinner with Seyhan so that he could play with her. Then I wasn't able to read to her enough because I had to make dinner for him and me. She had a fit—a full-out crying, clinging-to-my-leg, boogery fit.

He always has to bring up the close relationship that she and I have, saying that it is too close, that we are like one unit. It is easy to say such things, but how did this situation occur? He doesn't care to recognize that he chose not to be part of this family for three and a half years. She and I had to rely on each other without him. You can't decide to become part of a family after that long and expect to just slide into place. I, personally, think he is jealous and lashes out. He has gone out with Seyhan now and is probably relaying how Mina has serious psychological issues because of mother issues. She is always with me, so her problems must stem from something I have or have not done. It just infuriates me.

November 5, 2010

Just a quick note today. After I left Mina, screaming, at preschool, I headed to Starbucks to read and relax. Linda stopped by my table, and we chatted a bit. She asked me about my time frame for the personal chef business. I told her the beginning of the year. I can't have any extra income coming in before the alimony settlement, and I just want Mina to settle in after everything is finished. She said that she has two friends lined up for business! How wonderful! It is nice to know that I already have a cash flow even before picking a name for the business. What could be better than that?

I spoke with her about my icky feelings regarding the mortgage and filing. She was very comforting in the way she expressed herself. She said that we would all like to be able to execute our plans with the purest heart and intentions. However, sometimes life gets in the way. In order for you to protect your family, home, and investment, plans get a little cloudy, and lines get blurred. That's okay. You cannot be of pure heart all the time. You can only do the best that you can for each situation. She made me feel a whole lot better and less guilty about the matter. Time to put that concern to rest and move on.

I e-mailed the lawyer a few minutes ago and asked if she had some time Wednesday or Friday morning. In this technological age, it is so nice to be able to send a quick e-mail instead of using the phone. Too bad I can't text or e-mail Hakan: "Hakan, I would like a divorce, please."

November 9, 2010

Well, I did it. Mina went to sleep pretty easy last night. He had forgotten his wallet at work. When he came home, I asked him if we could sit and talk. I told him that I was still feeling the same as the summer and would like to proceed with the divorce.

He was much more upset this time than when we were in Turkey. He said that the two months had passed without us even trying to fix anything. I told him that he had asked for an extra few months to show me and Mina how much he loved us. There was nothing in particular he had done *wrong*; I just didn't see anything that changed how I felt inside.

He still wants to "hang in there" and try to fix things. I told him that it has been a long time for me, and I don't want to try anymore. I am a different person, and there are some things that have cut deep over the years that I can't let go of. Of course, he brought up the fact that he has let go and forgiven me for the hurts I have caused him. He was referencing a statement I made within the first week of meeting him. I was so enamored of him and liked him so much when we first me that when he asked me if I would ever move to Turkey, I said *yes*! He has held me to that one statement for ten years. "You said . . . !" I was newly in love, I had never lived away from my parents before, and I had not fully gotten to know his family yet. He has always wanted me to *want* to move back to Turkey as much as *he* wanted to. That is an unreasonable thing to ask of someone. I was willing to try. I saved money to move. I created a working binder on the aspects of moving. I created a moving budget. But I could not get him a job there. He said that if he had *felt* that I really wanted to go there, then we would have been there already. He is putting off blame onto me. He never networked with other universities like I suggested. He told me last night that he has forgiven *me* for speaking hastily. He wonders why I can't let go of such things. Basically, I think he believes that our problems all stem from that statement made when we first met. Since I didn't really follow through with my word, he got depressed and isolated himself from me and later from Mina, which led to inadvertent hurtfulness toward me. Backhandedly, I guess, I caused my own pain when I spoke in haste.

It is really sad, and I feel awful when he asks, "Where am I going to live? Will Mina still love me? I guess I will have to come here to love Sofia [the cat] too." I told him that he could take Sofia and that Mina would understand, but he won't take her pet. Mina has always considered Sofia

Hakan's cat, so I know she would understand. Beaner, well—that's *her* kitty.

The concept of divorce is not something just I have been thinking about. He admitted that he had thought about it as well but couldn't bring himself to go talk with a lawyer. I want a cooperative divorce, not an angry one—for Mina's sake. He agrees and will try to do his best. He wants to break the news to Mina right and not have this divorce completely devastate her. He is concerned that this will ruin her life and impede her growth and learning. I told him that would not be the case.

His mind is full of dire hypothetical scenarios: What if I don't get tenure and get a job in Missouri—would you move? What if we can't afford the house? What if Mina is scarred for life? How am I going to live here in Salt Lake City forever? How can we plan, plan, plan?

I told him that we need to take it one step at a time, and eventually, everyone will adjust and be okay.

The only request he has is that we both go to a therapist, together, to have one last talk. He said there is a 1 percent chance that I may change my mind if we are able to sit and hash it out with a mediator of sorts.

We did talk about his mother and his family. I told him that after his mom's last insult, I do not feel that I need to work hard on preserving the relationship. I've had enough after so many years. He thinks that because he "handled" her over the summer, that makes up for everything she has said. I told him that she never feels she has to apologize for anything she says, and it is just expected that it will be swept under the rug. He said that he was tired of me complaining about his family for the past six months. "Hold your horses, buddy!" I said. "You take that back! I never uttered one complaint about your family until the last week of August, and with good reason." He backed off. He said that his mother *did* apologize and say that insulting me was never her intention, but he did not tell me. That is kind of convenient to say *now*!

He said that he has distanced himself from his family and that they have backed off; what more did I want? I never asked him to distance himself from his family. I just didn't feel that it was my duty anymore to work so hard with communication. I never said that there needed to be *no* communication.

Anyway, he really doesn't see how we came to this point. He thinks that once I had Mina, I isolated her away from him, and he never was part of anything. I told him that he had selective memory and that he had refused to hold, help, or watch her. Because of his refusal to watch her, I had to cart her around to three stores when I shopped on Sundays because he wanted his comfort. I had to ask permission, in a way, to take a shower when he woke up—"Please watch the sleeping baby"—and he would not because he had just woken up, and so on. He was so insanely jealous of what we did during the day that I found that I had to hide what we did because it would create an argument. I could never say I was meeting this person for coffee, or Mina's friend was coming over. Our plans were always met with the same angry response: "Great! It's nice that *someone* has friends to have coffee with or come over to play! My only role is to work to pay for it!"

The one day I posted pizza party pictures online, he came home in a state and ran straight to bed, crying and ranting. Poor little Mina was beside herself, begging her father, "Please, Baba, let me have my friends, please! I love my friends!"

Whenever I would ask him to join us in what we were doing, he would just sit there and get teary. This wasn't how it was supposed to be, he said. "How can I enjoy this when my family in Turkey will never be able to?" If I shared something funny Mina said, he would counter, "Yeah, so can she do that in *Turkish*?"

I stopped asking him to join us, and we started living separate lives, isolated from each other. "Please do not say that I intentionally isolated Mina by taking over her care," I said to him.

Anyway, he took a Tylenol PM and went to bed. I was up most of the night with Mina and her sniffles, so I am pretty tired. I think it will be a pajama day, and Mina and I will just rest at home.

My Friday appointment with the lawyer has been moved to next Wednesday morning. Her case has not settled yet, and she needs to be in court Friday.

Hakan has been pretty snippy this morning, and I am just ignoring it. I understand that he is hurt and things just come out. Mina wanted to play that dress-up girl computer game, and he said, "Better enjoy it while you can . . . right, Elif?" Then after breakfast, he threw Saturday's Disney on Ice tickets at me and said, "Why don't you and a single mom go and see it!"

It's going to be a long month. I am glad that he has a conference in D.C. next week and that there is a possible climbing trip for him in the Tetons on another weekend. It will make the time move a bit faster.

November 11, 2010

It was a beautiful sunny day, and I felt good and peaceful as we drove to the marriage counselor this morning. We left Mina with Daisy. They were going to spend some time at the Natural History Museum.

Hakan went first and outlined his view of our situation and how we got here. He missed a big portion of the story: familial issues. I thought it would be wise to let him go first so that I could sit, process, and form my own responses.

Over the course of seventy-five minutes, we revisited a lot of issues, and I brought up a few more. I actually mentioned his mother's letter from May 2008 that listed all the things I had done wrong or not to her level of satisfaction. She had also sent this letter to my aunt to translate, so that I would understand everything "correctly."

By the end of the session, the therapist had a good idea of what was going on, and he said that he could help us if we gave him three to six months. My first gut response was an emphatic *no*! I felt that I needed to explain to the therapist that I am willing to come to these sessions only so that I can learn how to better communicate with Hakan and be friends.

I believe that I was very clear with Hakan last Christmas when we talked about all this at my parents' house. We agreed that we had problems that needed fixing and that we would both go to for counseling for a year, reconvene at the end of the year, and evaluate the situation. That was me, laying down the gauntlet. Now is the time to act!

I started counseling the first week of January 2010, but Hakan didn't make it to therapy until May. I cannot keep postponing my life because our personal timelines do not match up. There will always be something that will delay, at this point, the inevitable.

This marital counseling is not postponing my appointment with the lawyer next Wednesday. I might actually try to reschedule for earlier in the week since Hakan will be away from Sunday to Wednesday. This morning may have put Hakan's mind somewhat at ease with the situation, but I am still firm in my resolve. This is the right time for me, and that is what I have to keep reminding myself.

After looking all week through Hakan's desk downstairs for his TIAA-CREF statements with no success, I e-mailed my lawyer and asked if I could put down the account number from a very old statement. She said that would be fine, and she would subpoena the information. That word, "subpoena," has been prevalent in all the *Law & Order* episodes that I have watched over the years, but I never thought that that word would be used in reference to an aspect of my life. It is so alien, so foreign. It really brings it home that this is really happening, now, in real life and not on TV. It's just really weird.

I am looking forward to a few days by myself. He will be gone from Sunday morning until Wednesday night. I have already begun to line up some fun for myself: dinner out at the new Italian Restaurant with Daisy, homemade pizza and yummy wine with Marcia and Clare, breakfast at IKEA with Mina, and maybe a day to rest. It will just be blissful!

Oh my goodness! I almost forgot! I signed with the publisher today. It just goes to show that sometimes you have to ask for what you want. I asked Kyle if there were any good publishing deals coming up other than what was offered online. He gave me a $550 discount on a great package, and I am very pleased. The total package came to about $1,500, to be paid in three installments. Old habits die hard, though. I actually hesitated a bit when I gave my credit card number for my own special account. Hakan would see that much money come out of my birthday money account and would wonder. My heart beat faster with anxiety, but I *had* to—*had* to—take this step for me and for Mina. It is all about regaining control over my life again, right?

November 16, 2010

Hakan left for a conference early Sunday morning, and it has been so *still* here. We have moved through our days effortlessly, and Mina has gone to sleep easily, by 7:00 p.m. As much as the aspect of him actually, physically leaving will be difficult, the aftermath will not be so rough. There is a "freeness" in the way Mina moves through the house when he is not here. She can play her music early in the morning, and she can do her "theater" play with Nana on the Ojo at night.

When I talk about things "settling down," this is what I mean—the quiet and the stillness and the absence of the elephant in the room.

Bob, our maintenance guy, called today to check in on me. I had told him my plans before going to Turkey, and he was worried sick about us. He said that he will help me in any way he can, and I guess he is not charging me for taking care of the yard while we were away this summer.

It's his way of saying he cares. It is so nice to feel the love around you like a warm blanket. Kindness to others has a way of coming back tenfold to you when you need it most.

I did find out that the investment through Gaia's friend did not pan out as I had hoped. One bad apple really ruins it for the lot. Someone above Gaia's friend attempted to take the money and run. It has been a long road, but the payout is not forthcoming. However, I should receive my initial investment back next week sometime. I don't regret what I did at all. Having the opportunity gave me the oomph to risk and to free myself from feeling financially beholden to Hakan. Maybe I did not profit financially, but emotionally and spiritually, I gained more than I thought possible. And really, in the end, isn't that more important than physical money anyway?

Mina and I have been planning to go out to a fancy froufrou restaurant with Daisy while Hakan is away. When we do this, Mina sits up in the fancy chairs, orders her pasta, and gets a juice in a martini glass. Tonight we tried the Paris's sister restaurant, SeaSalt. I intended to get Daisy's dinner, but she was faster. It was so kind and appreciated!

Mina and I have developed our own rhythm around the house while he has been away. Maybe we don't pick up at night before bed, but we spend some time in the wee hours of the morning (we are up at 6:00 a.m.) cleaning up our mess. She has been instrumental in helping me with our Christmas presents for her teachers. After cutting the fleece, we had to edge it with matching binding, creating a lovely reading shawl. She has totally stepped up in handing me the pins and helping me with the actual sewing. Days with no naps go seamlessly. If I am working with the sewing project, she gives the dried leaves taped to the window a "haircut" with her scissors. She completely self-entertains. It is wonderful. The other wonderful thing about no naps is that she is in bed by 6:15 p.m. and asleep by 6:30 p.m.

November 17, 2010

I did it! I really did it! I set myself a goal, and I followed through! I held my appointment with the lawyer and filed today. With my having filled out the paperwork at home ahead of time, our meeting was brief and productive. She added a lot to the budget and brought the total up to about $4,200/month. I don't know how necessary all of it is, but I guess she knows what she is doing. I want to be fair, and I do not want Hakan to become destitute. I guess she probably is asking for more than I need so that I can get what I *actually* need as a result.

We came up with a parenting plan regarding custody and trips to Turkey. We decided I would go for sole physical custody and joint legal custody. I asked her to make a stipulation that Hakan cannot take Mina to Turkey alone until she is eight years old. I want her to be able to stand up for her beliefs and be able to call me or my aunt on the telephone or through the computer when she is there. I believe she will be articulate enough and physically able to do those things by that age. With regard to technology, kids grow up faster these days than when I was growing up. Also, I just want this coming year *off* from going to Turkey. I just want a break. The plan is that in even-numbered years, I will coordinate my trip with Hakan to Turkey, and in odd-numbered years, it will be up to me (1) whether I go and (2) the length of stay. I want to provide Mina the opportunity to travel to other places too. That is something that I have never been able to do. When I was a kid, our vacations were always to Turkey. It was always upsetting to me in school that other kids got to go to different places each year. Turkey may seem exotic and exciting to someone who hasn't been there, but when it is dictated that you go there for each summer vacation, it becomes a bit, well, tiring.

My mom asked me how I felt after I filed. Well, it is so alien to me at this point; it is some vague reality somewhere in the future, near future, but still somehow distant. The reality of it will set in after I tell him at our next therapy session this Friday. I think it is best to hold this news until there is a third, neutral party there to help him through. I am not here to hurt him or make him pay like other wives might feel when they are filing for divorce. I have dealt with my anger and my pain. I am willing to help him in whatever way he needs the help: finding an apartment, cleaning it, transferring bills, setting up a bank account. I want to make it as seamless as it can be so that, possibly, the stress level will be less later on. Do I need to do these things? No, but I can only imagine what he will be going through and how his feelings may transmit to Mina. Once the change of address occurs, we will all settle into our routines and figure out our new life. We will all be fine, eventually.

I have realized that when I feel stressed or anxious, I tend to give to others more. I have been baking and cooking and sewing up a storm.

Maybe I am trying to replace the anxious feelings with warmer feelings for others. It helps me get through the day. Today, I bought a book for my neighbor, Robyn, to put in her reading shawl. I wanted to finish it up today and bring it over, and I did. It was a good feeling to know that she will love it. In my own sort of craziness, it seems to balance some of the hurt that will be inflicted on Hakan. *I am not a horrible person*, I tell myself. My lawyer has been supportive on an emotional level. We spoke about the home front, and she said simply, "You do not need to justify your feelings to me or anyone else. They are yours to feel or not to feel." I almost burst into tears because someone said that it was okay to do what I feel is right for me.

So many women think that it is not okay to feel worthy of self-respect and to love themselves. I thought that for a long time. We do everything. It reminds me of a quote [about Fred Astaire] referencing Ginger Rogers: "Sure he was great, but don't forget Ginger Rogers did everything he did backwards . . . and in high heels!" Women are expected to do everything men do, except "backwards and in high heels." When I began to stand up for myself and my feelings, I began to second-guess them: Is this right? Do I deserve this? Is this the best that I can do?

Once I began to knock down all my doubts, I felt so much stronger and less afraid. I am not afraid of the future. Is it unfortunate that someone, Hakan (and his family), will be hurt by my decision? Yes, but where were they for the past ten years while I was being hurt emotionally?

My lawyer asked me if I had any questions at the end of the meeting. I asked only, "Do you think this can be finalized before Christmas and be my present from Santa this year?" She just smiled. Maybe, just maybe, I will be smiling this Christmas Eve and not crying. Wouldn't *that* be nice?

November 19, 2010

He came home, and I couldn't sleep the last two nights. I kept having an imagined therapy session with him and the marriage counselor. I guess I was practicing for the actual day. Last night, Mina had horrible teething pain, and I was up most of the night tending to her. Not exactly the most restful of nights, and I certainly didn't feel like going to therapy this morning with him and doing what I had set out to do. If it was any other day, I would have kept her home and in bed. Today, because I really needed to move with this, I pushed her a bit to go to school with the promise of picking her up early.

As we walked into the office and sat down, I just kept saying to myself, *This is the last bandage; just rip it off fast and be done with it.* I had been building this moment up in my head so much that I hadn't been able to sleep.

So this was the third time I said that I wanted a divorce, but when I mentioned actually filing, Hakan and the therapist were shocked. The therapist's main wish is to help people get back together. He still holds out hope for the future but will help us communicate better, which will help either way in the long run.

We sparred again, Hakan and I, about who has been hurt most by whose parents. I finally vocalized to Hakan that his mother has been very hurtful, and I wished that for once she would humble herself just a bit to say she was sorry. If she had expressed remorse to Hakan over the last incident, why hadn't he thought it important enough to mention to me?

The therapist basically said that neither of us is hearing the other. We each believe we have been hurt the most in this relationship, and we shoot down the other's feelings, almost invalidating them.

We talked about stress levels, stress cues, and "I feel" statements. If we begin our concerns, "I feel . . . when . . . because . . ." then our complaints seem less threatening to the other, and a conversation may be possible. The other should respectfully listen and reiterate it back in his or her own way, thereby validating the other's feelings and thought processes.

Hakan got very tense when we talked about the divorce process. He will not just sign something that he feels needs to be contested. He wants to protect *his* rights as well. How does the process unfold? How and when will he be served? What is in the envelope?

He expressed concerns over whether it was me calling the shots or me speaking for my father. He believes that I have not been able to control my own parents over the years and has felt hurt by their constant insults toward his country. I tried to set his mind at ease and said that if they had had their way, I would have been divorced four years ago. If my father had had his way, I would have filed last May. I am speaking for myself, by myself.

The therapist made mention of not signing the papers, but that would draw out the process and become more expensive in the end. The prospect of the expense will resolve this quickly, I hope.

Usually, I dislike starting a weekend with ickiness, but this was unavoidable. I needed to say it because he needed to hear it, and the papers are coming possibly next week.

I really just want to be fair and equitable all around. If things do not go the way that I would like, I am prepared to pack up what we love and move to Rhode Island.

NOVEMBER 22, 2010

Please stop the ride; I want to get off of this roller coaster! When is this going to end? When? I am tired, I am sad, and I am hurt. I need coffee.

I have been crying for a while with my parents on Ojo and have resorted to using an old dishtowel as a humongous tissue. Big problems = big tissues. My father just told me that they will not be coming out here for Christmas. So that means that I will have to see if Mina and I can go there, legally, or we'll just cancel Christmas. I can't even fathom that thought without starting to cry again. Mina needs some Christmas magic, and I need to feel it too. I want to feel the warmth of Christmas with my family. I wanted them here to help me get through this, but they think it will be extremely stressful on everyone if they are here. I am so tired that I don't even want to think about getting on a plane at the holidays. I don't want to have another stressful conversation with Hakan. It just takes so much out of me. Realistically, I see their point. I need a rest without Hakan, and it would be nice to enjoy the holidays without wondering how he'll be when he comes home from work, if he is still in the house at that time.

It would be nice to let him have the time to move things out of the house while we are not there so Mina will not see the physical transition. She would just have the absence of stuff to deal with. Maybe he will agree that it is for the best that we go alone to Rhode Island for Christmas. It is not really his favorite holiday anyway.

This past weekend passed relatively easily, mainly because our attention mutually has been on helping Mina get through the pain of a new molar. She was like a zombie on Saturday. After dinner, Hakan headed to the climbing gym and then out with Turkish friends for drinks. Sunday, it snowed, and he took his friends up snowshoeing from around 10:30 a.m. to 4:30 p.m. Interaction has been minimal and quiet.

He was surprised when I made him a sandwich for his hike. I am not a bad person. Why wouldn't I make him something to take? I want this divorce because the marriage is not healthy for me anymore. I still respect him as a person and as Mina's father. I am not going to start cooking separate meals for each of us or being mean about things. What good does that do in the end? Really, after the divorce, if I ever make too much for us to eat, I will probably offer him some then as well.

On top of all this, I am trying to regain my friendship footing with Samantha, again. I sent out a note to my friends about Friday's therapy session, filing for divorce, and the immediate aftermath. I got a note from Samantha that obviously has my best interests at heart, but the advice is not exactly what I *need* right now. Where does the friendship go from here? How do we move forward from this? This just adds yet more confusion to my life when I really don't want anymore. Here is our exchange of messages:

Sat, 20 Nov 2010

> Elif, I have been grappling for a bit with how to broach this with you.
>
> I am proud you are being decisive in your life. I believe you will benefit more than you know.
>
> I hope you can take this opportunity to communicate in an excellent setting and get everything you need from it.
>
> Here is the hard part . . . can you accept that you played a role? Not in a passive way but actively.
>
> I have found my greatest growth has been from naming my failure and actively changing my behavior, especially toward Dwayne. I am not a victim; he is not the villain. He was wrong, and one day he will own that, but by owning that I was wrong in how I spoke, what I expected, how I communicated, I am now better able to talk with him, and amazingly, just by changing me, our relationship has changed for the better.
>
> I wish the same for you.
>
> My humble advice is: try to act with an open heart.
>
> Samantha

Samantha,

I appreciate your honesty, but when you were where I am today, were you actually at that point? Or did you really just want to feel that your friends cared about you no matter what? I realize that I cannot feel free enough to just vent and talk to you about this stuff without feeling that you need me to *name* A, B, and C that I did wrong. Why can't I just talk to a friend? I am aware that I could have handled things better, and I am working toward standing up for myself and feel that I have made a lot of progress in the last year. I have recognized how far I have come through all of this and how difficult it has been for me to get where I am. I know that I have further to go, but maybe I do not need, at this point, a reminder of how much I haven't accomplished yet.

I know you love and care about me and want the best for me, but please, at this point all I need is someone to help bolster me up when I wobble. I am trying to remain strong at this point and get through.

I would like to feel that you have my back no matter what I say or do, but I completely understand if space is needed until I get to a self-actualized certain point.

Really, all I need is someone to say, "I am your friend and I am here for you however you need me." It is not like I am burying my head in the sand and saying screw it. I am going to marriage counseling to learn how to better communicate and work through these issues. Maybe at this point, all I want is to feel heard and validated by him and myself. You are three years removed from this. Can you look back and think about when your feelings were all jumbled up and you were going through all of this and about what you really needed from friends?

I really just don't know what to say. Yes, I was passive, and by being passive I allowed things to happen in my life that impacted me and now Mina. If I had stood up for myself and was a stronger person, much of this would not have happened. If I was proactive enough, maybe I would have taken heed of all those who sat down and told me to piss or get off the pot earlier. I didn't, but I am here now. If I was still being passive, I would have just fallen back into the routine after coming back to Turkey or after my self-imposed deadlines of October.

What is your timeline for me? Where did you expect me to be at this point in all of this? Really, I am doing the best I can at a day-to-day rate. I was really hoping that that would be enough for everyone to understand.

Elif

Sat, 20 Nov 2010 15:04:18 +0000

Elif,

To be honest I have been on your side and timeline and your bolstering listening post for ten years. For ten years I listened day after day. Now I am trying to help you be proactive in your healing. If that is not what you need, I am sorry, but it is what I am capable of offering.

S

Sat, 20 Nov 2010 08:29:25—0700

S,

I know that you are trying to help to move through this with your experience as a helping hand. You can offer a perspective that no one else can, but sometimes, I just feel that as much as I work through, it is not fast enough. Really, I am trying to move toward becoming that person. I am not sitting and stagnating anymore. I am really trying to be proactive. What more do you see that I am not doing to become more aware?

I know that you have been there day after day over the past ten years, and it must have been extremely difficult for you to sit and watch me. I know you are pushing me to grow beyond my comfort levels, but I don't work as fast as you. You have had three years of therapy to work through things, and you are doing great. I know that you are trying to pass on knowledge that you gained through difficulty in hopes that I won't have to go through what you went through to get to where you are now.

I want your friendship around me, but I don't want to feel judged by how far I haven't come yet. I am working to get to that point; really, I am.

You're my best friend and I care about you more than anyone . . .

Sat, 20 Nov 2010 16:02:48 +0000

E,

What I will say is that it is not a judgment. I sat on my opinions for ten years. I am not starting to judge now. I am sorry you can't accept what I am offering.

I will offer no more advice, but I don't know how I will feel in the end.

S

Now I am probably going to Rhode Island for Christmas—do I have to have added stress and sit down with Samantha to work it all out? Do I give her some space and hope that through talking with friends and her therapist, she can come around and at least see my point of view? Maybe not approve of it, but at least see where I am coming from.

So many lessons learned . . . it is wearing.

The sun is coming out, and I can see the blue sky. I guess I should shower and get out of pajamas by the time Mina gets home. She will probably ask me what I did all morning with out her. Quietly in my head, I will answer, "I cried, baby, because I am so sad that we all have to go through this." Out loud I will say, "Oh, nothing fun: laundry, dishes, cleaned the toilet—that kind of stuff. Now let's go and make a snowman!"

November 25, 2010

Happy Thanksgiving. I can't sleep.

Hakan is out with his Turkish friends again, and I had a difficult time putting Mina to sleep, and I am pretty drained. It was a difficult day all around. Thanksgiving has always been a hard holiday for us in general because it is all about family, and it has always been a reminder to him that he is *not* with his own family, in Turkey. It has been my least favorite holiday since being here in Utah because of the usual stress that it brings. This year was no different.

Apparently, he has met with a lawyer, which seems to be feeding his ego; he thinks that he will not have to pay much in alimony and that he has a claim to joint custody if he chooses to fight for it. I think the biggest problem I have regarding couples and divorce is that each person is usually thinking about him or herself more than the welfare of the child. I feel that he is thinking of his wallet, and it probably galls him that I may not need to work. What is more important: your wallet or the mental stability of your child during this transition? By not paying what is needed, you will be sending Mina to day care during the time she is not in preschool, I want to say to him. That will be traumatic in itself and also costly. It will probably cost more for a decent day care than to just pay me directly.

He wonders, if he pays me more for a short term, what will prevent me from moving to Rhode Island in five years when the money is gone and I cannot financially keep up with the bills? He would rather pay me less money long-term to keep me in Utah. If I have the money, he reasons, then I wouldn't need to move back to Rhode Island. I have a lovely life here, and so does Mina. Why would I uproot her if I didn't need too? Paranoia is creeping in, and he is scared of losing a lot. I really am willing to work with him for a suitable arrangement for all of us if he can get past this paranoia and think clearly about me as a person.

The joint custody battle may become another road block to moving to Rhode Island down the road. Again, he is thinking of himself and not Mina. He really doesn't want joint custody and wouldn't know how to handle it if he had.

His lawyer's version of what may transpire seems to contradict my lawyer's in some ways, and Hakan thinks that I may not have picked a good lawyer. In a backhanded way, it seems like he is undermining my decision. He doesn't understand how the house can just be transferred over to my name without proper credit. My name is already on the house, and the mortgage is done. It is a matter of removing his name. The lawyer said that if I had refinanced after the divorce was final, then it would have been based on my credit scores and income.

Hakan wants what's fair. Basically, he wants me to have to work. He doesn't want to continue carrying the financial burden alone. How is the money going to be divided—the assets, the equity on the house, the retirement? Really, I can't get my head around all that—that is for the lawyer to break down and show me. Let the lawyers look at numbers and put them on paper, and let me go over it. Since I do not deal with all that on a day-to-day basis, that is not a headache I want to have. Let the experts number-crunch and give me the bottom line.

His parents and family still don't know. His mother wrote a "Happy Thanksgiving" note to me and my family, so I felt obligated to respond. But I cheated—I copied and pasted a letter I had recently written to Hakan's aunt. It was the best I could do. Again, I am taking the step to repair the damage with his family. They can do and say what they want, and here I am stepping in to sweep up the mess to keep the peace. Damn. I am frustrated with them and with me. I am perpetuating the cycle with the hopes (ha-ha) that if I play nice, maybe he will play nice.

While I was at the bookstore on Friday for story-time, I picked up a book to read: *Parenting Apart: How to Parent after Divorce*. It was really helpful in advising how to break the news in an age-appropriate way, and it also gave many tips about how to set up two homes, change the terminology, and help the child through the aftermath.

The authors based a lot of their book on Kubler Ross's "death and dying" process of loss because divorce is a great loss to kids, and they need to learn how to grieve the loss in healthy ways. They talked about replacing the term "visitation" with "on-duty/off-duty" parenting and setting up a safe haven or two homes for the child. That way the child feels safe and comfortable in each environment, regardless of sole or joint custody. The safe haven doesn't need to be a whole room, but maybe a corner with toys, dolls, a pop-up fun tent, and so on.

Whoever has the kids is called the on-duty parent. That parent has rules and must *parent* the kids. It is his or her responsibility to be a parent while taking care of the child. Maybe the rules are different, but they work within that household.

The authors talk about a thirty-minute transitional activity between households, which makes a lot of sense. If the kid comes back hyper, play outside and release. If not, make a tradition of something quiet, like puzzles or book—anything to transition over from one place to the next. I was only able to skim the book, but I will pick it up next week during their holiday sale.

As I lay in bed after Mina fell asleep, I thought about the relocation issue. What if I sign the assurance that I won't move to Rhode Island? What's to stop him from moving to Turkey if his dream job comes up? What happens if he doesn't get tenure and gets a job somewhere else? I hate to use blackmail, but do I threaten to move due to financial difficulty unless I get the money I need to stay where I am? Do I want to stoop to that level?

November 27, 2010

Last week, I asked Marcia what she would do about the whole Christmas trip thing. I was going to try to weasel out of the truth, this once, and say that my grandfather was ill, which meant Mom was not able to travel. So I would be going there. Marcia told me to just tell him the truth. She was right, of course. I was just tired of all these confrontational conversations. Couldn't I escape just one, just this once?

I took a middle road. I wrote an e-mail. I took advice from the book I mentioned earlier, *Parenting Apart*. This is what I wrote:

> Hi there!
>
> I hope the snowshoeing was fun. I just wanted to talk to you sometime about Christmas this weekend. My parents do not want to add to a tense situation by coming out here for Christmas this year. I would like for you and me to sit down and figure out a holiday plan that works for all of us. It is hard to bring this subject up with Mina around, so I thought I would e-mail you first so you could think about suggestions that would work for you.
>
> See you soon,
>
> Elif

I gave him a night to think about it and brought it up after Mina went down for a nap today. He suggested that my parents make their trip a little later, such as around December 20. He would go see he brother in England from Christmas Day through New Year's. He and my parents would only overlap a few days, and it should be fine.

He is having a difficult day today. He is afraid he will only see Mina every other weekend, but I told him that wasn't my intention. I would love for the two of them to see each other as much as they can. I told him that she can stay all day with him and his parents when his parents come to visit. He chuckled and said sarcastically, "Where would they stay?" If he rented a condo or a duplex nearby, then everyone could visit as much as they wanted. Mina could walk to his house or apartment. I am really trying to think of ways for this to work for everyone.

Living close by in Sugar House is not what he wants to do. He is thinking of moving to an apartment closer to downtown, which tells me that he will not be up this way very often. I think he is finding it hard to keep up the connection with Mina. It is hard to build a relationship after so many years and so much harder to maintain it. It is proving to be more difficult on a day-to-day basis.

She is resisting him and his family, still. A lot of it is that she really just wants to play on her own, without anyone. She played on her own for almost six hours yesterday, and I sewed all day long. Today is the same way. I have been sewing, and she is playing. That is a great characteristic to learn. It is not that she is refusing someone, per se, but that she wants alone time with her toys.

Hakan's coping mechanism is to *not* be here in a constructive way: he goes out with friends, goes hiking, gets beer with friends, or goes to work or the gym. There is nothing in the way that he does it that is antagonistic or anything; it is healthy for him to release this ickiness. However, I believe Mina sees him as leaving her. She has resisted him more and more as he has made more and more plans out of the house.

Today was no different. After we talked about Christmas, he told me to go get my shopping down while she napped. I did, and she woke up early. She wanted nothing to do with, whether it was playing with him or talking with his parents on the Ojo. When I came back, I tried to help facilitate a bit of play *near* the Ojo. She completely refused by lying on her stomach and sticking her bum in the air toward the camera. Hakan got frustrated and remarked, "This is ridiculous," which in turn sent Mina to her room crying. "Baba hurt my feelings when called me ridiculous!" she said.

She and I sat on the bed and talked a bit about what had happened. Maybe her not saying hello to her grandparents had hurt Baba's feelings a bit, I told her. They missed seeing her and would love to hear about how school is. Scowling and with arms crossed, she said, "*Well*! I don't miss *them*! Humph!"

It sometimes feels like there is emotional ping-pong going on in this house between Mina and Hakan. "I don't want to talk to them!" *Ping*! "This is ridiculous." *Pong*! "I don't miss *them*!" *Ping*! "I am going to work and leave you two alone to have fun!" *Pong*! This whole thing makes me dizzy!

On a good note, my parents agreed to the compromise. I told them Hakan's proposition: December 20-January 1. My father and I bartered back and forth and seem to have settled on December 21-December 31 or January 1, depending on ticket availability. Phew! That was hard work, but in the end it will be worth it. Mina will have Christmas where she wants it and her grandparents to share it with. Hakan will be here for Christmas morning to see Mina's face opening her gifts and will enjoy New Year's out in England with his brother.

I am feeling accomplished: I have finished eight shawls in two days, am currently enjoying a cup of coffee, and will have a nice cold beer in a little while!

That's all, and that's plenty!

Second entry for the day, 9:46 p.m.

I would like to think of myself as a kind-hearted, compassionate person, and it really pains me to see another person in pain. It is so horribly painful to watch Hakan process what is about to happen. He is hurting and just about pleading with me to change my mind. "How can I survive on my own in this city where I have just about zero chance of meeting someone and starting my life over?"

How can I show him that it is in your darkest hour that you see the brightest light leading you to where you are supposed to be? I keep coming back to this picture book I have been reading to Mina: *The Quilt-Maker's Journey*. It revolves around a young woman who has everything she could ever want but who is not happy. She ventures into the darkness to find her purpose. When her candle goes out, another magically appears to lead her from the darkness to the outside. This is where I feel Hakan and I are today: in the darkness, but on different paths. One of the fundamental differences between Hakan and me is that I *believe* there will be another candle, and he does not. I don't know if I have written about this before or not, but I had a dream months ago in which I saw him, in Turkey, introducing a little baby boy to Mina. He was introducing Mina to her new half-brother. That dream gives me hope that he will, one day, find true happiness with someone he can really love. He can be the father and husband that he now knows how to be. How do I tell him about that dream without him thinking I am nuts?

Divorce really comes down to his life or my life. Do I live my life for him so he is happy, or do I live my life for me—problems and all—and make myself happy? I try to disengage a bit when he starts to cry because his road is not mine to travel anymore. He needs to stand on his own two feet and *live*! I want him to live! I want him to look at life and engage it! He has so much to offer, but he needs to believe that happiness is possible. I realize now that this is not a lesson I can teach him. He needs to learn it on his own.

Today we quietly talked about the future by the window in the living room. It is always so calming to sit in that chair because the warm sun pours in and warms you through, quieting your soul, and you can really hear each other's words.

He is scared to be alone. He sat in the chair, looking sadly out the window, and I sat on the footstool by his feet, waiting for him to speak.

He asked me, "What would you do if I just left and moved back to Turkey? I am alone in this city now. I don't know if I can do it alone. All I can guarantee is that I will try to stay. But if after a year, I am so sad, I may just have to go home and be with my family."

I put my hand on his leg and looked at him. "You are never alone. You have Mina and me, but we will just have a different sort of family structure. It doesn't have to be bad. If you moved back, I would understand. I would have to sell the house and move back to Rhode Island and in with my parents."

Am I scared? Yes, but I just have to keep believing things will get better. Does believing make you cry less at night? No, I need a tissue right now just sitting and typing this. I want to run home to my mom and my dad and just sit there and cry and cry and cry and ask them to make it all go away. Just make the hurt stop—just hug me and pet my head and tell me everything will be fine in the morning.

Okay, now how do I *not* laugh right now? My cat is licking my tears off my face. I laugh, I cry—the two become intermixed.

I would love to be able to write a sequel to this book a year from now and title it "Happy," crossing out the "Mostly" part. I want to be happy, I want him to be happy, and most importantly, I want Mina to be happy.

When will there be a stop button to this emotional roller coaster? I feel like a blubbering yo-yo at this point.

November 30, 2010

Mina and I had a good day. We "Elf-ed" the bookstore by hanging little sewn ornaments filled with chocolate-covered apricots. Mina made them herself over the weekend. Her friends came over to make candles for Christmas, and she painted her grandfather's Christmas present. It was a nice day.

Hakan came home full of bluster. He had talked with his Uncle Mehmet, the one who has a lot of money and his own business. There was an air of confidence about him that seemed a bit cocky. He told me that Mehmet was going to tell his parents about the divorce tomorrow and that I should ignore any e-mails I get from them if they don't "behave." He said that we needed to "chat" more over the weekend.

I felt my heart skip a beat, and the anxiety hit. All these "what if" questions kept bombarding me while I was putting Mina down to sleep. Of course, Mina took a loooong time to get to sleep, so my mind was racing over what could have been discussed, how it would affect Mina, how it would affect me, and so on. Then I took a deep breath and said to myself, *Stop!*

I need to try very hard not to engage his remarks that hint at less or no alimony. Whatever his uncle has cooked up, I will be okay. I need to keep saying that mantra over and over when I start to feel the anxiety creep in: *I will be okay. I will be okay.* Life will provide; it already *has* provided a path for me to follow.

I had a visual in my head of sitting in a little bubble, quiet, while he blusters all around me, unable to penetrate my little calm capsule of serenity.

Am I going blindly into the future? No, I just need to stop the "what if's" from taking control because that just upsets the path. Each "what if" question is a rock on a trail to trip over. Every time I concentrate on something that I can't control, I am throwing rocks or boulders in my own way. I just need to stay centered and breathe and trust.

Now that I have myself back in check, I recognize that the tug-of-war over finances is the ugliest part of divorce. Does he love having money more than love from his child? Finances have always been an issue with us. He felt I should have participated more in making money for the household. Now he is faced with paying me alimony to stay home and possibly not work after divorce. That must be so infuriating to him.

I don't know how else to tell him that I do not want the money so that I can sit around the house and eat bonbons while Mina is at school and he works. I want to help my child ease into this transition. Her father leaving and her mother dropping her at day care all day would be a double abandonment for this sensitive child. She was crying for an hour tonight about being left at school alone tomorrow, and she *likes* it there. I just want enough to help ease her through everything for a couple of years. Really, I am willing to even settle for three years' alimony instead of nine—just until she is in school most of the day.

Calculating what I should be minimally entitled to and what I am willing to settle for, it looks something like this:

$1,500 × 12 months × 9 years = $162,000

$2,500 × 12 months × 3 years = $90,000

My lawyer is asking for five years, and that would still be less ($150,000). I thought that he would have worked this math out already and would *want* to save money. I think he is so blinded by frustration that I may not have to go out and get a "normal" nine-to-five job that he doesn't see that I am willing to save him money in the end!

DECEMBER 1, 2010

After getting a lovely cup of coffee, I decided to walk across to Tony Caputo's Italian Deli before going to the bookstore for story-time. I needed olive oil desperately! While driving back from dropping Mina off at school, I'd had a great idea for a kids' taste-testing class for their store. They have so many adult taste-testing classes for their food—why not for kids? My mind was on cheese—how to get the kids to eat their yummy cheese? Then it hit me! Grilled cheese! Have a variety of grilled cheesed sandwiches cut out in different shapes to differentiate the different cheeses. Ted, the owner, thought it was a great idea, and he is going to go out and get a panini machine to do it! Maybe this is the start of working a bit with them as well. He said that making grilled cheese sandwiches would be a great way to use up the little bits of leftover cheese in the cases.

I said that I noticed they were making fresh soups these days and asked whether he would be interested in an easy red lentil soup recipe. "Sure!" he said. I think I will make up a sandwich bag with the lentils, bulgur, and spices and provide the recipe for him to try out.

Of course when my mind starts thinking, it just doesn't stop. While I was putting Mina down for a nap, I had yet another idea for a kids' class: Make, Take, and Bake Pizza. We could have the kids make their own pizzas in a tin foil pie plate, using their own pizza dough, sauce, cheese, meats, and so on, and take them home to bake.

I think I will write these ideas down, bring them in, and give them to Ted. He can do what he wants with them. If he needs help implementing them, he can give me a call.

This whole friendship shake-up with Samantha has had me pretty pensive the last week or so. It has been mentioned in so many words in her Facebook status updates, and that has been a bit upsetting to read. I don't want a ten-year friendship to just fade away, but what to do?

I had her Christmas packages to mail today, so I decided to include a little note. Inside, I wrote that I was aware of the friendship impasse between us and was willing to work at repairing it. I paraphrased one of her Facebook status updates: I don't want our friendship to continue to be an emotional mess and would like it to continue growing in the same direction. However, I said, if she felt that our friendship had come to a fork in the road and needed to change course, I would understand.

Bottom line, the friendship is important to me to work on. I hadn't realized that I might lose friends as I move through all of this. I hadn't prepared myself for that.

DECEMBER 2, 2010

I can't seem to help feeling relieved and resentful at the same time. These days, Hakan comes home for dinner, kisses Mina goodnight, and goes out with his friends until about midnight. I feel a bit relieved because I do not have to sit through uncomfortable silence together in the living room. Yet, I can't help feeling resentful that he can just take ten years off the clock and go out and have fun all the time. I usually rein myself in by telling myself that I really do not want to be out at all hours of the night anymore partying, but having the opportunity once in a while would be nice.

He asked me if I had any plans for the weekend, and I told him that Daisy and I had signed up for a three-hour wreath-making workshop at Red Butte Garden starting at 9:00 a.m. Saturday morning. He first responded, "Well, what if I am out really late the night before?"

I just sighed and said, "Forget it. I will figure something out." He quickly backtracked and asked what time he needed to be up. We shall see if he is up by 8:30 a.m. Saturday morning because Daisy will be picking me up at 8:40 a.m. I haven't told Mina yet. She will be a teary-eyed mess when I leave. He will have to handle her for three hours on his own. It will be a good learning experience for both of them.

After yesterday's entry, Sofia wrote and suggested that I give myself a break from thinking of Samantha and our friendship issues. If she is to be a good friend, she will be there for me in the end. She said that I had other things to turn my attention to. She's right, but it is hard. Last April, my therapist told me to mourn my marriage and the man that I married. I did, and it has made this process easier. I wasn't prepared to mourn a friendship as well, and that is eating me up inside. I could imagine not being married to Hakan, but I hadn't even given a thought about life without my best friend. It is so easy when living so far apart to let the friendship just float away. I worry that so much time will pass that it will seem too difficult to cross over if one of us feels the urge to reconnect. I need to release this too, I guess. What was that old saying? Something about releasing a bird, setting it free. If it returns back to you, it is meant to be.

Abby and Megan, at the bookstore, really loved their shawls. I told them that I wanted them to know how much I appreciated their love, support, and hugs over the past year. It really meant a lot to be able to go to the bookstore and feel part of a family, especially since I live so far from home. Abby looked at me, gave me a big hug, and said, "You *are* loved! Don't forget it!"

December 7, 2010

It is a good day. I was smiling before I even had my coffee. Checking my phone as I was waiting for my coffee to brew, I saw that an old friend had found me through Facebook. I should clarify a bit more: my first boyfriend had found me after twenty-one years through Facebook. He is married and has a lovely family, but it was nice to write back and forth and live in the past for a little while. It reminded me what it was like to feel something for someone—the butterflies, the tummy flip-flops, and so on. I don't feel that with Hakan anymore, and all these little things reaffirm my decision.

I was a bit anxious going into the weekend because Hakan had said that he wanted to talk with me about things, but that conversation never happened because he just wasn't around.

Finally, last night after Mina was asleep, we talked a bit. He has chosen *not* to go to England (oh, dear) to see his brother and will stay a few days with Seyhan. He asked about the duplex for rent, and I told him that he had waited too long. It had already been rented. The Christmas break will provide him the opportunity to buy a car and look around for an apartment before classes start.

We also chose not to go back to therapy again. He said that we seem to be handling things okay and moving on. If we begin to have a communication breakdown again, we can always go back.

Hopefully, I will get those darn stipulations from the lawyer today or tomorrow so we can begin the bargaining. Hakan would like to have all the bargaining banter over with by the time my parents come on December 22 or to put it on hold until after they leave. I also would like it done as soon as possible because that means everything can be finalized sooner.

My mother-in-law sent us both a heartfelt e-mail the other day. She and everyone else are saddened that we have chosen to separate. They were all waiting for us to work it out somehow, but she wished us both happiness for the future. Honestly, I was too tired to write a new letter to her, so I used the letter I had written over the summer, which I hadn't ended up giving her. Why waste a good letter? I had worked hard on that one. I felt good about sending it. It provided a certain amount of closure for me.

The Christmas treat baking has begun, and I spent a lovely morning baking up some Turkish treats, listening to some funky African music, and lighting holiday candles. I feel like I am finally getting my act together. I have more energy to do things, and the house is a lot neater too! When you don't feel so oppressed, you can get so much more done with very little effort.

DECEMBER 8, 2010

> I don't want another opportunity to learn & grow, she said. I
> just want to eat crackers & watch Oprah & pet my cat.
> —StoryPeople

DECEMBER 9, 2010

I need to stop, stop, stop thinking about him, my old boyfriend. My mind is all aflutter, and I can't concentrate on anything! It has been a long time since I felt this attention and heard such compliments. Today, Mina and I went to Gardner Village with Marcia and Clare. I knew I would get my picture taken at some point, and I went through three or four outfits before I settled on something. I even went downstairs to look at some coats I hadn't worn in *years* and pulled out my vintage electric blue Valentino coat from the sixties. Someone is looking at *me* again, via Facebook photos, and I wanted to look good. Mina just stood there in the hall this morning asking me what I was doing as I ripped through one of the drawers in the hall linen closet—sheets, towels, and whatever else flying behind me. I was actually looking for my *makeup* kit from years past. She had never seen me put on a full face of makeup before—eye shadow, eyeliner, the works—and she studied it carefully. Then she ran and got her makeup and eagerly set up her makeup station and did the same. For the first time in a long time, someone had made me feel beautiful again.

I need to feel good about myself because it will be hard to feel anything positive once Hakan is served. I finally got the stipulations from the lawyer yesterday, and he is going to freak out when he reads it, especially the alimony part. He is already starting to get a bit antsy with the waiting. That leads to sarcasm and nastiness. For example, "Maybe I will get with *my* lawyer and send you *my* stipulations" or "Guess I will be living in a dump after this is all over because that will be all I can afford."

Breathe in, breathe out—that's all I can do because I am really trying hard not to engage because it just makes matters worse. He asked me if I had told anyone yet and said that it was "okay" if I did now. Thanks for the permission! He actually asked if I had told Daisy and asked if she would she tell everyone at work—you know, spread gossip—so he wouldn't have to do it. He is finding it hard to tell his boss that he is getting divorced. I told him that I would tell everyone that the feeling was mutual, but he thought that people might think that he was leaving his kid, and he didn't want them to think that. At this point, I don't care what or how he tells it. Tell everyone that I filed, and they can say, "Poor Hakan."

He has already started looking at ads in the paper for apartments but mostly in the Avenues area. He won't be around much if he is going to live over there.

We are both at the point of wanting to move on from each other and be done with all of this. It is the damn stipulations and negotiations that are really just going to suck, and I am so nervous about them.

The days go by easy enough, but the nights after Mina goes to sleep are difficult. We just sit there on opposite sides of the living room, on our own computers. My lawyer said that we could wait until after the holidays, but I just want to get it *over* with and stop dragging it out. Let's get back to ripping off the bandage and dealing with it so I can move on.

My house is trashed again—completely stress-related. A few days ago, I felt in complete control, and now as I feel like I am beginning to spin, my house is nutty. It is that frenetic energy that scatters stuff everywhere, and you just can't see it while you are spinning!

The only place I can enjoy myself is in my dreams. This makes it so hard to wake up in the morning. Last night's dream was so *real!*

It was summer, and K, my old boyfriend from Turkey, and his son, Ege, were here at my house. The kids were bigger, maybe six. We had all been outside in the afternoon and were slowly getting things picked up before making dinner. I had told the kids that they needed to pick from the garden what they were going to eat for dinner and then pick some raspberries for dessert. They had their own baskets, and they were overflowing with carrots, cucumbers, tomatoes, and squash. Mina was trying to explain to Ege that *her* cherry tomatoes tasted sweeter because she had put a lot of love into growing her plant from a baby seed. Ege was adamant that *his* were sweeter, and they stood there going back and forth tasting each other's tomatoes. They couldn't decide, so they went to call on Selleck, the little boy who lives next door. Selleck matter-of-factly told them that their tomatoes tasted *exactly* the same and went back inside.

Mina and Ege just looked at each other, shrugged their shoulders, and then went to pick some raspberries. But there was more giggling going on than picking because they were *eating* more raspberries than putting in the baskets, and they thought that was hysterical.

I was in the back garden doing some sort of digging or planting and had somehow gotten dirt on my face as I brushed the hair out of my eyes. K was comfortably sitting on the back deck with a drink, taking in all the craziness.

With a look on his face that said he had an idea, he turned and went into the house and then came back out with an umbrella. I looked up and wondered what he was going to do with an umbrella on a hot summer day, but he had a plan. After pulling out the garden hose and laying it on the grass, he called me over. I was a little suspicious that he might spray me with the garden hose, but he reassured me that I would like it. Trustingly, I came close. K sat on the grass, motioned for me to curl up on his lap, opened the umbrella over our heads, and turned on the water. I asked him what he was doing, and smiling, he said, "We are going to hide in plain sight under our waterfall." With that said, he pointed the hose, running with water, at full stream straight up in the air. *Wooooosh*! The water shot high up in the air and then came down with a *splat* on top of the umbrella, falling all around us. Underneath our waterfall, K kissed me and tried to wipe the dirt smudges from my forehead.

We had a few moments alone under the waterfall before the kids noticed it and wanted to come under too. Somehow, we all crowded on K's lap under the waterfall. The kids loved to stick their hands in the water as it fell down and make their own waterfall from their hands.

DECEMBER 12, 2010

I am tired and emotional and nervous and whatever other adjective in that genre you could add. We have had a busy few days with Mina's holiday dance performance, the kids' workshop at the bookstore, and the Polar Express concert the next morning.

While we were at Mazza Friday night for dinner, Hakan started to get sarcastic and nasty, and his facial expressions expressed more than his words. "Are you *happy* now? What are you going to do in that big house?" And there was something about me being selfish. I am really trying not to hear or acknowledge these outbursts because it will just escalate. I could tell whenever he had thought of yet another irritating thing; his face showed it loud and clear.

He is being very proactive in looking for an apartment, mainly close to the university and downtown. However, he said that he was hesitant to sign anything because he didn't want to give up his rights to live in his house. Nevertheless, he took the checkbook with him yesterday when he went out.

He rented a movie after dinner, but I just didn't have the energy to be alone in a room with him, so I fell asleep with Mina around 7:30 p.m. It is total avoidance, I know, but I am so tired of battling. If things are this edgy before he gets the papers, I can only imagine how it will be after he gets them. Daisy told me that if it is too much for me to handle, Mina and I are welcome to stay at her house.

Then I got an e-mail from his Aunt Canan, who is so upset about this turn of events. She doesn't know how all of this got so mixed up. They all thought that he had made a big change, and we would be able to work it out. How, she wondered, did this all get to this point? She wrote about how Mina needs to be the most important thing now and asked how she is going to deal with this and blah, blah, blah.

Mina will transition better than all of us, and to be honest, that is the least of my concerns at this point. She does not ask about him when he is not here and easily says goodbye when he leaves. Of course, the immediacy of it will be difficult: transferring of household items, furniture, clothes.

Last night, Mina tripped over Sofia in the hallway and banged her knee. She already had a little pimple-like irritation that had been progressing the last few days, and when she fell, she landed right on that irritation. It burst and bled, and she cried and cried. Hakan looked at me and asked me how she would deal with the divorce if she couldn't handle a small cut.

He and his family seem to be looking at me like I am out to hurt my child and don't care about her feelings. I don't have the energy to even respond. I just have to let it go.

I was reminded today of a dream that I had months ago, way back in the summer. I can't remember if I wrote about it here or not, so I will write it again.

I cried when I woke up from it because of how I felt in the dream. In my dream, there was this man and his children who were in my life. I could never see his face, but he had dark, sort of curled hair. What I remember most is how much I was *loved* and cared for. We were all having a picnic somewhere. The grass was so green, and the sun was so bright and warm that I could not fully see this man's face as he sat down beside me. We sat all curled up together watching the kids play, and I was happy.

Mina woke up at that point, and I couldn't hold onto his hand anymore, and it was like he was falling away from me.

I felt that dream all through the day and wished to the stars above that night to send me someone who would want to hug me back when I hugged him.

I have started actively dreaming again—the type of dreams that leave you feeling so tired when you wake up because they were so real. These dream realities almost feel like little parallel universes that I can tap into only when I am sleeping.

These days I feel pulled into escapism. I just want to escape normal reality for my dreams, but then I am so tired upon waking that I want to just roll over and go back to sleep after the dream is over. My dreams are a wonderful gift to see every night, but I feel like I need to wear my sneakers to bed to keep up with how fast-paced they are. There are dreams where I am activly engaged in the storyline. There are also dreams which are presented to me like a play, enacted before me as I sleep. The following dream was presented in a "book" form with turning pages and moving images on each page. Was I reading a book or was I watching a film? In a dream, anything is possible.

Last night's dream:

There once was a man who asked his girl across the other end of the world what she wanted for Christmas this year. Her simple answer: "Send me a message on the wings of the bird so I might get his message on Christmas Day."

There was a place where the birds come along a magical inlet of the Bosphorus. That was where he must go to find the right bird. He was celebrating the day with his son, and hand in hand, they buy bags of seed from the bird lady on the corner. One bag they throw aimlessly at the birds to get their attention and bring them closer. They come by the hundreds! When they fly up, the man and his son almost can't see the sun through all the dark wings. Now comes the hard part: sitting still with seed all around them, luring that special bird closer. It needs to be close for them to whisper in its ear. Sitting still was especially hard for the four-year-old boy who wants to jump and chase them, but he was curious to see if a bird will come sit on his hand . . . and it *does*! As he stared in wonder and amazement at this huge bird on his small hand, his father stretches out his hands, full of food. Slowly, the bird inches his way over and makes himself comfortable in this man's warm, comfortable hands. The man was amazed at this bird staring straight at him, and he knows that he had found the right one.

Bending his head slowly, he whispered his message in the bird's ear and sends the animal off into the sky. All the birds rose up in unison, and in an instant, they are all gone.

This bird, unbeknownst to the man, told the story to another bird, and that bird told another, and so on. Soon, a whole flock of birds was entranced and wanted to help bring this message to the girl across the world.

On Christmas Day, the sun rises all pink and orange over the snowcapped mountain, and there is a bit of magic in the air as the girl opens the window shade and sees *hundreds* of birds on her lawn. Upon seeing her, they rose up at once and begin their dance from the lawn to the tree across the street and back again. It was sort of a circular motion that creates a soft wind. The wind whispered ever so softly the message: "Merry Christmas. We are bound in time and space and will one day find a place. In this life or in the next, upon your pillow my head will set."

When I woke up from this next dream, I felt as though I had sand falling from between my toes!

> It was nighttime, and the kids wanted to camp outside on the beach. We put up the tent, and they loved falling asleep while looking up at the stars through the screen top. K and I pulled a blanket and a pillow outside and lay down next to each other on the beach. The sand seemed to envelop us and hold us in its big hands. It was so dark except for the millions of stars above us. The inky darkness of the water contrasted with the sparkling stars. The moon was full and so close that it seemed we could scoop out some moon ice cream and fill ourselves up on moonbeams. Suddenly, a shooting star broke out across the sky, and K turned to me to ask me if I had wished for anything. What else could I have wished for when I had everything that I could ever wish for right there on the beach? He smiled, and we just lay in silence because there wasn't anything more that we needed to say.

DECEMBER 14, 2010

My mind has been preoccupied lately with the word "fit": how people fit into each other's lives, how I fit into everyone else's lives, how working will fit into Mina's and my new life. It applies to everything and everyone. We use the word all the time without really thinking about it: "Those two just fit together like they were carved from the same stone," or "There is so much going on in my life that I can't fit you in."

This all made me think of puzzles and puzzle pieces. It seems to me that people are born with an empty box, and we all go out in search of puzzle pieces to put in our box to make our life puzzle. Easy ones to find are mom, dad, family, but the harder ones are friends, lovers, work, hobbies, whatever makes you *you*. Sometimes, we find some that fit, and somehow, as we are putting the pieces together, a few accidentally get scattered under the couch and lost for a time. It is not until we start cleaning out all the other junk that has built up over time that we find them and hope they still fit. Some still fit, but some pieces, because they are made out of wood, you know, warp and bend. They don't fit in your life puzzle anymore and fall out or need to be removed. When you find the people that are supposed to be in your life, you just *know*. I think the interesting thing about this puzzle is that it is never just one picture. Events move around as you experience different things. Right now, I feel people who love me moving in and around in a circle. At the end of our life, when we look back, we will have this huge, huge puzzle to smile at and remember.

When we rediscover the pieces that got lost under the couch, we don't know how to fit each of them in our puzzles. We know they fit somewhere, but we haven't found that connecting piece yet that will let us say, "Aha! I know where this goes!"

I feel the gathering of friends around me this week, and it feels like my puzzle is shifting into a circular shape as everyone holds hands with each other in a protective circle, with me in the center. I saw Daisy on Saturday. Linda came by Sunday with a bottle of wine. Jane yesterday morning. Gaia in the afternoon. Linda came over in the afternoon and brought me a bag of lemons with a note that read, "When you have lemons, make lemonade!" Sofia is texting from Hawaii. Marcia called to see how things are going. Heather was going to come down this morning from Bountiful, but she got sick and will have to postpone. I even have a new friend, Toni (from my 29 Gifts blog), who is willing to drive down from Farmington if I need anything. However, there is one person missing, and it pains me to not feel her presence in my life anymore.

Gaia and I were able to sit and chat for over two hours yesterday. Mina was fantastic and played the whole time on her own. Gaia has a way of succinctly articulating what I may be trying to express.

She said that too many people say, "It's because I love you that I am telling you this," but it is what *they*, whoever they may be, think you should be doing in a certain situation. It is better to say, "How can I help you and support you? I may not understand what you want to do, but how can I help you get there?"

So many preach advice and then pat you on your back and say, "Okay, now go do it!" In this fast-paced society, we are expected to move through things fast, fast, fast to get to the next best thing. I am more like the turtle than the hare in this case. I move really slowly, and sometimes I even go back in my shell and hide for a time. Maybe that helps me heal. If I remember the fable correctly, slow and steady wins the race, so I think I will continue and be a turtle for a little while longer.

DECEMBER 15, 2010

The papers arrived in the mail yesterday afternoon. My lawyer officially filed on Monday, December 14, just about three weeks after I met with her. Seriously, if I had known that it would take three weeks to draw up the papers with all the information we talked about way back when, I would have gone to see her when I got back from Rhode Island. Thirty days from now, it should be final.

My heart started to palpitate when I saw the papers because I didn't know how the night was going to go. Would he open them right when he got home? Would he wait until after I went to bed? What would he do, and more importantly, how would he react? I needed a glass of wine and was drinking it by 3:00 p.m., followed by beer at dinner.

It was time to clean! Time to work off this nervous energy! Mina was excited—she loves to clean floors. We are slowly preparing for Mina's Razzleberry Raspberry Pizza Party this Saturday afternoon. She invited her schoolmates over to make dessert pizzas and do a holiday project.

When he came home and saw the papers last night, he said that he shouldn't open them at home. He will open them today at work, alone. He is not feeling inclined to agree with the short-term alimony. He doesn't know if he can afford it. He will not have grant money coming in this year to cover summer salary. We talked calmly in the kitchen about why it was important to me that I have more up-front. I tried to explain that I was thinking of Mina. I don't want her to feel that she has lost both parents if I have to leave her in day care and go to work. I just want enough to get us through the next few years, until she is in school full-time. Honestly, at this point, it is not about the money for me. It is about my daughter's mental stability. I am at the point where I would forgo money long-term just to be done with this involvement.

My parents don't want me to give on how much I need or the duration. They want me to get as much as I am owed by law. That's completely understandable, but I want to work out a deal that works for us all so that I can move on.

Hakan was also concerned about how the savings account was going to be allocated. Would there be special consideration that he was starting his life over, and would he get a bigger share of that pie? We have about $60,000 in the savings at this point. Thirty thousand dollars is not enough for him to start his life over?

He will be out of the house starting on Christmas Day and permanently by January 1, 2011. So even though the divorce will not be final for two more weeks, we will have started our new lives apart in 2011. That is exactly what I have wanted.

Before putting Mina to sleep last night, I had a very vague chat with her about life. She was upset about something, and I took that as an opportunity to talk to her about feelings. We talked about feeling sad, happy, grumpy, and lonely. It is okay to feel all those things, I told her. We can always sit and talk through the feelings together. There are so many people, near and far, who love Mina. I listed them for her and asked her if she believed me. She nodded her head. I asked her if she trusted that I would never do anything to hurt her. She nodded again.

I wanted to talk about feelings before they all got mixed up with everything that will happen next week.

2:14 p.m.

Thump-thump-thump-thump goes my heart. Hakan read the documents, and he is pissed. He is so furious that he is willing to go to court and may even file for joint custody. I was pretty calm actually and told him to write up what he wants; let's come to some sort of agreement, I said.

I am so not looking forward to dinner tonight. I just need to keep breathing, in and out. At the moment, I feel like I am going to have a heart attack!

My lawyer said that she has worked with his lawyer before and that those cases settled out of court, so I have hope we can do this.

At the moment, I have made myself a tall cup of coffee and am taking some time for myself.

2:44 P.M.

Okay, I have finished my coffee. Now I am sitting at the dining room table praying for a miracle. Even though I have a lot of friends and support, I am feeling pretty alone. I am the only one who can live this and go through it. People can be there for you to help you up if you fall, but they can't move through the darkness for you. At the end of the road, when you finally come out of the darkness and feel the bright sun on your face again, you feel empowered that you were able to persevere to the very end. Knowing the end does not really make the darkness more bearable, just acceptable as a stepping stone to the place where you need to be. I am feeling pretty cold at the moment, and I can't get warm even with all these layers on and warm coffee in my tummy.

8:20 P.M.

You know, the build up to this point was much worse. I have to say that I feel strangely peaceful. My life may be blown to bits as Hakan blusters, but in the end, I will still be standing. Why do I let myself get all worked up about all of this?

He was enraged at my stipulations. He called them ridiculous and said they needed to be thrown into the garbage. He is putting on his boxing gloves and is ready to fight. But what is he fighting for? Money? Visits to Turkey? What?

He is going to write his own stipulations, and I am to compromise with *him*. I think he is using the custody card (the threat of joint custody) to scare me into settling for less money. I really don't feel scared, or maybe I am beyond it at this point. Once you open the floodgates, you really need to just put on your swim fins and floaties and see where the deluge takes you. The more you try and control the raging current, the more exhausted you will become.

I don't feel anything: anger, hurt, pain, sadness. Nothing. Maybe I am numb, or maybe I have moved past some of it and am beginning to feel my own self-worth again. His opinion doesn't matter so much anymore and doesn't define my emotions or me. I used to crumple or tremble if he looked at me with disdain, but now I just shrug my shoulders and walk away.

I do need to working on eating better. I have been cooking up a storm but not eating so much of it. It is the *act* of cooking that seems to be feeding me. Today I have had a banana, a handful of almonds, and a bit of a salad.

The first night is over, and now we can move past it. It was horrible in its own way, but the anticipation is done now. Maybe I can sleep tonight. Wouldn't *that* be nice!

December 17, 2010

I escaped into my alternate reality last night when I fell asleep. Just two short and lovely dreams, but enough to empower me to keep moving forward:

1. In the dream, I had taken the summer off from going to Turkey and rented a house right on the beach in Rhode Island for a month with Mina. K and Ege came for two weeks to stay with us. Mina called to Ege to go outside and dig in the sand with her while K and I made breakfast in the kitchen. I was cooking up some vegetables to make an omelet and was stirring them. K came up behind me, put down his orange juice (with ice), and gave me a kiss on the side of my neck; the coldness of his lips was startling, but it was nice. He remained standing behind me, and I just seemed to fit in between his arms. With one hand, he held my stirring hand, and we stirred together. His other hand was around my waist. Time stood still in that moment.

2. There is a direct flight from Salt Lake to Paris, and I dreamed that I took Mina to Paris for her spring break in April. He met us there for one day, one night. Our meeting spot was under the Eiffel Tower. Mina and I were waiting, and K saw us before we saw him. He came up behind me, turned me around, and kissed me. As we walked back to the hotel, Mina was tired, and he carried her back. She fell asleep before we even made it there, so he and I decided to just sit on a bench in Paris, Mina sleeping on our laps, and just *be* and enjoy the short time that we had.

That's it. That is what kept me up until 1:00 a.m. last night.

Today, Hakan asked me if I had changed my relationship status on Facebook yet to reflect our divorce. I had thought of doing that, but out of respect for him, I'd decided I shouldn't do anything until everything was final and signed. He would like me to change my status tomorrow. Honestly, that's fine with me . . . it's just weird for him to ask me to do it.

We discussed the car and how to handle it when my parents come: who would be the one to rent? I left the decision up to him because it really doesn't matter to me one way or the other. Personally, if I were him, I would rent a car to go search for a car, buy said car, and return the rental. He needs to get a car anyway. Get it; be done with it. He came to the same conclusion around lunchtime and called to tell me that. Of course, he had to add that whatever value our current car has would be deducted from my share of the savings and go to him. Just take the money from the savings and put a down payment on a car, Hakan. It is as simple as that. I am not trying to rob you. I have let go of controlling the money. Let it flow toward me in unhindered abundance, however it comes. I cannot receive anything if I have my arms closed tight, hoarding what I have!

On an exciting note, Mina decided to take her nap in her bed this afternoon, and we will have her all set up to sleep in it tonight! She crawled in *on her own* and fell asleep! This is such a relief. If I can get her to sleep there at night, then I can slowly move myself out into my own bed over the next month or so.

We are in good shape for Mina's Raspberry Pizza Party tomorrow afternoon. Seven of her school friends will come over around 3:00 p.m. and make yummy pizzas. I was very proactive and looked in the freezer before making anything. I found half of a chocolate cake, a zucchini bread, and puff pastry. Instant food! I fixed up Mina's favorite spinach, herb, and egg-filled puff pastry and will put that in the oven tomorrow. Since we have been picking up and organizing little by little over the past few days, there was not much left to do today.

I am glad that I started early to get ready for the party because Hakan and I are going to try to go to the required divorce orientation class and divorce education class tomorrow morning at the courthouse. Gaia said that she will come by and stay with Mina from about 8:30 a.m. to around 12:30 p.m. If she can't, then Hakan can go on his own, and I will go when my parents come. We are not required to go together.

All this dialogue between K and me has really validated me in many ways. There are times when I can be a bit goofy. When Hakan and I first got married and moved here, I really enjoyed doing little, funny things for his lunches. I made up fresh fruit salads, a little container of sliced cucumbers, carrots, and a skyscraper-sized sandwich and topped it all with a little note. I remember meeting him at the cafeteria with the lunch, and he would never take everything out and put it on the table because he was embarrassed for others to see our picnic. I would tell him, "Let them see! I am sure they would love to have a wife who would make such love-filled lunches or just even a sandwich in general. How many of your colleagues' wives make their lunches?"

Today, I had a resurgence of silliness and put a birthday candle in the middle of Mina's spinach spanakopita for her party. I took a picture and sent it to K with a note that read, "Happy birthday! I made you a spanakopita cake, but I couldn't light the candle because it was melting from the bottom up! Ha ha!"

He was so touched that he wrote back immediately and said that my thoughtfulness had made him feel so special and rendered him speechless.

December 20, 2010

I have been very melancholy lately. The weather hasn't helped, with it being so grey. We went to the divorce orientation class and the divorce education class. There were so many people there and so many had kids under the age of six. It's so sad to see so many relationships end this way.

One thing they did stress was to try not to be so vindictive or controlling toward the divorcing spouse because it really hurts the child more in the end. I don't know how this affected Hakan's intentions, but at least there are no more looks anymore, and things have calmed a bit.

He came to me yesterday to talk about the savings account and the allocation of said funds. He was calm and clear, and I listened. He had looked up the value of the car ($8,000) and calculated how much we bought when we moved in ($4,000). He proposed that we divide the savings in half, and then he would get $12,000 more than half and I would get $12,000 less. Basically, he would end up with $42,000, and I would end up with $18,000. I thought about it and what was more important to me. I am trying not to be so afraid of not having enough money. It is that fear that sabotages things. All I want is enough alimony so that I can stay home and be there for Mina while she deals with all of this. That is more important to me than savings. I am hoping that with my being so amenable to his request, he will relax a bit about mine. It's a gamble, I know, but I am really trying to be open to receive.

We are nearing the end of all of this, and it is so very sad. We had our last Sunday breakfast together as a family, and he has two more dinners at home before my parents arrive. Come Christmas Day, he will be a nomad until January 1. He has been packing all weekend long and has taken a lot of stuff to his office. He has decided to take only personal things and the office furniture, which belongs to the school anyway. He asked that we take Mina out for a few hours next week so that he can come by and get them without her seeing.

There are ways to make old things new, and I will be heading to IKEA to do that very thing after Christmas. A new cushion for the IKEA chair and a new couch cover should make the room feel a bit fresher.

I'm still not eating so well—or sleeping, for that matter. Mina made me breakfast the other day. She put her little hands on her little hips and looked up at me and said, "Mama! You need to eat, you know!" Then she went into her snack drawer, pulled out a packet of oatmeal, poured it into a bowl, and got hot water from the bathroom sink. Yes, I ate it. The next day, she asked if I had eaten dinner after she was asleep and what I had eaten. We have officially reversed roles, and she is now mothering me.

I am not feeling motivated to do much of anything today except sit. Linda brought me some lemons last week to make "lemonade," but I thought that lemon cranberry cookies might be nice. When life sends you lemons, make lemon cranberry cookies! Ha!

THREE

BREATHE DEEP

Balance, heal, transform.

DECEMBER 23, 2010

It has been a tough few days. I am having a hard time wrestling with all of this. I hate that this decision is so painful for so many others, like Hakan and his family. Hakan has been slowly moving things out of the house after I put Mina to sleep. I can hear him rustling around downstairs, in his room, around the living room. He is hurt and angry. That is completely understandable. I just hope in time we can all come to some sort of acceptance. He would like to meet next week and see if the two of us can work out negotiations on our own, without lawyers, and save money. I asked him to send me his ideas so that I can be prepared.

He has pretty much moved out and decided not to stay here until Christmas Day. I had a hard time Tuesday night while he packed everything for the last time. I stayed in Mina's room and couldn't come out after she fell asleep. I admit it—I hid and avoided facing things.

Mina and I dropped him at his office Wednesday morning. He had one last suitcase and a bag. I really wanted to give him a hug and say goodbye, but I didn't think he would be receptive to that. I left it alone and just said, "Goodbye, Hakan," and he was gone.

As far as K, well, I believe the universe sent him to me for a short time to help me through the past few weeks. He has been just about my constant confidant through it all. He catapulted into my life like a meteor and was the last piece of my life puzzle to fit into place. His presence helped me remember what it was like to feel beautiful, loved, and special. I started to feel like *me* again and started to dress up and put makeup on. I had a few moments over the past few weeks where I just felt like sitting, crying, and feeling sorry for myself. I had this image of myself just curling up in a corner and becoming an emotional mess. But he was there, and he took both my hands and pulled me to my feet. He told me that he believed in me, that I was doing what was right for everyone—even Hakan—and that I was stronger than I thought I was. He pushed me back into the ring to fight for my life. We lived in a dream reality for a few weeks, and I was exhausted from dreaming by the time I woke up. There seemed to be a sort of gravity that kept pulling us back together though e-mails. The last dream was pretty poignant and summed up our lives perfectly.

This concept of magnetism and gravity pulls entered my dreams a couple days ago, on December 21. As a child, I played with my magnets on my parents' glass-topped coffee table. Sometimes, I would put one on top of the glass and see if I could pull the other underneath. They would be stuck together, but with a layer of glass between them. My dream somehow flipped this glass table on its end, and instead of magnets, there was us, pulled by some unknown force toward each other, separated by an infinite glass wall. We could see into each other's lives on the other side, but we couldn't hear each other or touch each other. The only thing we could do was match our hands and walk forward, forever walking hand in hand down this glass wall, looking for a door or a window or something that would allow us to actually meet.

We will always live parallel lives, and that is how it will be. I haven't heard from him in a few days, and you know, it's okay. He has a life to live, and so do I. It's enough to know that somewhere out there, someone cares about you and is there for you if you ever need it. He helped me find myself again. I had a dream the other night in which I was all dressed up, hair done, makeup just so, and I was waving both hands in the air and screaming at the top of my lungs, "I am back!" It's a good feeling to find yourself again.

I really feel loved by so many people, and that helps propel me forward. Linda came by the other day with a Christmas gift that her husband had made for Mina and me. It was a handmade wooden kaleidoscope! (She also included another bottle of wine in the gift bag—she thought I needed some more booze!)

We sat at the table and brainstormed names for my personal chef business. By the end of the day, we were laughing hysterically at some of the names we were coming up with. My brain is so fried these days that I kept coming up with silly names. The night before, I had kept seeing a head of lettuce with each leaf saying something else, such as "lettuce cook," "lettuce learn," "lettuce shop"—get it? I was laughing so hard I almost peed my pants telling Linda about it. Then she came up with her own: E.T. cooks! I guess, at times, I do feel like an extraterrestrial! We were on the floor rolling with laughter.

Oh! I bought myself a sassy dress from Anthropologie the other day! I got an e-mail with a coupon for an extra 25 percent off, and I found a fun dress to wear for the holidays and in the summer. My hairstylist is thinking up a sassy new hairstyle for me too! New year, new me!

December 24, 2010

It's Christmas Eve, and the weather has cleared a little, and my head feels better. If I said that it was easy letting K go, I would be lying. It's hard to go without talking with him (by e-mail). The other day, we decided to set up a "coincidental" meeting at a park while I am in Turkey this summer. He takes his son to the same park every weekend, and we talked about meeting up there for a quick hello—just for a few minutes. That night I had a dream that we were both at the park at the designated day and time, only when the time came, he chose not to take the chance and say hello. We just looked at each other, smiled, and moved on our way. These dreams seem to prepare me.

He must have mentioned me to someone who told him to just cut it off before it got out of control. I think that is just what he is doing. I understand, and I told him earlier not to jeopardize his family for me. It's just hard now that it's become a reality. I am grateful for the time we had and how he helped me through such a difficult time, though that doesn't make it any less sad when he has to go away. Do I wish that he never found me? No, this has made me realize what I want from someone and what to hold out for.

Another dream last night woke me up. It was another "goodbye" sort of dream. I have to let him go. Even though he was mine in the beginning, he is not mine in the end.

There was once a girl who had a little cottage on a little beach. She was a warm, loving girl and tended her little garden by the sea. She was the Sea Maiden who took care of the tides. Each morning, she would take her broom and sweep the tide out off the sand. At night, she would call it back, make little sand pillows, and put the sea to sleep.

One night, she felt lonely and stepped out onto the sand to sit under the stars. The sand was a magical sand. It was never cool, but rather always warm and radiated love up through her feet and gave her a tingling feeling all over.

She sat on the sand and looked up at the stars and the Man in the Moon. The Man in the Moon looked down and wondered why she looked so sad, and he asked her. Her eyes were the color of the sea and seemed to move with the current.

She wanted a friend. So he sent down stars to play with her up and down the beach. They danced and played, and the stars did acrobatics to make her laugh, but still she wasn't happy.

She wanted someone to love and someone to hug her. So the Man in the Moon whipped up a little sea breeze to come and wraps its sea-spray arms around her to comfort her, but still she wasn't happy.

She really just wanted someone to hold her hand. At that, the Man in the Moon himself left his seat among the stars and came down to sit next to her on the beach. They sat in silence on the sand, and he held her hand under the sparkling sky. At last, she was happy.

However, the Man in the Moon couldn't stay because it was the sun's turn to come out and shine. He had to go away. He was never hers to keep anyway, but he would always be with her, shining down and smiling. If he stayed with her, others would be sad. He said that one day, he would send down a moonbeam and swing her up next to him, and they would cross the skies together, but this was not that time. But she would be comforted that he was always there, whether she could see him or not.

And the girl was happy.

December 26, 2010

The holiday was filled with lots of mixed feelings. It went very well but was sad too. Hakan called Christmas Eve and spoke with Mina. He told her that he would be here on Christmas morning. He backhandedly asked if he could come and stay Christmas Eve, and I said no. We had originally planned for him to be here through Christmas morning, but he changed his mind at the last minute and decided *not* to be here. It is not healthy for anyone for him to keep changing his mind back and forth. He said that he would get to the house as early as he could, and he did. He was here by 7:30 in the morning, and I am really glad for Mina that he was.

It is amazing how people can change in a few days—physically, I mean. I was so startled to see that he is starting to grow a light beard or goatee on his chin. He was surprised to see me in my new dress too. We are both changing in our own ways.

There were a few moments where he got emotional and had to excuse himself. It is really hard for me to see someone hurting and not be able to do anything about it. He would like to see Mina for an hour or so this week, but it will be difficult to tear Mina away from Nana. I will try to get her to go to the bookstore with me, and he wants to meet us there.

I did call his mom on Ojo to say hello and to show her that Mina was enjoying the beading present she sent. It was really, really awkward. She didn't even really look at us and didn't really want to talk to us. How am I going to work out our trips to Turkey? I am at a loss as to how to handle it. Hakan has said that he does *not* want to coordinate trips with me and Mina to Turkey. That means he will not spend time with Mina in Turkey, and the responsibility will fall on me to make sure Mina gets time with the whole family. Where are we going to stay? My aunt and uncle will be in Ayvalik, at the summer house, and not in Istanbul. As nice as it would be to spend all our time there, that will not be possible. I guess I could stay at the Istanbul house on my own, which is fine, but how am I going to get Mina across the Bosphorus all the time to see his family? If we can't even talk on the Ojo or phone for a few minutes, how am I going to be able to stay, comfortably, at their house for two weeks? My friend Hayri called me the other night to see how I was. I jokingly told him that Mina and I will stay with him when he moves back to Turkey at the end of January. Mina is comfortable with him, and he would have a more central apartment. He laughed and said that that might actually work out!

Yesterday, I wrote to K and said goodbye. I said that I completely understood that he needed to distance himself. I wished him well and told him that I would always be here for him if he needed anything. Of course, after I did that, he began writing again. We have agreed that I will still send my dream-stories, and we'll leave it at that for a little while. I sent him the description of my latest dream, from last week:

> It was a beautiful Saturday morning, and I was reading on
> the bench in the park. I saw K and Ege come into the park,
> but I kept reading. They had brought a ball, and the ball got
> away from Ege, and he ran after it toward my reading bench.

He and I started talking. He told me his name was Ege, and I said, "Oh! So *you* are Ege! The fairies who wake up the flowers in the morning told me all about you! After they wake up the flowers here, they fly around the world to my house to wake up my flowers! I heard them talking one day about this sweet little boy from the park. When I asked them who they were talking about, they told me of this sweet, kind, thoughtful little boy who comes to this park with his father each weekend. I happened to be near the park today and thought I would stop and read here for a while."

We sat a talked a little bit, and then I asked if he wanted a story before I had to go. I asked him if he knew of the Man in the Moon and the Sea Maiden story. He shook his head, and I started the story. He sat, and I acted out the story as I told it. He asked for another story before I had to go, so I asked him if he knew how magical he was. "No," he said.

"Well, you have magic that starts from the tips of your toes and goes all the way up to the tips of your hair. You are so magical that you can make others feel loved by just hugging them." I asked him if sometimes his father comes home from work, lots of things on his mind, and just sits quietly on the couch. "I bet that when you go over and climb in his lap and put your head on his chest, he feels better and smiles at you."

Ege shook his head yes.

"There is a fun, colorful, magical way you can share your love with others. Do you know how to make love balls? No? Well, let me show you how, and then you can make them for whomever you want."

So we all sat cross-legged on the grass, and I opened my arms big and wide. I took my hands and pretended that I was feeling the outside of an invisible ball shape. "This is a magical love ball," I said. "It can be as big or as small as you want it to be. In it, you pull colors from all around you and stuff them inside with all your magic and love."

I waved my arms like I was grabbing different colors as they flew around me. I stuffed them into my ball, shaping the ball in a big round shape as I went. I put in green and pink and blue and yellow, with a sprinkling of rainbow dust.

"And when you are done, you give the designated person the heads-up—'Baba! Here comes your love ball!' And you throw it to him and *poof!* He instantly smiles and feels so much better. You can make small ones and put them in pockets to take with you when you feel scared. When you reach into your pocket, you can feel all the warmth and tingling from all the swirling colors!"

He sat so seriously and made his first love ball and asked K which colors he would like. After Ege was done, he threw it to his father, and they had the biggest smiles on their faces.

I told him to never forget that his love is magical, and even a little smile can make the world brighter. Then I said I had to fly away myself. I was like the leaves—when the wind picks up, I must fly away home. He asked for more stories, and I said, "Maybe next year, if the wind is right, it will send me back here one morning." I told him that it was so nice to have met him and that he was just as sweet as the fairies said.

Then it was time for me to go, and I looked up at K, smiled, collected my things, and got into a taxi to go home.

DECEMBER 29, 2010

Mom and I have been doing some cleaning and clearing. It really helps to have an extra set of hands to work through everything so much faster. I finally pulled out the boxes of my wedding china and used them. They had never been used and were still in the original mailing case! I had forgotten they were so pretty! You can't imagine how nice it felt to pull out the decade-old everyday dishes and replace them with the beautiful china! I plan on celebrating every day by eating on these dishes, not just special occasions!

After clearing that space, it was on to my closets and the back pantry. It is so nice to have Mom here to help get it done. With all this going on, sometimes these small projects can seem really daunting. Cleaning is cathartic and emotional. During the process of going through my closet, I came upon my jewelry box. I found wedding gifts (necklaces, pearls, etc.) from his family with the original wedding notes tucked inside. The gifts were special-occasion pieces, and I had never worn them. I feel like I let a decade of my life go by, waiting for that special occasion. Why? Why did I wait to live, to celebrate *life*? We never used the china, I never wore the jewelry, and I held onto special dresses. I still have the outfit I wore after I changed out of my wedding dress. It still fits. I am going to wear that outfit one sunny spring day, even if I am only going to get a coffee at Starbucks!

I gave the jewelry to Mom to take back to Rhode Island and put in their safety deposit box for Mina. What else could I do? I also took my engagement ring and wedding band and gave them to her as well. I had inherited the diamond ring from my Great-Aunt Margie and had a new setting made for the stone. I still remember going with Mom to get a setting for it. I loved that ring. It's beautiful, but there is no reason to have a ring worth over $30,000 sitting in my house when it would be much safer in the family security deposit box. I also found old ticket stubs and letters from Hakan from before we got married. It makes me cry to read them now. How did we get to this point?

It really is the small things that power you forward. We have a battery-operated thermostat in the hallway, and the battery has been low for months. I remember mentioning it to Hakan. I thought I could just change out the AA batteries and be done with it, but Hakan put me off by saying he would have to reprogram it, and it would take a long time. I never did it. There was enough juice in the batteries to signal the heat to come on, but not enough if I wanted to turn *up* the heat. I solved that problem by just putting on another sweater.

Well, Mom gets chilly and wanted to turn the heat up, and I told her it needed more batteries. So she went downstairs, got two, brought them up, and handed them to me. I have to say, I actually stood there in the hallway looking from the batteries to the thermostat, wondering what would happen. Silly me—nothing happened. The thermostat retains enough charge to allow you to change the batteries without having to reprogram the whole thing.

This little thing is such an example of my life: needing to change but frozen in action. I can't tell you how great I felt after changing those two damn batteries! Who would have thought?

I met with Hakan yesterday around lunchtime to see if we could come to some sort of agreement. It is interesting how the universe speaks to you in different ways. As I was parking the car, a song by Roxette from the eighties came on—"It must have been love, but it's over now!" the woman sang. I had a few minutes before our meeting, so I sat and listened to it. In a way, it gave me some extra strength.

We sat, we discussed, and he laid out his ideas. I really do not know how much fight I have left in me. He is agreeing to give me enough money to stay home with Mina for the next few years, but the bare minimum. Here are his ideas:

1. Alimony

   He wants to keep Mina comfortable in the lifestyle she is used to until she gets to first grade and said that he would pay adequate alimony that would gradually step down each year for five years until Mina is in first grade. He said that I will probably be working by then, and he doesn't want to give me more that what is actually needed. He said that the judge would take into consideration minimum wage and that I might only get about $850/month alimony from the judge (according to his lawyer).

2. House

   Even though the current value of the house is almost the same as what we owe, he is considering the money we put *into* it as equity. There was a $20,000 gift from my parents, $30,000 from his parents, and $10,000 from us, for a total of $60,000. The current retirement account is $136,000. He proposed that we subtract $60,000 from the $136,000 and divide in two the remaining $76,000 from the retirement. In other words, in exchange for what we put into the house, he would want a bigger chunk of the retirement, and then I would have the house free and clear. He was confused about how it could be completely in my name without refinancing. His lawyer said that in order for me to have the house completely in my name, I would have to refinance and that the bank wouldn't do it with my having no income. Hakan said that he is fine signing something that says the house is mine, and he wants no claim and we can keep the house papers as they are. But, he says, this prevents him from buying another house with his name still on this mortgage.

3. Mina

He agrees that sole physical custody is the best for Mina right now, but he is not happy about the joint legal, with me having the deciding vote. He wants a clause put in that says we will revisit the physical custody situation when Mina turns ten years old and possibly change it to joint custody. My goal is to get Mina to the point where she is comfortable staying with him overnight and for days at a time. I am not looking at sole custody as keeping Mina from him. As long as we can sit down amicably and talk things out and make this a comfortable environment for Mina, I am comfortable with setting our own guidelines over the coming years.

4. Turkey

He will put it in writing that he will pay for my and Mina's tickets. I said that I was willing to compromise and have every third year off from going to Turkey: two years going, one year off. I want Mina to have the option of not going somewhere if she doesn't want to. The same will apply after she turns eight years old.

We are having a difficult time figuring out how to share time with Mina in Turkey. I had been up nights thinking about it: maybe I'll stay with my cousin Esra, who lives right on the Metro line near his parents; maybe I'll stay at my Aunt Binnaz's house and take the ferry over each morning; maybe I'll stay with his parents and leave each day. He said, ideally, we would all stay at his parents' at the same time, but he would stay in another room. Yes, that is what I am striving for too.

5. Savings

We already divided the savings and closed that account. My parents are in the fighting mood and want me to go to court if I have to. I am thinking of asking for a bit more, like $2,500, but it is hard when his mind is set on the minimum he has to pay. He said that if I still insist that the house has no equity, he would fight to keep it and rent it to us. He is willing to go to court and fight if my reply is "ridiculous" again.

4:07 P.M.

My lawyer responded really quickly and is helping me to stand my ground. I have sent off his negotiations to a few friends to get their reactions, and those have been mixed. I want to be fair, but I also do not want to fail to protect my and Mina's rights. I understand now why so many women would rather just settle for less than enter into more battles. When women—and moms—get to the point of filing, they have already fought so much within themselves. We are worn down emotionally, physically, and psychologically. I would rather get something similar to what I wanted than fight to the death. My lawyer wrote the following:

> Well, at least he is talking! I stand by my alimony calculations, but it is a crapshoot, and negotiation is never a bad thing.
>
> The equity in the house will simply *not* be determined as he is trying to determine it. If there is a battle, it will be determined by getting an appraisal and subtracting the mortgage obligation. Period.
>
> The court will not give him the house and have you rent it from him. Period. So that threat is empty.
>
> The court presumes that joint legal custody is in a child's best interest. Then, being the primary physical custodian, you will be given the tie-breaking vote. In order to revisit a custody order, there must be a material and substantial change of circumstances. You can always agree to change things, but do not agree to put it in the order as a requirement. That only sets you up for a fight when Mina turns eight or ten.
>
> Perhaps he is ready to attend mediation?

December 31, 2010

It is New Year's Eve, and I feel like I have grown much more than I ever thought I would. This year has been full of unexpectedness—good and bad. I had hoped to have this journal finished by today so that I could start the new year completely fresh. The best-laid plans of mice and men, eh?

I forgot to write the other day about the money situation. When I spoke to Hakan about paying off the car repairs and using the next paycheck to clear the credit card, he informed me that he has pulled his paycheck deposit from our mutual checking account. There will not be any more deposits going in. I was shocked because I had written to him, specifically saying that I wanted to keep it open and joint until all our financial disputes were legally settled. I did not want to dip into my emergency savings account for basic daily needs. He promised to pay me back payments once everything was ironed out, but how do I track that? What date do I start from? I had no idea. So I e-mailed my lawyer.

She said that I should not have to dip into savings and that we could file for temporary relief and then get me alimony. This might actually work out in my favor. I need to write to Hakan anyway regarding his other negotiations, and I will add a note explaining that the lawyer thinks it's best to go the temporary relief route rather than try to get back payments.

Last night, when I was putting Mina to sleep, she looked up at me and asked, "Mama, if I am making snow angels and Nana and Dede are not here to pull me out of the snow, who will pick me up?"

"I will," I answered her. At that, she was able to roll over and go to sleep.

While my father was here, I asked him to work on a website for my personal chef business: www.kismetcooking.com. He set up a nice template and showed me how to add to it. I have finally committed to the name Kismet Cooking. "Kismet" in Turkish means "fate," and that is really how all of this somehow came together. Somehow, fate or destiny or whatever you want to call it brought many elements together to help me through all of this. I can start meeting with people next week, work on that website, kick-start the Etsy site again, and start accumulating appropriate licenses.

January 1, 2011

Happy New Year!

We had a lovely time out with friends last night and came home just in time to cuddle, read a book, and see the New Year arrive.

It has been an interesting energy shift with everyone gone. Even though I took care of Mina on my own over the past four years, there is a different sort of energy that comes in when there really *isn't* anyone there to help. Hakan is not here, my parents have left, and it is just me and Mina. The house is so quiet, so still. I can't seem to explain it right, but the house feels different. It is palpable. It is like a train conductor pulling a lever and changing tracks. There is a bit of jerkiness, and then the train chugs along a different path.

Hakan came over this morning for a little while and read to Mina while she took a bath. I would like to say that I was able to take advantage of the time to do some work around the house, but Mina asked me to sit with them in the bathroom as well. She kept monitoring where I was and what I was doing in the kitchen when I wasn't in the bathroom. She was fine with him here and was okay when he left. He was expecting a furniture delivery at his apartment and had to go but will be back tomorrow afternoon sometime, and we will tell her together about the divorce.

Sofia, the cat, actually had a very distinct reaction to Hakan being here. She bit him! She was *mad* that he hasn't been here.

Today, since Hakan left, Mina and I have had a quiet day at home. She wanted to make a cake on her own for her doll's birthday. I let her. She pulled out whatever ingredients she wanted and went to town measuring and pouring. It has been an all-day activity. After it was cooked, she started putting candles on it, singing happy birthday, and cutting her dolls pieces to eat. I have been able to have a cup of coffee and write a bit. I really think she will be fine.

Hakan asked me to write him responses to his proposed "negotiations," and I have to do it. I need to write out everything the lawyer said and what she is planning on doing this week. He is willing to meet sometime while Mina is at preschool and talk over things more if we need/want to. I guess that's helpful. I am just tired of talking. I just want it *done*.

January 4, 2011

Hakan came over on Sunday afternoon, and eventually we told Mina. When he first came in, she was pretty aggressive toward his affections. I think she was a bit confused at the big outpouring of hugs, kisses, and sentiments. Her aggression and somewhat refusing manner seemed to make him want to love and hug her more. This became kind of a vicious cycle. He let her be for a bit and ate his sandwich, and then it was time to talk to her. She had come to sit by my chair in the dining room. Hakan said that he missed her very much and asked if she missed him. She matter-of-factly said, "Yes, but I miss Nana more."

I told her that we had something to talk about as a family and asked where we should do it. She wanted to stay right where she was, and she wanted me to continue hand-sewing the doll dress as I talked. We talked about how the family unit was changing and about puzzle pieces. There was a time when Mama and Baba's puzzle pieces fit together well, but over time, we grew in different ways, and our puzzle pieces don't fit well anymore. Then I had a big slip of the tongue—I said that when some puzzle pieces don't fit so well, it's time to find pieces that do. Oops! That was so not intentional! Hakan's headed whipped around toward mine, and he asked if that was what this was all about—was I looking for another puzzle piece?

It was interesting to watch her mannerisms before telling her and then after. It was like a *huge* weight was lifted off her shoulders after we told her. *Now* she knew what was going on, and that was such a relief to her. All she asked was whether she was staying with Mama. Once she knew that, she was able to relax and then said, "Okay, Baba, now let's go play in my room."

Hakan just looked at her and said to me, "Either she is taking it really well, or she is hiding it well."

He later wrote and asked how she was after he left. She was fine. She asked for a yogurt, and we read and then sewed all evening long. At dinnertime, she asked about the situation again, and this time I used a food analogy. I asked her if she would eat avocado pizza. She scrunched up her face and said, "Yuck!" Right now, I said, Mama and Baba are an avocado pizza. They don't go so well together. But if we separate them, would avocado and pizza taste okay? Mina nodded yes. Well then, Mama and Baba will be happy and better separate like the food. Her eyes lit up, and you could almost see the cartoon light bulb go on over her head. She *got* it.

I was concerned that it would carry over into school the next day and that drop-off would be a nightmare, but it wasn't. Getting up and off to school was so calm and relaxing. We were done getting ready so early that we were able to sit and read a few books before getting into the car. She didn't cry in the car about me leaving her. I am not saying there wasn't some whining, but not to the extreme that I had seen way back in

October. When I picked her up later, they all said she was great and did fine after I left.

I finally wrote my response to Hakan's negotiation proposals.

> I have been doing a lot of thinking about all the stuff you came up with, and these are me thoughts.
>
> I wrote an e-mail to my lawyer to get ask her a few questions. She said that it is a positive sign that we can negotiate the alimony. We were talking about Mina's school, and I revisited my budget. That wasn't included in the budget, just household and food, etc. If we wanted a revolving money door, then we could increase the alimony to cover the school. Or you can just pay it off your credit card as is.
>
> The $2,100 would go through Mina's year at kindergarten (because it is half-day four days a week). That would make it $2,100 until May 2013, then stepping down to $1,500 for two years and then $1,000 for the last year. I would feel more comfortable if the alimony was $2,500, then $2,000, and then $1,500 because of unexpected possible expenses.
>
> I asked the lawyer about how equity is established in the house. She said that the way they determine the house value is to take the latest evaluation of the house. When the city sent out the taxes, it said our house value right now was about $288,000. Equity is determined by subtracting what is owed from what it is worth: $10,000. Having your name on this house does not prevent you from having another house or mortgage. The $70,000 figure came from what we, as a couple, put into the house. Adding the $10,000 in equity brings it up to $80,000, which would divide to $40,000. I don't know if we can recalculate retirement in this way with house figures or not. I would be willing to talk about this formula: $136,000 (retirement) − $40,000 = $96,000 and $96,000/2 = $48,000 (retirement share). I would get $48,000 from retirement, and you would get $88,000.
>
> I wrote to my lawyer about how to keep track of expenses for future back payments and such. I told her that I was using savings to start paying for things. She said that applying for temporary relief for me would be easier.

He came to visit Mina today and to talk more about negotiations. To say he wasn't pleased with my answer is an understatement. He doesn't trust my lawyer and thinks that she is after extra money. He thinks that my lawyer is trying to make me think that Hakan is trying to screw me over. He asked why I felt that I had to go to court to get temporary relief. Well, he pulled the paycheck from the checking after I specifically asked him *not* to do anything with that account until the dust settled.

I think he felt frustrated that I had a bit of mistrust of his back-payment promises. He said that he would transfer half of his paycheck into the checking account until everything is figured out if I tell my lawyer *not* to file for temporary relief. Done. I e-mailed her right then and there and called off the dogs.

Next was the alimony. He didn't understand why I would ask for $500 more than what I need. When I explained it was for "unexpected expenses," he asked, "What sort of 'unexpected expenses'?" Well, that's the thing—they are unexpected. You don't know what they are until they drop down on you like a bombshell.

I asked him to negotiate with me because I had come down $500 from my lawyer's original request and said that he needed to come up a little to meet in the middle. It is called bargaining.

I hadn't wanted to talk about all of this stuff with Mina around, but he kept bringing up the conversation in the kitchen because he was upset. Mina was *not* happy about it at all. She would get in his face and scream, she would tell him to stop talking, she would growl, and she would run up onto my lap. He realized that he was pissing her off, and now she was mad at him, but he just couldn't stop talking about the house value and the retirement. He really wants an extra portion of the retirement in exchange for the house equity. I need to go downstairs today and find the appraisal that was done a year ago when we first thought of refinancing. I believe they appraised the house at $312,000. Then in the fall we got a notice from the city saying that our house value was about $288,000 when compared to recently sold houses in the area. If he wants to bring another appraiser in, let him. I can't imagine the house has gone up dramatically to support his $70,000 house value claim.

I had a lovely phone call with my friend Sema, who lives in Rhode Island and has three successful Etsy businesses. She told me to call her so she can help me kick-start this business again and move some product. I told her to give me a week to get my act together, and then we can talk product marketing. She said that I sounded a hundred times better than when she talked to me back in Rhode Island last Christmas.

Since Mina had a great day at school yesterday, I promised her breakfast at IKEA this morning. So after I finish up a bit of sewing and maybe some yoga, we are off for a fun day!

JANUARY 6, 2011

I am about three hours into my twelve-hour "work" day. Now that Mina doesn't rest, it is a full day wearing the mommy-hat. Tuesdays and Thursdays take so much patience to get through these days. Trying to get Mina to understand that I have work to do around the house is sometimes difficult. I used to be able to do a lot of stuff while she napped. Now, I need to reorganize the day to do my work in the morning while she is agreeable and not in the afternoon when she is grumpy and sleepy. I feel that, at times, I am harder on her than usual because I am trying to nip some needy behavior in the bud. I can't be sidelined by tears and pleading.

This morning, in order to get some stuff done, I set up the table for her to paint at 6:00 a.m. While she painted, I drank my coffee and cut up vegetables to cook later.

She is a vivid dreamer, like me, I guess. She is working through her fears at night with her dreams. She woke up this morning and told me two of her dreams. Both revolved around kites. In the first one, she, Hakan, and I were at the slide park. Hakan was a kite, and a wind blew him away into the trees. Another gust came by, and she was afraid that it would blow me away too. In the second dream, we were at Sugarhouse Park near the pond, flying a big kite. It was really windy out. Hakan and I both grabbed the kite to keep it from blowing away, but a really strong wind blew Hakan, me, and the kite away, and she couldn't hold onto the string. She was left all alone and scared.

Dealing with Hakan has been the surreal part. He came over the other day, and we sat at the dining room table drinking beers, eating chips and dip, and talking about dividing up sheets and towels. Then I made up a shopping bag of Turkish packaged soups, nuts, olives, and tea for him to take to his apartment. We still haven't come to any agreement regarding the house. He has been coming by just about every day this week and will be tapering off visits to every few days once school starts for him.

I think the most calming thing for me has been being able to make our own schedule. We wake up and have coffee (well, I do!), and I do yoga while Mina plays on her own. It is such a nice feeling to relax into the morning and not feel rushed. Today we were up at 6:00 a.m., and by 7:30 a.m. I had finished yoga and was watching the sun rise over the mountains, all pink and fluffy. We still had an hour before we even had to *think* about leaving for school.

At the moment, I am getting irritated that she is not letting me finish writing this. I am really trying to be sensitive to the fact that she needs more attention, but I feel like I am being manipulated a bit to do things, and that it highly aggravating. There is no need for me to sit next to her while she picks up her quarters five feet away in the living room.

Now I have a crying child next to me, and I really just need some space at this moment because I shouldn't have to jump and get her drink for her when she can get it herself.

7:45 P.M.

My day has just ended, and I am tucked up on the couch wearing Mina's ice cream snuggly with my second glass of wine. The day was interesting. When people ask me how Mina is handling all of this, I usually say, "Pretty well." But there are odd moments when the littlest thing will become the biggest disappointment and cause the greatest upset. You can't plan for them because they are so random. Take today, for example. We met Marcia and Clare at Red Butte Garden to feed the ducks. It was a lot colder than I thought it would be, and there were *no* ducks anywhere to feed. Mina was absolutely devastated. She was beyond disappointed and cried and cried and cried about not being able to see the ducks, not being able have her snack by the ducks, not being able to use the same path to the ducks (due to ice and snow). She was a mess. Once she calmed down, she was fine and wanted to get Clare a little present in the gift shop. She dried her tears and picked out a wind-up ladybug toy to give to Clare.

The rest of the day was really good. We created a new toy (completely out of her head), and she was so grateful. She had spent two days painting "space grizzlies," fronts and backs, on two different papers. After they dried, we sewed them together and stuffed them. They resemble a painted paper pillow. This little girl came up to me, put her hand on my arm, looked up, and said, "Mama, thank you so much for making my space grizzlies for me. I really appreciate it." This kid is four!

She sat at my feet and played on her own for almost three hours while I pinned up two more reading shawls. After the first one, I asked her if she wanted me to get dinner ready for her, and she said that she wasn't through playing yet, that I should continue sewing.

We cleaned; we organized; we danced. It was a fun afternoon, and I was able to clean and clear out a lot of stuff.

Then Hakan came over to visit. I knew from his eyes that I needed to avoid him. I had made up a little bag of baby stuff for Berna, things I had found while I was cleaning: CDs of Turkish lullabies, mothering magazines, other Turkish baby stuff. He looked at it and was exasperated. I knew from that moment it was going to be one of those nights. He was all riled up about something. He had been thinking about me and money and asked me whether I would be working when Mina was in kindergarten. I said probably part-time. He just chuckled sarcastically. As I picked up my iPad to surf Facebook, I heard him snicker or something, and I called him on it. "Why are you snickering at me? What did I do tonight?"

He is frustrated that I seem to feel "entitled" to sit at home and not work. Um . . . I can't leave my job as a mom. And it is super-hard to keep your cool when every "let's bug Mom" button is being pushed *all at the same time*!

His coming in with an attitude did not help the whole father-daughter bonding time. She didn't let go of my hand for about a half hour. Facilitating interaction between the two of them just tires me. Then he brought up talking with his parents. "It would be nice if you called my parents once in a while on Ojo." I told him we haven't called anyone on Ojo lately because we have been busy with school and cleaning. That kind of blew the wind out of his sails. "Oh," he said.

I really need to get used to all this visitation time. It's hard because it throws the energy completely off-balance. He comes and plays, she stays up later than usual and gets wound up, and then he gets to leave, and I have to put the wild child to bed. She was so sweet tonight. She wanted to put *me* to bed. She said goodbye to Hakan and set to work getting my pajamas out and taking my socks off and putting them away. She even patted my back, gesturing for me to get going to bed. "No, no, Mama, you lie down and rest. I will turn out the light!"

On a completely random note, Samantha called today. It was "how are you?" and "how are things?" and so on. We talked about where I was in the whole divorce process and how things had been going, but I felt a bit guarded. It is so easy for me to just forgive and forget. After almost six weeks of not talking, I am afraid of getting hurt again.

JANUARY 11, 2011

Last night, I went to bed a bit early. I have tried to get into a sort of routine where I go to bed before I am tired and just slowly let go of the day. It's when I send out lots of love-filled energy to all my friends and to myself. As I lie there quietly, I try to be aware of the sort of things that pop in my head. Boy did something come to me last night! It was a wild ride of an idea about living—you need to fasten your seat belt because this ride goes fast!

Yesterday I was reading something about kids and "growing up." I think as parents we see it as our job to help our kids "grow up" and grow older. What if the learning is supposed to be a two-way street? As we teach them life lessons, they are teaching us to grow *younger*. I think that is the secret to a happy, long life—to remember how to play, laugh, and have fun with the little things. We may think that their little brains and bodies are empty vessels to put knowledge in, but what if they are meant to help us *release* some of the junk we have accumulated in our vessel over the years? After laughing until it hurts in response to something your kid did, don't you feel lighter—like you let go of some yucky thoughts that were stored in your baby toe?

It is when we live through the kids' eyes that we become younger. We can sit on the floor and get messy, get our hands all painted, or make mud pies in the backyard. We see things differently and slightly off-center, and that makes the world more fun, I think. I am actually looking forward to our edamame bean-shooting contest. It will be fun to see Mina squeeze the edamame pod and how far the bean will shoot into the air! I want to make a bulls-eye for the wall or many bowls and buckets to aim for. So what if the floor is scattered with beans? I have a broom, and Mina loves to sweep!

This summer, when we were visiting Binnaz at her summer house in Ayvalik, Mina wanted to take a bubble bath in her jet tub. The jet bubbles are so dense when you put bubble soap in it, and she wanted to make bubble crowns for herself and my aunts, my cousin Ekin, and me. We all laughed so hard we were crying! Can you imagine Binnaz, so serious, with a mound of bubbles on her head like a hat?

I think that the secret to everlasting happiness is to really, truly learn to be free to play with abandon like a child. I think they are here to teach us what we have forgotten while doing all that important "growing up" stuff.

It is January 11, and Hakan got paid on the seventh. He said that he would transfer half his paycheck to my checking account, and so far, the balance is $150—no more money has come through. His lawyer has contacted mine regarding my financials and setting up mediation. I have such a headache today from all of this. I called the health insurance company to see how much my COBRA payment would be every month, and the amount just blew me away: $508.67! I really had no idea it would cost that much. I rarely need to go to the doctor, and it just about knocks the wind out of my sails to see this figure. I knew it would be a couple hundred dollars, but I didn't know how high it would actually be.

I was able to get on a budget plan for our heat. Instead of $80/month or more during the winter, I have it down to $40 every month for the whole year. Our first grocery shopping endeavor went very well; it is amazing how low our grocery bill is now. We will definitely be able to keep to our $500/month grocery budget.

Deep down, I know I am going to be okay. It is just so hard sometimes to keep the faith when you are dealing with the day-to-day stuff. Linda has been such a blessing in my life that I really don't know how I would have been able to get this new business off the ground without her. She is now throwing a brunch for my existing "clients" as well as some more friends. I will do all the cooking so that everyone will be familiar with what I do. It comes down to karma in this case and "what goes around comes around." I can't believe all of this generosity stems from me and my cooking at the Tea Grotto more than three years ago!

I had a realization the other day with regard to Mina and the subject of divorce. I think sometimes we as adults have a tendency to "overtalk" a situation. We want to make sure that the kids understand, and we talk *at* them, not *with* them, about the situation. However, the times we feel are best to talk to them may not be the time they will be receptive. I have learned that if Mina has questions and comes to me for answers, she is more receptive and understands the concepts faster. When I spoke to her at a different time, she wasn't ready to talk about serious stuff, and she got really quiet and sad and didn't really understand what I was trying to tell her. I am not saying to avoid the conversation, but to let the conversation begin with them.

JANUARY 12, 2011

It has been interesting to observe and listen to Mina with regard to Hakan and his visits. Monday was a good day for us. We got a couple packages from family, and it felt like Christmas all over again. I got a fun knitted hat that somehow made me reconnect to the artsy student from so long ago. India Arie was singing, *loudly*, as I cooked in the kitchen, and Mina played on the floor of the living room. Hakan called and asked me to ask Mina if she would like him to come over in the afternoon. I didn't even have to tell her who was on the phone or say anything. She looked at me and calmly said, "Mama, I don't want Baba to come today. I really just want to play on my own tonight."

Hakan heard it and was taken aback. I don't think he wanted that answer or thought he would get that answer before the question was even asked. He said he would prefer to come because his schedule would be tight on Tuesday. "Well, come, but you will have to deal with Mina when you get here," I said.

You should have seen her face when he came in after she had asked him not to. I think for a minute she felt not heard and her opinion/wishes not respected, and she did not hold back. "Baba, what are you doing here? I didn't want you to come today." After a while, she relaxed, and they had a good time playing.

That night, we actually used the Ojo for the first time in about two weeks. We had a lovely time having dinner with my parents. Mina was relaxed, playful, and secure. Yesterday, we had a lovely day at home, and it was super calm. Mornings are filled with ballet dancing and yoga. This morning, Mina got me breakfast again after yoga. She went to the fridge, took out a few clementines, put them in a bowl, and brought them to me. She told me to relax and sit in the chair by the window, and she would peel the oranges for me. After peeling them, she fed me, piece by piece, and made sure I ate them all. The teachers have remarked on how different and secure she is this semester.

By contrast, tonight, when Hakan came, she became very insecure, afraid of monsters and the dark, and set up game boxes around all of us for "protection" and was very needy at bedtime. She told Hakan that we lock up the door tight when we go to bed. He asked if we should lock up now, and she matter-of-factly said, "No, Baba, you have your *own* home. We will lock up after you go home."

Once she relaxes, she enjoys being with him because he is actually *playing* with her, and they are having fun together. That is all I have ever wanted for them.

When he left, she whispered in my ear, "I love it when Baba comes and visits me." Playing with him and having him all to herself is probably what she has wanted for a long time.

Before he left, he went over some more alimony calculations. He has come up some from his original figures, and I am really tempted to take them. I need this to be over, but I want it to be fair.

I need to look at my budget, but I think I can make things work with this alimony and with paying health insurance. If I get rid of the cable and the phone (which I had been considering anyway), I will be able to meet my budget.

There are other things to consider before all of this can be signed off on, but at least he has not dug in his heels at the first figure.

JANUARY 15, 2011

Seriously, where do I begin? I have felt charged up to write for the past few days, but things are coming from so many directions that I haven't known where to start.

Thursday was a fun release for Mina. Her friend Ashlan came over, and they got to make a royal mess of the place by shooting edamame beans at the drawing of Bullseye (the horse from *Toy Story*) all day long. The girls roared with laughter as each edamame popped.

Even though we spent the day laughing, the monsters came out to play too, and I played hardball back. Mina was convinced there were monsters in the kitchen and in the bathroom and wouldn't do anything or go anywhere without me near. It became a huge fit, but I was not about to give in to it. These monsters were not slow to develop; they had materialized only the day before. As I listened to her plead with me to go with her to the kitchen to get more ice cream, I thought about how others might coddle or do what she asked because "poor little girl, she is dealing with the divorce." But on the other hand, I do not want to coddle and start a bad habit that will be doubly difficult to break. Oh, and she pulled out all the stops to pull on the heart strings: "Mama, if you loved me, you would want to make me happy and go with me to the kitchen. I can't do anything right to make you love me. I don't want to be your kid anymore or live with you."

I put my pajamas on, made myself comfortable, and waited out the fit. Forty minutes later, Mina decided be brave and venture into the kitchen. "Guess what, Mama? There are no monsters in the kitchen. I think I will go back and get some almonds now." Feeling even braver, she ventured into the bathroom—again, no monsters there.

I thought we had vanquished the monsters, and then tonight came. After Hakan came over, the protection boxes came out again. Hakan asked if they were going to play monsters. Did she need him to protect her from them? Then when he left, he asked if he should come at monster time again. Now it needs to be a discussion. I do not want to have a fear fostered. If she brings it up on her own, fine—go take care of the monsters. However, if she has not even mentioned them, let's not bring that fear up again to the consciousness.

When he came yesterday afternoon, he mentioned that I had continued using the mutual bank credit card. Uh, yeah—I needed to get the car fixed, and yes, I used it once at Joann's to make a purchase. Why did I use the credit card? Well, I didn't know if there would be enough money in the account to cover the charge. He looked at me and said, "Isn't the savings account *money?*"

Oh, and by the way, I asked him, where was that money that was supposed to be deposited into my account?

He said that he was about to deposit the money the week before and asked his lawyer about it. His lawyer said that he would call my lawyer to see if that would be okay, but that my lawyer hadn't gotten back to him with an answer all week long.

We were sitting with Mina so there was no way to have a *real* conversation about it, but if he knew I was waiting on the money, why wouldn't he have sent me an e-mail at the beginning of the week explaining why it was delayed?

I told him that I would accept his numbers, but that I expected to have what I used from the savings replenished with back payments starting on January 1. Have your lawyer write it up and let's get on with it, I told him. He is still asking me why I am doing this and if I still want to continue. Yes, and I don't need to keep going into why I am doing this.

Let's switch gears a bit to all the support I am getting from every direction. After writing notes to my neighbors, I have gotten phone calls and visits from my neighbors telling me that they are there whenever I need them. My neighbor Ann, up the road, came down and rang my doorbell at 7:30 p.m. tonight! She had gotten my note saying that Hakan was not living here anymore and then saw him come into the house. She said she sat and waited at the window until he left to come down and check on me. After chatting, it felt so comforting to know that everyone is looking out for me.

I actually asked for a favor today. Since I had only two things to get at Costco, I asked Daisy, if she was going there, to get me juice and salad mix. She was happy to help and brought the stuff by later in the day. It is so hard for me to ask for favors. It is that independent streak that I have. People want to help but won't know how unless you tell them. I just need to relax and let people help me.

Are you ready for the last bit of the day? My mother-in-law called us on Ojo this morning. She was actually really nice and pleasant, like it was last year. I don't know if she has come to terms with everything and is willing to try again. I really can't begin to understand people, their emotions, their motivations, or their agendas these days. I just have to fall back on my great-grandmother's advice: When people are nice, be nice back. When they aren't, leave them alone.

Mina didn't want to talk to her, so my mother-in-law and I chatted for about thirty minutes before we had to go to the farmer's market. I think this was the longest I have spoken to her since leaving Turkey last August. She missed talking to her girls and thought she would give us a call. I gave her a brief overview of our days, Mina's school, and so on. "You know . . . life moves forward," I said. My last comment wasn't met with hurt, sadness, or sulking regarding this whole new life. She smiled, nodded in agreement, and said, "Yes, my dear, life does move forward in its own way."

I didn't expect that reaction.

January 16, 2011

Dreams, dreams, dreams . . . so many dreams last night. I had a pretty vivid dream of being a foster mother to all sorts of kids when Mina got a bit older. We all went everywhere together, and I even took them all to Turkey when summer came around. I felt like I was raising a mixed-bag Brady Bunch household, and it was fun. I guess it is something to think about down the road.

Then my dream shifted to a puppet show in the springtime. There were big white rabbit puppets and flowers; maybe it was around Easter. K was sitting next to me as we watched the show. Our hands were lying on our own laps, just barely touching at the sides. Then there was a moment when he looked down at my hands, and a memory from years ago seemed to hit him—of how he had liked tracing my fingernails with his finger. I remember him holding my hand flat in one of his and tracing around my fingernails with his other hand. It was a quiet, loving memory.

In the dream, once the memory unfolded in his head, he tentatively reached out to reenact it. It was a very strange, coming-full-circle moment. Holding my hand, he asked where we were going to go away to for the weekend: Greece or some other island. To me, going away to an expensive place is not so important as the time I spend with someone I care about, I told him. He looked at me shocked, surprised that I didn't want to go to some expensive place, but then smiled.

I woke up both rested and exhausted this morning, if that makes any sense. It has been a few days since K and I have written. It seems to ebb and flow. He retreats a bit every now and then, not because he doesn't care, but because he begins to feel too much. Our last e-mail thread revolved around dreams that we both had but couldn't share. He said that it has been a long time since he has felt this way—that he is special.

January 17, 2011

I reread and finished *The Secret* last night and was amazed at how I have utilized it over the past four years. There are very specific instances that I can trace back to using *The Secret*. I remember being really impressed by the story of the man who got into an accident and couldn't move, who could just use his mind. Each day, he visualized himself walking out of the hospital, and eventually, he did. They called him the Miracle Man. I used that in my own visualizations for my hip. I visualized brand-new hip bone growing and healing itself. I remember now that soon after, I went to the doctor, and he used the words "possible regeneration" when describing my hip condition. It was a sign to me to keep doing what I was doing, that I was onto something! I also stopped talking about my hip problems and drawing attention to the negativity. All of this has worked wonders!

In August 2008, Mina and I spent a few weeks in Rhode Island. Samantha was painting her apartment over, and I went to the paint store with her. While we were there, I saw a green paint color that I absolutely *loved*! I took the paint sample strip and said, "I would love to have a room in my house painted this color. Even if I have to paint a closet, my house will have this color somewhere." When I returned to Salt Lake City and began house-hunting, we walked into *my* house. I knew when we walked in that it would be my house: the whole living room, including ceiling, was painted that green. It was kind of beyond our budget, and we made a lowball offer. The owner took our offer immediately—it was so easy!

It was everything that I had ever wanted in a house. I remember telling friends it was like someone had read my list and presented me the perfect house, complete with chickens across the street in the community garden!

All these instances reaffirm my own belief that I will be okay, better than okay, if I just keep believing. Things have come into my life over the past few months that I never would have thought possible. When it is right, it moves easily and freely. Life becomes fluid, moving you toward the person you are supposed to be.

Oh, and regarding my dream the other night: K said that after reading my dream, he was instantly taken back to that memory he had forgotten. He could immediately "see" the memory in his head and was amazed how fast he could relive a time so long ago.

JANUARY 19, 2011

I have been really enjoying my new India Arie CD, and the song "Beautiful Day" just sums up things perfectly.

"Beautiful Day" should be played by everyone every morning to start the day. It is so uplifting and motivating. Mina and I dance to this song every night over and over again. What a beautiful way to end the day, honor it, and welcome the coming day with a smile:

> Life is a journey,
> Not a destination.
> There are no mistakes,
> Just chances we've taken

It is funny how a little music can really lift you up and keep you going. As we were going into school this morning, Mina saw that someone had littered out the window and reminded me of that cleanup project we were going to do in Turkey. It got me rethinking the project and how I can create an environmental group from here to help clean up stuff over there. I think there many environmental people to talk to around here about how to start a project of such magnitude. It would be nice to use proceeds from this book to fund this idea. I don't know if I really would have seen the realistic potential if I hadn't reread *The Secret*. If my mind, unconsciously, brought so many things into my life, what could I do if I really, consciously put my mind to it? What could we accomplish? We could name the project MINA:Mindfulness in Action.

I actually got motivated to work on that nagging problem of separating the bank accounts. Ugh. I decided to go to the bank on the way home from dropping Mina at school. I thought it would be a piece of cake once I had a bank representative do it. Well, is it ever easy? No. The checking account and savings account that I want closed are linked to each other and linked to the mortgage. I need to call a mortgage representative on my own and separate it from one savings account and attach it to the other. Then the accounts can be closed. As far as closing the bank credit card, I have to call yet another phone number and do *that* separately too. I did leave there having accomplished something: I was able to reset my PIN for my new debit card! I have to look at what I was able to do, not what I was not able to complete. There is always tomorrow, and the sun is coming out. Time to go out and recharge!

January 20, 2011

As I sit and watch Mina and Hakan interact, there are times I hold my tongue because I do not want to create tension. I have this little conversation in my head: should I say something, or should I just leave it alone and let it resolve itself? For example, as I have written before, these days Hakan comes in proclaiming how much he loves Mina. I think that is wonderful, but it is overwhelming because all these proclamations are still so new. He just never said it so much to her before. It seems to me that he wants her to proclaim her love for him in the same way, but kids don't work that way. I do not think that it is okay to constantly ask a child how much she loves you or anyone else. Love is not a competition. If you choose to ask a child how much she loves you, then you need to accept her answer for the moment, whether it is "a lot" or "a little." You shouldn't take it personally because their emotions change regularly.

So that is how it was last night. He proclaimed his love and asked her how much she loved him, and she put her fingers close together (a little bit). Then the questions continued.

"Well, what can Baba do to make you love him *this* much?" he asked, opening his arms out wide.

To that, she answered, "Nothing."

He turned to me and asked, "Whose fault is this that she says she only loves me this tiny bit? Not *my* fault!"

It took a lot for me to bite my tongue, and I sighed. I did get a bit defensive and retorted back, "*So* . . . do you think it is *my* fault then?"

I really wanted to scream out, *You rarely took any interest in us for over three and a half years, and you expect the same love as we share. It is wonderful that you are taking such a loving interest in her, playing with her, and getting to know her. But you need to give her time to feel secure in your love.*

They play well together now, but she still will not go anywhere alone with him. He asked her to go to the slide park around the corner, and she immediately added, "With Mama too!" It must be difficult and frustrating for him to hear this, but a child's love and comfort take time to establish. If you are willing to put in the time and work, you will be so pleased with the results. Security and trust do not happen overnight!

This morning, Mina and I are headed down to clean up and organize the basement. We are reclaiming the house as ours and pulling our personalities out of storage to put out on display! It is time to let our inner selves shine and let it pour out of every corner of the house.

January 21, 2011

Last night, as I lay down, I had a bit of an epiphany. Samantha and I have been talking again and mostly about newly found old loves. Conversations beginning with "if only" and "what if" are futile when you can look back on the journey: "if only he could have found me x years ago" or "if only we didn't lose touch." I began to see our life's journey like a sculptor looks at a block of marble. Inside this block is our "David," and we are our own Michelangelo. Beauty is yearning to break free, but first big chunks needed to be hammered, chiseled, and sanded off, and that hurts. The only way to really become who we are is to go through these life trials and emerge wondrous. Where would be the appreciation of the good without the bad? How would we learn? How would we grow?

Once you begin to open yourself up, all sorts of things can come to you. I spoke about *The Secret* the other day. That night, I remembered a photo that K had sent me in a letter and was wondering where I had put it: did I leave it with the letter in the envelope, or did I put it in a photo album? Wistfully, I said to myself, "I wish I had that old photo he sent me."

Yesterday, something interesting happened. As I was going through old college photos, something slid out, completely unrelated. It was a twenty-year-old photo of K! Not the one I was thinking of, but one he had sent in another letter. I was shocked! How did *that* get here, in *these* photos? Every little thing like this makes me even more convinced that I am on the right path, that something is guiding me to better things. With him or without him, I am growing into the person I was born to be. I just have to be open to the flow: the natural, effortless unfolding of our lives in a way that moves us toward wholeness and harmony.

As I near the end of this saga, I am pretty worn out. I am hoping to sign papers in the next week or so and have it all finalized by February 1. I have taken steps this week to get Mina back into her bed, and it has been so easy. I sat down and talked with her Sunday night about starting the process of getting her back into her bed February 1, but she wanted to get started right away. Okay then! Let's go!

We set up a reward system: For each night she goes to bed easily, she can put a sticker on the calendar. Once she fills fourteen days, I will giver her $10 to go to the toy store and choose whatever she wants. She climbed right up into bed and was asleep in ten minutes, no crying! Great on one hand, but not so great on my end. I haven't been able to sleep well all week long as she tosses, turns, and flips out of bed. I cannot relax into sleep and instead just crash around 2:00 a.m. She has been waking up around 4:30 or 5:00 a.m. Do the math—I am not getting much sleep. I had to come up with a creative solution and sewed her a bumper that attaches by Velcro to each side. That seemed to help a bit last night. Maybe I will be able to finally relax and sleep tonight. I am so tired.

I found myself a new book at the bookstore today, and they let me charge it against my house account. It is called *Soul of a Citizen: Living with Conviction in Challenging Times*. In many ways, it is comforting because it demonstrates how one person can make a difference. Each of us has something to give to the world. Each of us has a gift. It is surrounding ourselves with those who lift us up to see what is possible that helps us do more with our lives.

Time to fill up another glass of wine and read a bit before sleepwalking to bed. G'night.

JANUARY 22, 2011

Today, I feel glorious. That is the word of the day: glorious! Maybe it is the second glass of wine, but whatever it is, I feel good. You can't even imagine how empowering it feels to be in control of your mind, your thoughts, and your life again and really *live*. My mind is finally clear, and I can think again and really *feel* what it is to be alive again.

I have been reading this book, *Soul of a Citizen*, and I have gotten through a third of it, and I just keep finding myself saying, *"Yes!* This is it!"* There are a few segments that I want to share, so bear with me as I copy them:

> When it's over, I don't want to wonder
> if I have made of my life something particular, and real.

I don't want to find myself sighing and frightened,
or full of argument.
I don't want to end up simply having visited this world.

—Mary Oliver, "When Death Comes"

Oliver's images go to the heart of the matter. Will we remain mere visitors, planetary tourists? Or will we recognize that the earth is our home, and create a common future with our fellow inhabitants? Only by choosing the latter course will we realize, in the words of a young Atlanta activist, Sonya Vetra Tinsely, "That you shape the world as much as it shapes you.'" (Loeb 39) Being brave does not mean being unafraid. It often means being afraid and doing it anyway"(50). I love this!

"As for who we will be, the answer is: We don't know . . . But we do know that growth comes from saying YES to the unknown" (64-65).

After reading the whole time Hakan was visiting with Mina today, I realized that I do not want to be afraid to live anymore and do not want to be a visitor anymore. I am ready to engage life, and I feel like I am about to burst on the scene with all this crazy energy and ideas. Too long did I resign myself to a life that was less than spectacular. Well, no more. That is not the example I want to show Mina. I don't want her to feel that she has to settle because that is what is expected.

Growth happens when you stretch yourself further than you thought possible, in a good way. Tonight, Mina and I danced crazy dances in the hallway in front of the mirror, and we were just silly. I feel so free, you can't even imagine. I am tearing up thinking how important that is—to feel free to be yourself, however that is. You should always feel free to be silly and goofy whenever the moment hits you and not feel that someone will judge you and make you feel embarrassed.

At the moment, I am laughing because my cat is snoring so loudly that I can't really hear myself think! Last night, I couldn't sleep with the cat snoring on one side of me and Mina snoring in her bed next to me.

January 24, 2011

Ugh! I really need sleep! One of the reasons I resisted putting Mina in her bed for so long was that it was going to take me a while to get used to the new routine as well. Now that we have resolved the "falling out of bed" issue with my homemade bumper, I should be able to relax and sleep, right? Nope. My body got used to being awake until 1:00 a.m. I am really exhausted and fighting a cold at this point.

I was able to pull off a lovely brunch for Linda yesterday. How could a day be any better? Blue sky, champagne for lunch, a new client party set for February 26, 2011, a regular client, and an unexpected $200 check in my pocket! I had told Linda I wasn't going to charge her because of all she was doing, but she stuck a check in my bag anyway.

Over the past few days, I have been on the phone with various utility companies getting Hakan's name off the bills. Interestingly enough, I cannot remove his name from the gas bill until the final divorce decree. I actually have to send the gas company a copy for them to remove him. How random! Each time I called the phone or electric company, they asked who my employer was. Each time, I replied, "My husband." Then I would explain the situation. I decided, for now, to keep the house phone rather than unbundle everything. If I disconnected the phone line, I would only save $10-15. Not really worth it. I was able to bundle in my cell phone and save a bit of money that way.

Today I received Hakan's stipulations. Maybe that was why I didn't sleep very well last night. The alimony is straightened out, but now we are entering into the issues of the house and the Turkey trips. He is asking me to refinance the house within five years or sell the house. He wants his name off of the mortgage. Understandable. I did a bit of research online while Mina ate lunch and learned all my options. Refinancing is one option, but another is called bank assumption. If approved, it would remove Hakan's name from the home without my having to refinance. It is application-based with multiple rounds of approval. First, you fill out the initial application with a $14 application fee. If approved, you pass to the next level, where they ask for more credit and financial information. Another fee: $900. One of the main questions is income, obviously. I asked if alimony is considered income if it covers the mortgage payments. The bank representative told me that they prefer to see an application come in after twelve months of alimony payments. It is stronger and has a greater chance of acceptance.

I need to call the bank and talk to someone about general refinancing after getting alimony. Then I think I can make a more informed choice.

There are other issues that need to be addressed, but I am just trying to work through one at a time so I don't feel overwhelmed.

My new book has really helped open my eyes to other ways to grow and give. It speaks to me on so many levels. I was reading a section about helping inner-city kids and how to revamp the system to help them better. Just reading this small section got me thinking about all those kids in Istanbul who sell little tissue packages for pennies. When was the last time they read a good book or had a book read to them? I thought of talking to a few of the kids about a weekly story-time on the grass somewhere. I could bring the books, a snack, and some juice and lay out a blanket for them to sit on. If I could inspire one of those kids to read or go back to school, wouldn't it be worth it? Maybe all they need is for someone to say "I care" by spending some time with them. I think we could have a lot of fun!

Once you start to open your self-imposed boxed thinking and see what's outside, *woosh*! All sorts of possibilities present themselves to you. As I have begun researching environmental groups in Turkey, I have been able to make a list of possible contacts to write to. Mina keeps asking me if I have worked out her cleanup plan yet. I am trying to remain optimistic and realistic and not surround myself with those who are pessimistic about the possibility of actually making this project a reality. I have started down the road toward social activism, and I am curious where it will lead and who I will meet.

January 27, 2011

Last night, Gaia called and left me a message about her banker. She said maybe he could be helpful and asked if she could give him my number. Absolutely! I need all the bank help I can get! He called within fifteen minutes, and he was so helpful. He closed accounts, set up new ones, set up a savings for Mina, and will speak to people about mortgage and house stuff. It was wonderful to just say, "Here, handle this." And he did.

It is so nice to feel so many people coming around to help me get through all of this. Did I mention that I was asked back by the museum to do tours? Amy e-mailed me and said the team missed me and asked whether I was able to come back now that Mina was in preschool. I gave a resounding *yes*! Immediately, an e-mail went out to the team saying, "Elif is coming back!" All the supportive e-mails from all my old friends came flying in! Little by little, I am finding all the dispersed threads of my being and weaving them back together into a better version of the old me.

Hakan came by this afternoon, and the weather was beautiful. He made some coffee, and Mina wanted to dance outside on the lawn. He is frustrated because all he gets to do is watch her do stuff like dancing outside to her *Magic Flute* music. He wants to actually interact and play with her. I can understand his frustration, but this is where she is right now. She likes to play alone but with someone on the sidelines. Today, I participated by being a "plop" sound effect when she dropped a doll. Not exciting, but there it is.

He has noticed that her Turkish has diminished, and she finds it difficult to converse with him in Turkish now. Well, he chose to speak to her in English over a month ago. I never thought it was a good idea because it is always harder to go back to something hard when you know you can do it a different way more easily. It is much easier for her to express exactly what she is feeling in English.

He is upset, and it saddens him. "Are you enjoying this, Elif? She doesn't remember any Turkish since I have been gone."

"It isn't the fact that you have not been here," I replied. "It is the fact that you chose *not* to speak to her in Turkish when you *have* been here. You made it easy for her to speak English, and she got used to it."

Hakan would like me to be more involved in making her play more with him or go places alone with him and in interfering when she needs to stop behavior A to do behavior B. I don't believe that I have to be in the middle so much because the two of them need to learn their own way of interacting. If she needs to stop behavior A with him, then he needs to get her to stop and not give in. I can facilitate them being together, comfortably, and move to another room or go inside. The rest is up to them, I think. As Mina would say, "Don't you agree?" or "Isn't that true, Mama?"

I finally wrote my responses to his stipulations and sent them to my lawyer to go over. She will review the original stipulation, look at my responses, and get back to me. I have agreed to most of his propositions, but there are a few minor things that need tweaking, in my mind.

These were my revisions to Hakan's stipulations:

1. Traveling with minor children
   a. Notice of travel must be given at least one month ahead of time.
   b. Notice of grandparent visits given to the other as soon as known to prevent overlapping of grandparent visit.

2. Child support full amount is $987.00, to be made in weekly installments of $246.75 to account for months that have five weeks instead of four.
3. Extracurricular activities and higher education will be shared equally with a private school cap of $20,000/year. Petitioner is not considering private education for elementary due to excellent public school nearby, but possible middle/high school at the Realms of Inquiry because public high schools are not ranked well.
4. Real property: Petitioner will refinance home in own name by May 30, 2016, upon alimony termination.
5. Tax exemption: Respondent will claim child in odd-numbered years, Petitioner even-numbered years.
6. Physical custody: Petitioner is willing work toward a greater allotment of parent/child time with respondent. Petitioner is willing to allocate extra time when family visits from Turkey. While family is visiting, the Petitioner will drop Mina off after school, each day, until 7:00 p.m. On days that there is no school, Mina will be dropped off for 9:00 a.m.-7:00 p.m. Family is more than welcome at Mina's home all day, any day, and Petitioner offers up her residence if they wish to stay for a portion or all of visit.
7. Revisiting physical custody when Mina turns eight will not be necessary due to liberal time-sharing of child.
8. Travel to Turkey: Respondent may go to Turkey anytime, as often as he wants. Petitioner and child may only go to Turkey two out of three years. Once Mina turns eight, she still has that option to go or not to go on that third year. The trip to Turkey will use two weeks of Respondent's and two weeks of Petitioner's alone/vacation time with Mina. Respondent will pay both Petitioner and child airfare.

9. The custodial parent retains position in joint legal custody. Petitioner will work with mediators if a dispute arises that cannot be handled between the two parties.

FEBRUARY 4, 2011

This process moves soooo slow! It makes me feel like I am stuck in mud with no motivation to do much of anything, much less write here. Yes, I have been avoiding this journal because of the lack of momentum in any area of my life. No word from the lawyer, no word back from potential clients, frustration from Hakan, just lots of nothin'. I needed to do something to kind of kick-start my motor and get me going again, and that usually means that I need to sew something. Off to Joann's I went to take advantage of their winter sale, and I found cute, cute, *cute* mermaid material to make some little girl dresses. Tuesday, I spent the whole day sewing three dresses for Mina's friends Anna and Ashlan as well as for Mina. My goodness! It was so rejuvenating! It cleared the cobwebs right out of my head! I was able to think clearly again and started to make my way down my to-do list. I got my mortgage payment set up to come out of my new savings account, which will enable me to finally close out the mutual checking and savings accounts in both our names. I e-mailed a few potential clients for the chef business. Mina and I cleaned the whole house tip-top clean and vacuumed everywhere! I cleaned and cleared my space to allow stuff to come my way, and come my way things did!

I had made a mental list of things that I needed or wanted for the coming year, such as a new bed and a composter. I think I mentioned in a previous entry that Daisy is giving me her old rotary composter for free, and now Sofia is giving me her queen sleigh-bed headboard for free.

On top of that, I have been offered a job, of sorts. As I was picking Mina up at school today, I saw Zephyron, Anna's father. He mentioned that their nanny had abruptly quit, and they were looking for someone to watch Anna after school until 6:00 p.m. on Mondays and Wednesdays. He said he would compensate me for my time. Wow! I may get paid to take care of Anna in my own home. I am sure it won't always be a piece of cake, but wow! This could pay for my health care!

My lawyer did finally get back to me and said that I had made some good compromises. She mentioned that the courts do not usually favor a step down in alimony allocation and that usually it lasts as long as the marriage did or until the death of one party. I told her that she needed to have that conversation with Hakan's lawyer because if I brought it up with Hakan, he would think I was fishing for more money. She said she would draft a letter to his lawyer and send it to me for approval. I am still waiting. Waiting on the lawyers is especially draining.

I had a very empowering day on Wednesday. I took the first step to return to the museum as a docent. I hadn't been there in about four years, since Mina was born. Even though it is familiar ground, it was still intimidating. But I don't know why I was even worried—it was like coming home. It was my home for most of my time in Utah as either a volunteer or a paid employee. When I walked through the doors and saw all my Wednesday teammates smiling at me, I felt like I had found another piece of my life puzzle and clicked it into place. So many of the ladies are my mom's age, and the hugs sent a very clear message: "Welcome home; we missed you!"

I touched base with my publishing company the other day and met my new representative. She made me feel a bit better about writing my biography section of the book. It's funny—even though I am writing a very personal book, I am finding it really hard to write about who I am in the biography. She told me that they have a team that will mold what I say in a way that will represent me and who I am in the best way possible on the back flap of the book. I did try to elicit help from friends on Facebook! I posted a question on my wall: "What would you write about me?" I got really interesting feedback:

"Amazing cook of pastries, tea connoisseur, one who thinks out of the box, earthy, loving, generous, smiling mother!!"

"The Ekins make the bestest chocolate chip cookies around town . . . fabulous gardener, seamstress, friend, and mom."

"My comment for you would be free minded thoughtful and kind woman who also is a peace keeper and a great mom."

While on my 29 Gifts blog page, I reread my status from a while back, and that really speaks to who I am as well: "'Treat people as if they were what they ought to be and you will help them become what they are capable of becoming.'—Goethe"

Why is it so hard to write about who you are—all the wonderful things that make you *you*? Does it seem unbelievable to you when it is written on paper? I guess it goes back to not really feeling special for so many years and getting used to it. When you can see how wonderful and special you really are, you stop and think, *If I really* am *this special, why couldn't he see it? Why couldn't he make* me *see it?* How is it that someone I haven't seen in over twenty one years can see it and make me believe it? In almost every e-mail, K reiterates the same mantra to me: You are special. I feel it, I believe it, and it shines from every part of who I am now. I am finally doing things I have wanted to do but have been intimidated to do before. I set up my appointment to have some blue put in my hair next month. I went to a pizza parlor that I have wanted to try for years, and it was sooo good!

Our neighbor Ann, up the street, wanted to check in on us and see how we were making out, so she invited Mina and me to come up and read stories at her house last Tuesday. Mina thoroughly enjoyed herself and loved playing with all her interactive imagination games. Ann remarked to me as we watched Mina play that this was not the same child from last fall. She said that Mina is so much more comfortable, outgoing, and willing to have a long, in-depth conversation with her. She is more open toward people and not insecure. Ann was amazed. Now, this woman knows kids—she is the woman who started the fine arts preschool that Mina goes to. It is so validating to me when people see it and say those things to me. It makes me so secure in my decision.

February 5, 2011

Clean! Must clean everything! We were up early, and I made up my mind to clean the empty bedroom. It had never felt like mine because I never spent any time in that room except to pick out my clothes. I had been avoiding going in and clearing out stuff and cleaning. I had actually closed off the door since he left so that I wouldn't be reminded of what needed to be done. Today, I opened the door, went in, and scrubbed every inch of that room. I moved the mattress against the wall, positioned the frame, moved a dresser downstairs, and moved some of my clothes into the closet. In terms of energy, it feels more like mine and less like his now, if that makes any sense.

It is amazing what happens when you start moving and cleaning—you can't stop. Over the course of the day, I did four loads of laundry, washed Mina's coats, baked a pumpkin, made pumpkin bread, cooked a *vat* of applesauce, cleaned the guest room, unloaded and then loaded the dishwasher, cleaned the bathroom, cleaned the litter box, and then sat down with a cup of coffee to relax. Most of this was done before 10:30 a.m.!

It is almost like I need to clean every inch of this house—walls, floors, baseboards, and so on—to make it *mine*. I need to clean away the arguments, the sadness, and the frustration from every surface because it is like an invisible film that can creep up on you when you least expect it. I want to paint the walls with positivity! I want happiness, laughter, joy, and pure silliness to sneak up and tickle you senseless when you come to visit. When people come to my house, I want them to feel this *life* bombard them and make them feel alive.

It is so exciting to decorate again! My bedroom is a blank canvas just waiting for me to make it mine!

February 7, 2011

Yesterday, Mina and I went to the aquarium with a few of Mina's school friends. As the kids played, Annie, Mary Jane's mom, and I sat chatting. She wanted to add me as a friend on Facebook, so I told her how to spell my name. When she found my profile on her phone, I looked at the main screen, and it was so weird. The only thing underneath my name describing me was the one sentence: "Elif is single." I don't know why it hit me as bizarre, but why was that the only thing to describe me? Being "single" doesn't define who I am; it is just an aspect of me.

After talking with Zep yesterday, I realized that I do need to just leave Mina with Hakan and let them figure it out, good and bad. I have been preoccupied with allowing a comfortable playtime between them and creating a relaxing environment for them to play in, but it is not "reality." Zep is right. I am backhandedly reinforcing Mina's insecurities by *not* leaving. Time to change that. I am going to go to Costco while Hakan is here today. He will have to handle it, and she will be okay, after a while.

It has been so nice to feel taken care of by so many new friends. So unexpected and so, well, nice. Mina and I picked up Zep and the girls (Anna and Bella) and drove to the aquarium. Zep bought our tickets, and later, Amy, Anna's mom, invited us to stay for dinner. It was such a lovely, fun, free day. We all sat down to a lovely meal, lovely wine, and lovely conversation.

FEBRUARY 11, 2011

It was pretty tough last night dealing with Hakan after he received our responses to his stipulations. He was extremely antagonistic toward me. He kept looking at me like I was evil.

"You are a liar! I don't trust anything that you say again!" He spit the words at me with such hate, and I was really, truly confused about what I had lied about. "You lied to me about the custody! When you and I had met at Einstein Bagels before Christmas, you told me that you might consider revisiting the custody issue when Mina turned eight. You changed your mind and chose *not* to reconsider that avenue, so you are a liar! Just like when you told me in 1999 that you would move to Turkey with me."

He kept calling me a liar in front of Mina. He sat down on the couch and looked down at Mina and me sitting on the rug in the living room across from him.

"What you need to understand, Elif, is that Mina is *not* your property, and you should stop thinking that you own Mina! I should have some control over things too, especially education."

I really kept my voice calm, level, and not emotional at all and simply said, "Since you are not legally required to pay anything for Mina's school, you shouldn't have the deciding vote on it."

He didn't like that answer, and I didn't like the way he was speaking to me.

He retorted, "I am not angry; we are just two people, talking."

"Well," I said, "your tone is very antagonistic, and I don't appreciate it."

Poor little Mina had to stand up for me again. When he got a phone call, she came up to me and said, "Mama, when Baba is mean to you and calls you a liar, you don't have to listen to him or even look at him. Just ignore him."

He came back into the room and asked, "Mina, what did you just say to your mom just now while I was on the phone?"

She stood up, pulled herself to her full height, looked him in the eye, and said matter-of-factly, "Baba, when you speak meanly to Mama, she doesn't have to listen to you. She doesn't have to listen to you calling her a liar."

He shut up.

He is also upset about having to pay the last mortgage payment and was upset that I had used the credit card (to pay for the car brake repair and four tire replacements).

"You are really unbelievable, Elif. Unbelievable. I am eventually going to pay you over $100,000, and you still want an extra $800 for the mortgage. You really live in a fairy tale if you think that you won't have to work like everyone else in the normal world. I will take you to court for custody of Mina, and I have a good chance to get her since I have a good job and stable housing."

Mina wouldn't stay alone with him while he was here and made me sit next to her on the couch while they read books for a while. She is just not comfortable alone with him. I actually did leave them alone on Monday afternoon to start getting them used to each other. I went to Costco. He was pretty annoyed that I was going to start transitioning into that so soon and that he would have to deal with her being upset. I asked him what *was* a good time to start separating me from this visitation situation—at 5:00 p.m. when she would be sleepy and want to go to sleep? She was so upset that I left, she was shaking and screaming for me in the window. This doesn't happen when I leave her with friends or at school.

After I came back from Costco, we told Hakan about what we had done over the weekend—about going to the aquarium with Mina's friend Anna and her father. Hakan became nasty and said, "Well, it's nice that Mina spent so long with Anna's dad and not her own!" Then he turned to Mina and said, "Mina, I am not really feeling the love lately. There are no hugs or kisses for Baba when he comes. If I don't start feeling the love soon, maybe I don't come over so much."

How can that be an okay living situation for this child? She has been extremely verbal about how she feels and told him *not* to come Tuesday because she really just wanted to play alone. Sometimes she wants just Mama time, sometimes she wants Baba time, and sometimes she really just wants to play alone.

He has been late coming a few times this week. He was supposed to come at 11:00 a.m. last Saturday, and he showed up at 11:45 a.m. Then Tuesday, I had to call him at 5:25 p.m. to see if he was coming (he was supposed to be here at 5:00 p.m.). He was still at work and wanted to know why I needed to know right then whether he was coming. Well, if he was coming, I would keep her up. If not, then I would start putting her to bed—she was asleep by 6:00 p.m. on Monday night and slept thirteen hours. He said he would leave work and come.

Later last night, Mina had some questions about the "grown-up talk," and I asked her what she wanted to know. She said that he and I were talking about her, but that she didn't really understand.

I told her that Mama and Baba are trying to figure out theirs lives as separate people, and that means we have to come to some compromises. Sometimes it is easy, and sometimes it is not. I told her that we both love her very much and want the best for her, but that sometimes each person has a different idea of what "the best" is. I told her that right now, she stays with Mama all the time, and Baba comes here to play. Then I asked her to think of how big Emma (our eight-year-old neighbor) is. Mina said, "Super big!"

I said that when Mina was super big like Emma, we might have Mina stay a few nights with Baba too. Baba loves her very much and would love to have the opportunity to put her to bed too. Mina's little chin crumpled up; she got teary and said that she wasn't comfortable at his house.

I got a bit teary and upset too, and she calmed me down. She said, "Mama, you protect me because you love me, and I protect you because I love you! We protect each other!" Then she told me to go wash my face, and things would be better in the morning.

I called my parents and told them what is going on, and they said that what he is doing is harassment and intimidation, and he needs to stop. Everything that I had all bottled up inside came out, and I was pretty hysterical. He had played the custody card, and I was scared. Mom called Linda to come and sit with me until I calmed down. I did stop my father from calling Hakan and yelling at him. That wouldn't help anything.

I called Bob, my handyman, to have my locks changed, and my friend Linda will be coming to keep me company during Hakan's next visit tomorrow at 11:00 a.m.

He will be talking to his lawyer today and probably asking him to get ready for court for a custody battle.

February 13, 2011

Bob and Greg came over straightaway Friday to change the locks. I am so blessed. They had such a busy schedule that day, but Bob told Greg, "I don't know the whole story, but we *have* to get those locks changed ASAP." They are so wonderful.

Linda did come on Saturday to spend Hakan's morning visit with me. Hakan and Mina stayed inside while Linda and I enjoyed our coffee outside. Hakan actually got upset that Linda was there "disrupting" his time with Mina. It just goes to show that nothing will ever please him. I told him that I thought it would help because it would give me an excuse *not* to be in the house, and he could be alone with her. Whatever.

Mina and I celebrated Valentine's Day early today. I wanted her to be able to enjoy the day. We made heart-shaped pancakes and read her new book: *Shakespeare for Kids: Romeo and Juliet*. We sat and read the whole play, and she loved it.

We spent most of the day outside in the gorgeous spring weather. First, we met Daisy down at Starbucks, and she was just infuriated that he hasn't given any money, not even the calculable child support of $987.00. She said that his pissy level is way up at work, that his antagonism is not aimed just in my direction. His pessimistic attitude has reached a whole new level at work.

Does it help to know that it is not just me he is angry at? Yeah, kind of. He is just angry at life in general.

After leaving Daisy, we went home and had a lovely day outside. It was positively *hot*! Oh, and the sun felt so good on my face, so rejuvenating! Mina gave her Hello Kitty phone a bath in the plastic tub outside and decided to strip down and get in too!

It was just a lovely, lovely day—she was so happy and danced her crazy galloping dance around the house all afternoon.

February 15, 2011

We had a fun-filled day yesterday with Anna. I planned a lovely Valentine's Day surprise for her parents. The girls made up fresh pesto and pizza dough and chocolate-covered strawberries. Anna had instructions on how to make the pizza dinner for her parents, and her mom was thrilled.

Today, Mina and I are pretty pooped! I did get to finish my new book, *The Power*. It is the follow-up book to *The Secret*. It validated much of how I have been handling this whole process, using love as a foundation. It was nice to see my ideas expressed in such a succinct way and nice to have little reminders of how to take it further. Much of what was written, I had read before in many different places. Having it all together in one book helped me focus on what I could still do to improve things.

There are moments that make you feel helpless and powerful at the same time. This morning, as I was taking out the garbage, the recycling garbage can fell over (onto my toe—*ouch*!). The can is so big that I could probably fit in it, and I didn't know how I was going to get this damn can straight and up without spilling everything all over the place. I felt pretty helpless at that moment, really alone. My neighbor, Mark, was out and offered to help, but I said that I could handle it. He let me fight with it but stayed outside in case I got into trouble. Well, by golly, I somehow righted it and got it up again! Little things to empower you through the day can really make a difference in your mental state!

I e-mailed my lawyer to see if Hakan's lawyer had tried to contact her, but no, no contact yet. I am not going to fall into thinking negative thoughts and will put forth only positive images toward the outcome. I have had a "talk" with myself, and I will not keep talking about how things are not going well, but instead will talk to myself about how wonderfully everything is turning out.

I may not have control over how Hakan will react or how everything will turn out, but I do have control over my thoughts. By removing my attention from the bad, I will look to all that is good and remind myself of all the good that has appeared through this process. This will all be over soon and is such a small speed bump over the course of my life. I am going to take the morning for myself and not go to the museum. I need to rest my head and spend the morning with a coffee at the bookstore.

Mina is napping today, and I am enjoying the unexpected quiet to collect my thoughts—my *good* thoughts—and count all my blessings.

8:17 P.M.

I went into this visit with good intentions, and it worked out. While they played, I put on my music and swept the house. I swept the house for two reasons: (1) it needed it, and (2) I wanted to prevent negative energy from festering. I remembered a scene from the movie *Practical Magic*. The ladies had to get rid of some nastiness in the house, and after they grabbed their brooms, they all swept in one direction toward the door and "cleaned house" in a way. Well, I thought that might be a good idea too, keeping the nastiness from taking root. I felt better after clearing my space. And I even gave Hakan some chocolate hearts that Mina and I had made yesterday! How's that for goodwill?

February 24, 2011

Can life feel stuck in the mud and moving really fast at the same time? There is still no movement on signing papers. I e-mailed my lawyer after a week and asked what was going on. She said that she was waiting for Hakan's lawyer to contact her, and he hadn't yet—still after yet *another* week, no contact. She said she would call him to check in. Seriously, I am ready to go to court myself to get this thing signed. It is hard to get motivated to do anything when you feel like you are at a standstill in one portion of your life.

I decided to make a list, a list of *everything* I want to get done in the house, in life, in work, everything. That was just the thing I needed to get a fire under my ass and get going! The first thing I did was revisit the Etsy sewing projects down in the guest room closet. On Saturday, I pulled out all the unfinished ponchos and other half-done items. After separating them into piles, I got down to work and sewed up everything there in about an hour! *Wow!* Then I decided to create a space for my work downstairs and converted Hakan's old gear closet into my product stockroom. The space was perfect, and the shoe rack on the wall was the ideal place to hang the ponchos! Over the next two days, I cut out more ponchos from remaining material. All in all, I was able to whip out more than fifteen ponchos and six baby doll carriers, and I created a stockroom! I felt so energized to keep going!

Soon after, I got an e-mail from Christee, a potential cooking client. She not only wanted me to cook some food for her this week; she wanted me to cook up a dinner for four for this Friday. Now I had that food order on top of the party for forty Saturday night. Life is good, and I will have two nice checks in my hand by Friday!

I have not internalized any negativity and have put forth a lot of love. I went to the International Market the other day to get some olive oil and cheese. I asked Hakan if he needed anything, and he said no. But while I was there, I saw some things that he would like and picked them up anyway. I came home and put them in a bag along with a Ziploc of the fennel tea he likes and two Ziploc bags of Mina's soup mix with a recipe card. He was surprised and asked if I needed any money toward the stuff. "Nope," I said, "it's all set—enjoy." He looked at me quizzically but didn't push it.

He has been better and not moody when he comes over. I still haven't received any money from him, and I just don't understand why there needs to be such a power struggle over it. I find it funny that he asks when I am going to remove his name from the car insurance because it will save me a lot of money. He is concerned about me saving money, yet he won't give me the money stipulated? I just don't get it. Honestly, the car title and insurance are the least of my concerns at this point.

The other day, I wrote to K about lessons I had learned over the year:

> As I sit here and watch the snow fall with my big cup of Dragonwell tea, I feel very aware of everything: past, present, dreams for the future. There are so many things that I have come to learn, and I just thought I would share. If something makes you stop and think, great . . . if not, that is okay, too.
>
> I see myself, in my head, sitting on a bench with a cup of tea watching my life movie play before me. It is not that I am not engaging life, but that I have released a tight grip of control over it. If I have learned anything, it is this: Things happen in your life when you are ready for them, and not any sooner. You have to go through hell in order to have your eyes opened to see the good around you. Too often, we have an idea of how we want our life to be *right now*, but maybe we are not ready for whatever that is yet—we still have growing to do in order to appreciate the gifts.
>
> So many people feel as if they know your life better and have all this advice on how to fix problem A or B, but maybe you are not ready for their suggestions. Life changes when you, yourself, are ready for something more, something better.

People can express concern and ask how they can help you, right now, but forcing advice never works.

I have made a conscious effort not to put negatives into my ideas or dreams. If I can dream it or think it, then there is a way for it to happen. *How it* will happen, I don't know, but I have stopped telling myself that I will not be able to do this or that or have this or that. Looking back on the past six months has shown me that things, people, and events happen in your life. They answer your questions in the weirdest ways.

I have started to say thank you more for what I have rather than always looking at what I do *not* have. When you focus so much on what you don't have, your life feels empty. Each person has so much good around them to be grateful for, and the more you focus on or draw your attention to *those* things, the more aware you will become when something else that is good comes into your life.

I was reminded of a story out of Japan a few years ago. A man did experiments on emotions and their effects on water. This man took words like "grateful," "funny," "sad," "angry," and "jealous" and attached each to a bottle of water and left the bottles overnight. He came back the next day, put a drop from each bottle on a slide, and froze the droplets. When he looked at these frozen droplets under the microscope, he was amazed at what he saw. These water droplets attached to positive emotions created beautiful frozen shapes that contrasted with the water connected to negative emotions, which had jagged, angry shapes. If just a piece of paper with a word written on it might have affected the water, what do you think our thoughts do to us when we think negatively? Our body is mostly water . . . something to think about.

It is important to honor your feelings, good and bad, because they are part of who you are. If you feel like doing something nice for someone, then do it because you want to and not because you expect something of equal value given back to you. Good always comes back to you when it is given from your heart. I am just realizing that now. It is hard for me to believe that Linda remembers me giving her free treats at the tea grotto when I cooked there. Much of her help goes all the way back to a free cookie or two and a smile. When you put love and goodness out into the world, it comes back like a boomerang to you even bigger.

There is nothing better than a good hug. I have a friend, Gaia, who gives the best hugs in the world. You really feel that she cares when she gives you a hug hello or goodbye. It is so easy to make someone feel cared about when you give a really good hug.

Let love lead you where you need to go. There is a wonderful life out there waiting for you to take a look at it. I know it! Feel it! I hope that you never forget that you are a special person with many gifts to give others. If you have to work late, invite your wife and Ege for a picnic dinner with you at work. It might be like an adventure for Ege to have a picnic in your office. Anyway . . . I want the best for you, and I want you to want the best for you. I am finally waking up to life after sleeping for so many years, and I feel like I am playing catch-up. You only have one life to live . . . live it to the fullest, so at the end you can say, "Woooo-hooooo! What a ride *that* was!"

Interestingly enough, he didn't feel like he deserved all the nice things I thought about him, and that bothered me, and I told him so:

Okay, so I am going back to the "deserve" or "not deserve" part of all of this. Every person, no matter what, is special and deserves to know it, to feel it. What is it about you that makes you think you *don't* deserve the things I think about you? Seriously, do you leave the toilet seat up all the time, do you fart too much, do your feet smell after a long day's work? Who cares? Being special is not conditional on such little things.

This I *do* know: When I needed someone to listen in December, you were there. When I felt like sitting down on the floor and crying and just giving up, you reached through the computer screen, grabbed my hands, and pulled me up to my feet and told me that I was stronger than I thought and would get through this. I am sure that I am not the first person in your life you have helped get back on their feet.

A few questions to think about:

What would make your life "scream out loud" good? What do you need to make it even better?

For me, it was simply the freedom to be myself and not feel ashamed of who I was inside. It wasn't money or a house or new clothes. Those things help, but not where it really counts, inside your heart.

Do you need to get out and do more things outside, like diving or rafting or hiking? How can you rework your schedule to fit in *your* needs to make you feel full and happy inside?

When you take a look at your life now and look at Ege, what *more* do you want for him when he grows up? What thoughts enter your head when you read that question? "I hope he doesn't have to do this or deal with that"? Well, if you are thinking that Ege shouldn't have to experience this-and-that like you, why do *you* still have to experience those things?

For me, I didn't want Mina to live in a marriage without love. I didn't want her to think that was okay. I grew up in a house like that, and look what happened. I needed to stop the cycle from repeating itself and give Mina the opportunity to experience something wonderful.

You need to remember that you *deserve* the best life you can make. Everyone does. Life is not passing time until we die! Life is about experiencing, loving, playing, laughing, playing in the mud, and getting dirty with your kids' fun. You can't go back to the times you missed, but you can make sure you don't miss the days coming up.

Just live—that's all, just live.

Time for some breakfast and off to say goodbye to a friend My best friend, Sofia, is moving to Hawaii. Good for her, sad for me. But hey! Now I have a place to stay in Hawaii! Looking at the good side of things, right?

Well, I need to get rolling . . . literally! I need to go roll about a hundred grape leaves for the party on Saturday! Hope my fingers don't get knotted up!

Well, he has been here for fifteen minutes, and already, I feel a corset tightening around my chest. He and Mina went downstairs to play, and I guess they had a conversation about Mina staying with Hakan sometimes, overnight. Mina remarked that Mommy said she would never have to do that. *Stomp, stomp, stomp*—up the stairs they came to ask Mommy. He just sat there with this look on his face, the one that makes me feel intimidated. I told him that I never said such a thing; all I said was that for right now, Mina spends her nights with Mommy. He didn't believe me. He said if he wanted to push it, he could have her all day and night every other weekend. After a few more probing questions, Mina admitted that I had never said it and that she had made it up because she was scared to spend the night alone at Baba's house.

I am irritated and tired of having to defend myself against him. My lawyer got back to me this morning and said she would try to speak with Hakan's lawyer. If there is no response, she is going to file for temporary support with the court.

February 26, 2011

I am having a difficult day. I plummeted after Hakan left today. It actually had been a good few days around here. I made some money. K made me feel so special yesterday when we were chatting online at Starbucks. Just lovely, lovely thoughts, and it left me floating among the clouds for most of the day.

Even this morning was good. Mina and I put on some light bluesy music and set the table nice for breakfast. My mother-in-law called on the Ojo video phone, and we had a nice conversation. She was very touched that we had made her a reading shawl and sent it over. Hakan's father liked the shirt that he got too. Really, a pleasant morning.

Hakan's visit was fine until he told me that his lawyer had sent me something in the mail and that we should take some time this week to chat on our own. That just sent knots throughout my body, and the corset began tightening around my chest again, so I couldn't breathe. He says that my lawyer hasn't returned his lawyer's calls, whereas my lawyer says she hasn't received any calls. Who is to know who is right at this point? I just want it done. What do we need a couple of hours to discuss other than custody? The thought of another highly charged interaction with him just sent my head spinning. At the same time this was going on, he looked at me and told me I look tired and asked if I was feeling okay. Really? Yeah, I am tired. I am emotionally drained and trying to establish a business because I can't count on you to give me the money you promised!

All this brought back a dream I had the other night. In the dream I was in court talking to the judge about alimony. Out of the corner of my eye, I saw a cobra on a pile of rocks near Mina. Before I could warn Mina to back away, the cobra bit her on her back. Somehow, she had no shirt on, and you could really see the puncture wounds. Interestingly enough, her body repelled the venom, and it bubbled out of the wounds. All that was left was an empty fang-like hole, and we put a small Band-Aid over it. She was fine. I think the dream was a warning that there was still more yucky stuff to go through, but that Mina would be okay.

Not feeling particularly good, I texted Vanessa to see if she and Ashlan wanted to meet us for coffee later. They came out, and it was nice for Mina to have someone to play with while I pulled myself together. I feel like I have been on the verge of tears all afternoon, and I am tired of this shit. I hate to feel weak, and I feel like I am possibly being pushed to sign his way or go to court and then be the bad guy for bringing all this to court. I can just picture him saying that he was willing to sign, but I had to drag us all to court. I really need to get myself together because I am, possibly, going to court to stand up for something important: custody and the well-being of my child.

I feel pushed into considering meeting him on Thursday to "discuss" things. Half of me says "no way," and the other half is still—can you believe it? *still*—trying to avoid confrontation by acquiescing to his request. The fact that I am still making decisions based on his responses and emotional potentiality really pisses me off—at myself!

I wrote to my lawyer and told her what was going on. She needs to get to the bottom of all of this ASAP before I make a decision one way or the other for Thursday. Would I love to open the mail and see something signed by Hakan, just requiring my own signature to finalize things—yes! Is that even a remote possibility at this point?

March 2, 2011

I cannot believe it is March already. My lawyer did receive a fax from Hakan's lawyers with *his* responses to my responses. Goodness, it gets so confusing! A lot of the verbiage is quite defensive, coming from extreme emotions. There are things that he has conceded (great) or modified (fine). The big-ticket items are custody, trips to Turkey, and the deciding vote on education. He still wants his right to revisit the concept of joint custody when Mina is ten years old. His position on the trips to Turkey actually doesn't make a lot of sense to me. He believes that a judge will allow him to take Mina on his own to Turkey if I elect not to go. He says that I am "electing" to travel, on his dime, to Turkey. If I want to be able to see my family, then I should take a separate trip.

That's just plain silly. Mina will not even go out for ice cream with him. She would not go alone to the toy store, knowing that she was getting toys. She did not want to even go across the street to see the goats alone with him yesterday. How is a judge going to allow him to take her, alone, to Turkey? How can he think that a judge would? Also, even if he is paying for the tickets, what right does he have to dictate who I do or do not see?

He mentioned the other night that he might not even want to travel at the same time as us, so how does that all work out? How does visitation work out while we are over there and he has his time alone with her? I offered to stay for two weeks at his family's house, for one week at my aunt's summer house, and for one week at my aunt's Istanbul house. It is just hard with both our families living on different sides of the Bosphorus. I cannot see Mina being okay with me taking her over on the boat, handing her over to him, and leaving like that. She is not comfortable going in the car with him in her own country, in her own neighborhood. How will she be comfortable with him, alone, in a different country? My parents think I should just skip this year, but I have to figure this all out at some point because he wants it written in the settlement. He also said he may not go over for a long time this year, maybe just two weeks. It is all so confusing.

As far as the deciding vote on education goes, I do not think that he should have the deciding vote if he is not required to pay anything toward it. I believe I mentioned his fears in an earlier entry, and I feel like I need to write down what I will *not* do to assuage his fears: I will not homeschool

Mina. I will not send her to an alternative school. I will not send her to a high-end, pricey, private school.

I was actually okay once I read the fax my lawyer sent over. It is the unknown that makes me crazy. Once it is written down, I can deal with it.

Hakan came over last night and was pretty defensive. We were all in the kitchen. I was getting some food ready for Mina's dinner, and Hakan was sitting on the floor with Mina.

"You know what, Baba?" she said to him. "Nana is coming to visit me soon for a week! I am so excited to see her and play with her and take her to the park!"

I played down the visit by saying that it really would be only five days if you don't include the travel dates. Why do I still feel like I have to justify my mom's visit or play down how long my mom is staying?

Concerned, he asked, "Am I not going to be able to see Mina while your mom is here? How is that all going to work? You know she doesn't want to see anyone else when your mom comes to visit."

"I don't really think there will be a problem at all. Of course you will see Mina, but we may just have to adjust the day and times. We have to try."

At that, he turned to Mina. "So, would you like your *other* grandmother to visit?"

She looked at me with a deer-in-headlights expression and quietly nodded.

To me he said in a mocking tone, "Where exactly were you thinking my mom would stay if she visits: with me at my apartment or here with you and Mina?"

"Your mom is more than welcome to stay with us. For as long as she likes."

To that, he retorted, "Well, it looks like *everyone* is welcome in this house except me! Isn't that right, Elif?"

I turned away, ignored him, and did the dishes. When I did turn around again, he asked, "So you still want to go through with the divorce, huh?"

This time, I looked straight at him. "Yes."

He wants to meet alone tomorrow, but after yesterday, I am ambivalent. I do not want to get into a screaming match as we try to hash out the trip to Turkey. I was going to have Vanessa watch Mina, but Ashlan is sick. I am going with that as a sign not to meet and to write him instead. I need the time to talk to my lawyer and figure things out.

The other areas of my life are really starting to come together, and I can see that great things lie ahead. I have been so blessed to have K come back into my life with the support that I need to get through this. He just keeps pulling me up to my feet and telling me that I am strong enough to keep going. We spent Monday morning online, e-mailing back and forth. He was just ending his day at work, and I was just beginning mine. That time just works for us. I am enjoying the moments because that is really all we have right now. I don't know what the future will bring or not bring, and I will not preoccupy myself with what-ifs. If I do that, then I miss the moment. All we have in life is right now, this moment. I plan on enjoying every last second.

I took Monday as a "me" day and went window shopping down at Anthropologie. I enjoyed feeling pretty with all the lovely clothes. It is definitely an ego booster to see yourself looking good! I did end up leaving with something: my first pair of skinny pants (on sale!). I felt twenty-five again, and I looked it too!

When I was at the museum today, many of the ladies said that it is quite apparent that I am feeling really great! It shows, they said, in the way I hold myself.

Anne and I had coffee before our tour, and she told me of her trip to Austin, Texas, to see her first boyfriend. She hadn't seen him in almost fifty years. All she could say was "wow!" and that she had rented a fully furnished apartment there on a six-week lease. Her husband seems supportive because she just knows in her heart that she needs to do this, with or without his "blessing." Good for her! I asked her what she wore. Seriously, what do you wear to see your first love after so many years? I have gone through so many outfits in my head for when I see K this summer for our "chance" meeting at the park. I still haven't settled on anything yet. It's actually driving me crazy. It shouldn't matter so much, but it does. Samantha said that I could meet him wearing a trash bag, and he would still think I was beautiful. You know, she is right. I need to just relax about it.

I was able to scratch something off my bucket list today: I got *blue* put in my hair, and it is cute. Really subtle, but nice. I have always wanted some color like blue or purple in my hair but was always afraid to assert myself like that. Well, the new me isn't afraid anymore. Skinny pants, blue hair . . . hmm, what's next?

Mina has been dreaming these days. Her dreams come up when there is more tension between Hakan and me. She woke up the other day with a pretty extensive and elaborate dream for a four-year-old and was able to articulate it pretty well.

Her dream was set back in time "before Baba moved out into his own apartment." The three of us were walking to someone's house for dinner. She went in first and saw her friend Ashlan, but when she turned around, she saw Hakan and me walking away, down the street. She ran after us but couldn't find us. She saw a man on a bicycle and asked him if he had seen us. He said that we had turned the corner. When she turned the corner, she saw a Mommy and a Baba, but they were not us because the Mommy had long hair. She saw us up ahead and called out to me. I didn't recognize her. She saw me walk up to our house and pull on my sweater, but I didn't know her. Finally, she said, I recognized her and gave her a hug and brought her inside and cuddled her. She had found her Mama.

MARCH 4, 2011

I had a good day yesterday. Mina and I were out early to go to Joann's to get clasps for my ponchos. I am really trying to reinvigorate the Etsy business. I have twenty unfinished ponchos that I want to complete and get online. Every little step I take to complete them pushes me forward. I may not have done any sewing, but I took the steps to get clasps and pinned five outer and inner linings together.

Mina was just wonderful yesterday and played on her own most of the day, allowing me to really clean and clear my space. It really helps my head to clear my space before Hakan comes over in the evenings. I was actually banned from the dining room while Mina played under the table. I took advantage of the time to also handwrite expressions of gratitude in a journal. Somehow, it seems more powerful to actually write down my wishes, dreams, and gratitude—that mind-body connection thing.

While Mina was playing, I had the opportunity to also talk with my lawyer on the phone. That cleared my head a lot too. She and I were able to discuss a game plan regarding Hakan's latest notes. We are both trying to figure out how to word the trips to Turkey, and it is tough. It is such a fine line: I do not want be under his control over there if he buys the tickets, but I can't afford to buy them on my own either. We did decide to call his bluff about hiring a child custody evaluator. First, he will have to pay for it if he wants it. Second, she said there is nothing to fear because a judge will never allow him to take Mina to Turkey on his own if she won't even go across the street to see the goats on her own. As far as the final say on education, she suggested that we put in a statement saying that we would meet with a mediator if we couldn't agree. Also, we will stipulate what I will *not* do and just have it in writing.

She will take today and the weekend to draft a letter in response. I felt much better after talking with her; it put my mind at ease.

March 5, 2011

What a wacky day! K sent me an invite to join this site called Badoo, so I did. It's a singles site, people looking to connect and so on. Goodness, I signed up yesterday and added a photo, and I am getting all kinds of attention from all over the place. I am not sure about all of this: hey; hello; hola, mamacita! People are too familiar with people they don't know these days, I guess. Is this life in the singles lane? In the last four hours, I have gotten twenty-five messages from people named Hitman, Vampiro, and Test, among others. Ten people want to meet me, and I have had over a hundred hits on my profile. I have been told I look "delicious," "lovely," and like I "fell from the angels." Blah, blah, blah. Do women really fall for this crap? Anyway, I *did* answer one message: Claude, twenty-nine, from Switzerland. He finds me "pleasing," would like to get to know me, and so on. Sure, you seem harmless enough and pretty darn cute too!

March 7, 2011

I just spent the last two hours, thirteen minutes, and forty-nine seconds watching my first movie alone—another full-circle moment. It was *Eat Pray Love*.

I cried when I read the book years ago because I identified with so much. Now I cry because I see myself at the other end, on the journey back to myself. The moment when she is kneeling on the floor, praying to God for a sign, took me back to Christmas 2009—the fear of the unknown, the knowledge that every molecule of my being *knew*, just as she knew, that I didn't want to be married anymore. This wasn't the life I was destined to have. The guilt of shattering another person's world, the frustration of the journey, and the utter unknowable somehow never deterred me from the path. It is an awakening to feel *worth* it. Does that make any sense? I give and give and give, selflessly, in order to feel worthy and loved, but I don't give and give and give to myself in the same magnitude. *Now*, after all this, I am slowly realizing that I do need to shake things down to the foundation in order to rebuild. The concept of ruins and being ruined is completely subjective. Someone can go to see the Ancient Ruins of Greece and Rome and just see old broken rocks. However, if you look closely, you see that life builds up in and around the ruins, growing and blossoming in a different way. You just need to be open to it.

So many phrases from the movie hit home:

Richard from Texas says to Liz, "Groceries [his nickname for her], don't be afraid of love."

Ketut, the medicine man from Bali, says to Liz, "If you stop focusing your mind on the men in your life [good and bad], there is an empty space for the universe to—*bam!*—come in and show you possibilities."

Maybe I don't need to travel all over the world to find myself. Maybe I just need to trust myself more and trust the journey.

I met with Mina's teachers today for a parent-teacher conference, and it was so nice to hear them say that Mina is an example to them all with her love and her compassion. After hearing about our past troubles, divorce, and so on, her teacher was even more impressed at how well Mina is doing.

We have brought peace back into our lives by starting our own rituals. We celebrate each day now with a nice tablecloth and napkins, burning candles, and gratitude. Before, in order to get Mina to eat her dinner, I would read to her, thereby sacrificing my enjoyment of the meal. Now, with our special dinners, we sit together under the candlelight and talk about the wonderful things that meant so much during the day. We each tell the other our five tip-top events of the day. After we talk about them, she blows out the candles and finishes her dinner. For the first time in more than four years, I am enjoying my meals.

Mornings are filled with dancing as we welcome the day by picking only one or two candles to burn while we listen to *A Beautiful Day* by

India Arie or Sufi music. There is no rushing, just love swirling in the air as she twirls before her dolls.

Life can change in an instant, and you just have to be ready for it. It's like winter in Utah: I wore sandals to meet with her teachers in the afternoon, and now there is about four inches of snow on the ground. When I look outside, I feel like I am looking into a snow-globe scene with everything white, glistening, and quiet.

I am glad that I took the time to go up to Blockbuster video to get the movie because they were having a "going out of business" sale, and I was able to get the movie for pennies. All I wanted was that movie. I looked and looked (and believed) for it. I knew it was there; it was just a matter of allowing myself to relax and find it. Obviously, I found it—mixed in randomly with other DVDs. Miracles happen all the time in so many ways and are different for each person. We all have our own set of road markers that prove to us that we are on the right path.

Richard from Texas sums it up perfectly when Liz has grown tired of the journey being so hard: "You want the castle, but in order to get to the castle, you first need to swim across the moat."

The fear that I felt at the beginning has now been replaced with empowerment because I feel validated within myself. Two friends are starting their process now, and I can hear the doubt—I can recognize the tone—whether we are talking on the phone or via MSN messenger. Amy just moved her and her girls (Anna and Bella) to their new apartment over the weekend. My friend Esra, in Turkey, is packing and planning to move herself and her son Omer to live with her mother. I was not able to see her last summer and thought she had already divorced because she had changed her status on Facebook. She has told me now that she was all ready—had the job and a new apartment—but then her husband lost his job. She has been supporting them for the past six months, and she is waiting for him to get a job. She hasn't left because she doesn't want to be labeled the bad guy. The realization that I have come to is that the labels do not matter. What matters is being able to look yourself in the mirror, to *know* your heart and your own truth, and to be able to look your child in his or her face. That's it. When it comes to the point of contemplating divorce, you need to hold true to yourself, not sacrifice yourself, in order to participate fully in *your* life again.

MARCH 11, 2011

Wednesday, I planned a fun afternoon for Anna and Mina. In order to do all the cooking projects, I needed to stop by the market after dropping Mina at school. While I was there, I saw the chopped hot Italian vegetable relish that Hakan really likes. It has been years since I have been able to find it. I think I stood there, looking at it, for about five minutes: should I or shouldn't I get it for him? I feel that there is a constant battle inside me sometimes. Do I *not* get it for him just out of spite, I asked myself, or do I get it because he really enjoys it? Eventually, I did what felt right in my heart, which translated into buying it for him.

When I wrote to him about Friday's visit, I mentioned that I had found the vegetables and wished him a good day. He actually responded well, with a thank-you. And he also wished me a good day! It's a start, right?

My parents are quite adamant about my trip to Turkey this year. They do not want me to go. They are worried about where I am going to stay, the stress, the pressure, shuffling Mina across the Bosphorus, and so on. If we cannot come to some sort of agreement soon, we may not be able to find good tickets to go anyway. Tickets this year are outrageous! It does not even matter if you travel in May or July. The price is about $1,800 a ticket—*ouch*!

I did take time for myself yesterday when Hakan came over at 5:00 p.m. After they went downstairs to play, I poured myself some red wine; got my new book, *Everyday Sacred: A Woman's Journey Home*; and put on some mellow Sufi music.

What a great book! I was able to finish after Mina went to sleep. It begins like this:

This story is about a bowl.

> A bowl—waiting to be filled
> If what I have just written makes no sense to you, I am not surprised.
> If I had known in the beginning what I was looking for, I would not have written this story.
> I had to trust there was a reason I had to write, and I didn't have it all figured out in order to begin.
> I would find what I was looking for along the way.

The book is about one woman's journey to take a step back and see the sacred and the wonder of everyday happenings. Sometimes, when we are so caught up in ourselves and our problems, we forget to take a step back and look at the beauty, not the struggle, of our lives. So many of her ideas really hit home for me and resonated on a deeper level. While writing this journal, I feel as if I have kept saying that some circumstance has come "full circle," and now I can release and let go.

On page ten of the book, there is a big circle with a quote from Deena Metzger's *Writing for Your Life*: "Stories move in circles. They don't go in straight lines. So it helps if you listen in circles. There are stories inside stories and stories between stories, and finding your way through them is as easy and as hard as finding your way home. And part of the finding is the getting lost. And when you're lost, you start to look around and listen."

Wow! There were so many lessons in this book, but there is one other portion of the book that gave me an idea about how to destroy and rebuild myself in an artistic way. The author meets a potter who makes cracked bowls. He creates the bowl, destroys the creation, and then pieces it back together into something even more beautiful. It is somewhat a reference to the practice in many Asian cultures which revere cracking and chipping teacups by filling the cracks with silver, thereby celebrating the journey. Being cracked, chipped, and pieced back together only enhances the beauty of the cup and ourselves. Where would we be if we were not cracked or chipped along the way? It is what we use as glue that sets us apart: Do we fill in the cracks with love and seamlessly piece ourselves back together? Do we haphazardly fill in the cracks with anger or frustration and create a seam that oozes out the sides, creating a lumpy, bumpy, uncomfortable union?

Pieces, pieces, pieces . . . life is all about pieces, be they cracked or broken pieces or puzzle pieces. We build ourselves back up one piece at a time. Last night, as I was going to sleep, I realized a way to somehow reclaim myself and come to terms with the last ten years with Hakan. I am going to shred all our bank statements, ticket stubs, and letters and reuse the shredded paper to create papier-mâché bowls. It is my way of taking something that turned ugly and turning it into something beautiful.

MARCH 12, 2011

At the end of the day, I choose to laugh instead of cry. What had been a good day had the possibility to end crappy, *but* then the waiter brought me a sangria! Ole!

Hakan came over around lunchtime, and it was beautiful outside, but he was not having any luck getting Mina outside to play with him. Then I had an idea! I remembered that I had bought Mina a new ball at the bookstore's sale last month. I was saving it for Easter, but I brought it out anyway. When she wasn't looking, I gave it to him to give to her. He looked at me, puzzled, and asked, "Why? Why are you being so nice to me these days?" Well, why wouldn't I? It is best for Mina and isn't that the most important thing? Mina should have fun memories, not, stressful ones. She was thrilled with the ball and immediately wanted to go outside and play with him. Mission accomplished!

While they were playing, I thought I would take some time and get seedling pots ready. I asked Mina if she wanted to do seeds with Baba, and she thought that was a great idea. We all sat down and planted seeds together. These are things we should have done when we were together, but maybe I can give these memories to Mina now. He actually enjoyed himself and had a good time. If only, if only, if only he had relaxed enough earlier, so that he could have enjoyed us before it all had to come to this.

But being nice to him does not mean that I relinquish my independence. I will never admit difficulty, financial strain, or physical discomfort. He tried to give me money for the ball, asked me how I was doing these days, and asked how my hip was. *Really*, I thought, *none of your concern, thanks.*

It is insulting to me, actually, to have him offer to reimburse me for a $4 ball. Is he withholding the money to see me beg for reimbursement? I would rather not eat for a day.

Mina and I had a lovely afternoon at Disney on Ice with Emily and the kids, after which we went to the pizza parlor. Hakan called while we were there, and he was furious! He had just received my lawyer's latest letter and found it completely unacceptable. He said he is going to fight me all the way. As he was blustering away on his end of the phone, I remained cool as a cucumber. I don't have any more anger toward him, and that makes it so much easier to endure these telephone calls. I said, "I am sorry you are feeling this way, but I need to go now."

Then there was a choice to make once I had hung up: fall into the stress or laugh. I chose to not get upset, drink my sangria (or two), and have a good time. Emily and I laughed and laughed. It felt good to have someone there at that moment to laugh with!

I am sure that Hakan, suspicious and not trusting by nature, is thinking that I have been nice to him in order to get something from him, but that truly is not the case. Our problems should not even make it into Mina's atmosphere and affect her any more than they already do. If my being nice to him helps her to heal, then it is worth it in the end.

Today, Mina and I are headed to see a *Peter and the Wolf* concert downtown. I am going to attach a new memory to an old outfit. I am going to wear the special skirt and top that I wore on my wedding day after taking off my wedding dress. If I wear it today to this special concert with a sweater, I will be recycling and reclaiming a portion of myself.

MARCH 15, 2011

It was a tough visit last night. He is hurt and angry at the way things are progressing and is lashing out again. He sees what he wants to see. While I was out shopping, Mina asked Hakan if he would take her to the toy store to get a doll. When I got home, I was informed of this discussion. I didn't want any part of it because I didn't think she needed another toy, let alone another doll. I told her that if it was that important to her, she could go with Hakan in his own car. That didn't last long, but they got farther than before. She made it down the driveway, but then ran back in, crying. She said that she wasn't comfortable or ready to go out with him alone. He sees her playing house with her dolls and talking about dolls getting married and thinks that she wants a normal family life. He said that my family and I are delusional if we think that she wants this life, without him.

We were sitting on the floor of the living room facing each other with Mina on his lap, playing with her dolls.

"Mina," he said, "Baba would never do anything to hurt you. *Baba* loves you and will *always* do what is right for you."

His voice was so patronizing, with a nasty undertone aimed in my direction. What I understood him to be saying was that he wanted to keep the family together, but Mommy was willing to hurt her own child for her freedom.

"You know, it is inappropriate to say such things because I don't try to insinuate things about you or your love for her."

"I wasn't speaking to her; I was making a point to you."

At that point, I was just disgusted, so I got up and quietly walked out of the room and busied myself in the kitchen.

But he couldn't leave it alone. He walked around and through the other door, cornering me in the kitchen. "You know, Elif, you need stop using Mina as a weapon for blackmail!"

I immediately put down the dish I was washing and whipped my head around.

"*What?* You need to cease the conversation around Mina!" I said in a quiet voice because Mina was just through the door, sitting at the dining room tables, drawing. "You are being a bully!" I was not going to talk to him if he was going to continue to bully me. I will not be made to feel inferior in my own house!

He has a habit when he is being arrogant of looking down at me over his nose, and he did so at this point. "I am not raising my voice or yelling at you, am I? I am not behaving like a bully!" He was angry and chomping at the bit to really let it out. "*When, when, when* can we talk about this stuff?" I turned my back to him and went back to washing dishes. Exasperated, he stormed out of the room

If he is going to be like this, then I would rather our lawyers or a mediator handle it. I do not want to be attacked like this. If he thought that Mina was not aware of his behavior, he was wrong. After he left, Mina asked, "Mama, why was Baba trying to start an argument again?"

"Baby, it is not appropriate for you to hear the grown-up talk, and I asked him to stop."

"Yeah, like I had to do last time . . . remember, Mama, when I had to stand up and shush him when he was being mean to you?" The she sighed sadly.

I wrote to my lawyer and told her what happened. She said that Hakan is probably making it sound worse than it really is because he is not getting what he wants. Most likely, his lawyer is telling him that what my lawyer is saying is true. Truth hurts.

Even though Hakan wants this done, he wants it done his way. It is so frustrating that these problems are over such little things like trips to

Turkey and who gets the final say over Mina's education. It really boils down to just three trips to Turkey before Mina gets old enough to go with him on her own at age eight. All of this over three trips over the course of a lifetime? Sigh.

MARCH 17, 2011

I had a good chat with my lawyer yesterday morning. She reassured me that she will be right there next to me if this has to go to mediation. She said that the four of us (she and I and Hakan and his lawyer) would sit down in one room but might have to move to separate rooms if emotions got heated. She told me that I am doing all the right things in trying to help Hakan and Mina develop a relationship.

He was still waiting for a response about meeting alone to chat. After Monday's "weapon" remark, I really didn't feel comfortable. I felt that I would soon become target practice for his verbal outbursts. I feared would just talk *at* me and not *with* me, accusing me, judging me, and so on. Here I am after months of therapy, feeling strong, feeling like me again, and I still get knots in my stomach when I have to e-mail him something he may get upset over. Ugh! It is so frustrating for me to feel that he still has some control over my feelings!

Well, I faced it, and I did it—I wrote him a letter this morning:

> Morning,
>
> I have been doing some thinking over the past few days about us taking some time and talking. First, Gaia hasn't finished up her work in California, so she won't be back until the weekend and can't watch Mina today.
>
> Also, it seems that the items we most need to work out have a lot of emotions attached to them, which makes talking about them, calmly, difficult. We just seem to talk *at* each other and not with each other. Unfortunately, we may have gotten to the point where we need someone to help us work through this.

He actually agreed with me, and it looks like we are off to mediation. When I spoke to my lawyer yesterday, she said that she had spoken with his lawyer before calling me. Hakan and his lawyer were due to talk this morning. I am always on edge these days when he comes over because I just don't know what sort of emotions he is bringing in with him. Today was . . . all right. When Mina went downstairs and I sat at the table, he did walk into the dining room and give me one of his arrogant smiles before joining her. Okay, whatever, dude.

I actually spent the day working. Mina was a dream and played on her own most of the day. I finished up five ponchos, completely, and will photograph Mina in them this weekend to post on Etsy. We went down to see Marcia and Clare because I needed Marcia's help with my Kismet Cooking website. Now that I have a clearer idea, I can chug ahead with that this weekend when we are up at dawn!

Did I mention that the money I invested with Gaia's friend is being reimbursed with interest? Woo-hoo! Money coming back to me!

I am welcoming any money these days since there hasn't been any money since December, and the savings account just looks so sad. Linda was funny the other day. She asked if she should throw another party for me to make come cooking money. What a lady!

I am not crazy-worried about money coming in, but it is unsettling when it isn't. It is a control tactic at this point.

On a completely random note, Hakan mentioned seeing some photos of Mina on my Facebook page. He must have spent some time on my page and probably read all that I am up to. I don't really care because there is nothing there I don't want him to see, but it's hard for me that he has so much access to my "private" life now (as private as it can be on Facebook). He has completely blocked me from his profile, and that's fine. I give him access because of Mina, so that he can see pictures and videos of her. I wonder, what does he think when he sees us so . . . well . . . happy? We have been taking the time to enjoy the moments and celebrate them. We now have a special Tuesday morning breakfast and set the table nice with flowers and candles. We listen to Enya while we eat and have our juice in fancy wine glasses. We calm down at night the same way—we make dinner a special occasion and talk about all the good things that happened. Then we play mellow music, keep the lights low (sometimes just candles), and play quietly before going to bed. It works out so well for us. Can he honestly think that Mina is suffering or lacking because he is not around and we are not together as a family anymore?

MARCH 19, 2011

What am I doing? I am sitting at the table staring blankly at the computer screen with my head in my hands. I am feeling paralyzed and immobile. Mina is in the bath, and I have just about an hour to myself, and I can't bring myself to do anything except sit here and stare at this computer. These are the type of days—gray, cold, and stagnant—that I seem to internalize and embody. Doubts creep in and stir up my insides. My face has erupted like lots of mini volcanoes all over, and Mina has been using her nightlight to try to "connect the dots." Not funny!

Last month I was devouring music that seemed to emanate how I was feeling. Now I have turned to books. I am reading and reading, looking for answers in the pages. I know the answers are not there, but inside me. Still, I read and extract personal meaning from random anecdotes.

Maybe it is seeing Amy, Anna's mom, just starting this separation/divorce process that has a portion of me reidentifying with the initial fears.

As I sit here and write, I can see all our little seeds sprouting. Some just push right up, ready and willing. That arugula zipped right out of its seeds and is having a party! Others were planted upside down and seem to have had a harder time, pushing under the dirt only to right themselves toward the sun. Right now, I feel like the second type of seed. I'm ready to burst free, but damn, what's all this dirt that I have to dig through? On top of that, who is this little girl who sprinkled eggshells all over the dirt? Once through the dirt, I still . . . must . . . navigate . . . sharp shells! Somehow, these seeds do it each and every time. It is so instinctual.

A few other lessons have presented themselves to me over the past two weeks. As much as the experience with that singles social network, Badoo, was insane, I learned something about myself. To have someone like Claude (the twenty-nine-year-old) tell me that I was interesting and he was interested was nice. After chatting with him online, I realized that the great feelings I had for K were not as all-encompassing as they had been. It had been so long since anyone had expressed any sort of true affection for me or accepted me for who I was. I think I was in love with feeling loved and not with the person. It was reassuring for me to hear Claude say that my having a kid was not a problem but an added bonus. Whether or not anything comes of this is immaterial. It is the knowledge that there are men out there who will not shy away from a single mom, as my aunt told me over the summer, that helps. Maybe that was the whole point of all this men-business.

March 27, 2011

Can I tell you much I am so *done* with this divorce process? Goodness, it takes . . . soooo long to finish! At this point, I am loath to write anything because that means it isn't *over* yet! Phone tag between lawyers, e-mail tag between lawyers, lots of wasted air in trying to set up a mediation appointment.

Oh yeah, and did I mention I set up a father-daughter outing for Hakan and Mina with Zep and Anna? Well, I organized a little outing down to the children's museum at the Gateway shopping plaza. I drove Mina there and handed her over. She was comfortable with Anna there, and I was able to leave them alone. They all had a grand time, and we met up for ice cream three hours later. Woo-hoo! Father-daughter bonding.

I think I am feeling a bit pissy. Here I am, smoothing things out for them to have a great relationship, and I get no kudos from him, and he still doesn't trust me. I am really trying to keep myself together for Mina's sake, but I will tell ya, when he still comes out with zinger insults or insinuations, I just want to bop him one!

My lawyer is working on the whole temporary relief situation, so maybe, just *maybe*, I will see some money before my savings are completely wiped out. The situation has made me come up with two categories for purchases: essentials and non-essentials—for example, toilet paper (essential) versus Q-tips (nonessential).

I have even begun to rinse and wash Mina's disposable plastic straws from IKEA. This is crazy. I have cut back on so many groceries that I am down to about $35/week. I have been turning the heat off during the day when we leave and turning it back on just before Mina goes to bed. The lights are off until absolutely necessary. I use candles. I felt like I splurged the other day when I went to the liquor store to get some wine. Yellowtail merlot was on sale for $6 a bottle—I bought two!

Hopefully, my garden will yield enough food that I can cut the food bill down even more. I have started baking bread and freezing it rather than buying it. I feel like a friggin' pioneer. I have mixed feelings about it—it's great on one hand to do all this stuff with Mina, but I'm pissy that I *have* to do it in order to save money.

My question is this: what does he think he is accomplishing by withholding the money and making it this difficult?

We have made progress with Mina leaving the house with him. I feel that the situation has escalated in his mind, and there has been constant pushing to go to the toy store, go get ice cream, anything, just for her to leave with him. There seems to be a sort of urgency. It makes me think that maybe his lawyer is pushing him to get her to leave with him to strengthen their side in some way. When Anna and her mom came over yesterday, we left the girls with Hakan while we went to Costco. He was able to get Mina out of the house with him while Anna was there. However, once Anna left, and he asked Mina if she wanted to go to the toy store, to get ice cream, and so on, Mina looked at him and said (1) that she had enough toys, thank you, and he could buy her something for her birthday, and (2) that she had already had a big ice cream bar at home, and it wasn't healthy for her to eat too much ice cream this late in the day.

I have also, slowly, begun transitioning back into my own room, into a *bed*, at night these days! Wow! Sleeping in a bed is such a luxury—it could become addicting! Now I realize why so many people do it! I start off on the floor in her room but move to the other room if I wake up. She seems okay with it, actually. If she hears me leave, she just asks if she can come and cuddle in bed with me when she wakes up—no crying or fussing. I really need a new mattress, though. Some of Hakan's residual indentations are deep, and I feel like I am sliding into a hole. That sometimes makes me tense up, which makes my hip ache. I can't get a new mattress until I get some money from him. That is really the main reason I haven't fully transitioned over to sleeping full-time in the bed.

MARCH 29, 2011

Woo-hoo! Mediation is set for April 7 at 9:00 a.m. Can it be possible that all of this might be settled next week? It is really hard to fathom or internalize that possibility. I e-mailed my lawyer about how long the session will be and how much. It will take about four hours at $200/hour. The cost will be split between the parties, and she, the mediator, wants payment before she leaves. Between her fee and the lawyer's fee for those same four hours, it is going to be a pricey morning. Let's see how my math goes: $400 mediator (my half) + $1,000 lawyer = $1,400! Ouch! And they call this cheap? Well, comparatively speaking, I am sure it is cheaper than going to court. My job now is to figure out child care for that day from about 8:30 a.m. to 1:30 p.m. Maybe I can drop her at Marcia and Clare's house for the morning, with Daisy taking Mina out to lunch. It's a possibility.

MARCH 30, 2011

I took the morning to go hang at the Oasis Cafe, and it was so peaceful. There is a new age bookstore in one corner, and I did what many women do during times of flux—I went and got my tarot cards read. Years ago, my friend told me that going to a tarot card reader was cheap therapy. She is right.

It was an interesting reading if nothing else. She even took notes for me to consult later! With Mercury going into retrograde, it is a good time to finish old things. Signing divorce papers at this time would be a very good thing!

She told me to get up off my good-girl butt and get in the game: do what you normally would *not* do, she said. I was told to "see" and feel exactly how I would like the mediation to be or turn out. I am to step in and out of this energy and visualization three times, twice a day. So when I actually get into the mediation, I will feel stronger because I visualized it.

"What are you bringing in with you to help you through the session?" she asked. This is what I came up with:

1. My Armani suit as armor, for strength
2. My 3,000-year-old iron Mesopotamian bull's head pendant, for holding my ground
3. Special cards from my grandmothers, for confidence
4. Michael the Archangel, for protection
5. Hakan's name on a piece of paper, in my shoes—every time I walk, or stamp, on it, I stamp out his controlling energy.

April 1, 2011

What a good day! I made up some coffee and brought it down to my lawyer this morning after dropping Mina at school. It was a good meeting. We talked about what we were going to discuss next week at mediation. She was proactive and forwarded the mediator all back-and-forth stipulations to save time. I had her laughing about avocado pizzas by the time we were done. I feel really comfortable with her.

I still had time before story-time, and I thought I would head to Tony Caputo's for my Friday morning breakfast sandwich. Ted and his other worker were having Mexican breakfast soft tacos and made me a couple. Not only did Ted not charge me for breakfast; he told me my coffee was on the house! What a gift to me today!

Feeling energized, I headed to the bookstore and ran into a mom I hadn't seen in a while. Laura and her baby, Margaret, used to come all the time last summer, and she is not only a friend of a friend, but also my father's old student. She had moved to California, and I was surprised to see her! Guess what—she moved back to Utah and is filing for divorce too! I asked her where she was staying and offered her the extra bedroom downstairs if she needed a place to stay. Maybe I will set up the downstairs as a sort of halfway house for divorcing mothers with children! Ha!

Time to go out and play in the garden. We planted our corn, peas, beans, and arugula yesterday, and they need some water. I am excited to say that our peach tree is blossoming, and we might actually get peaches this year! Mina is doing such a good job helping me get the yard in order. We raked leaves and bagged them. I am glad she enjoys working with me in the yard. It will be a great help as time goes on. Now I am looking into drying our clothes outside in the fresh air and saving money (and energy) by not using the dryer. I am hoping she will love to hang clothes to dry, too!

April 5, 2011

We got the tax refund stuff back from the accountant, and it's nice. My share will be about $1,800, but here is the kicker—it is due to be directly deposited into the closed mutual checking account. Okay, now what? Then I got a letter from my bank telling me that I am conducting too many transfers from my savings account to the checking. This has incurred transaction fees, and they may change my savings into another checking account. It just frustrates me because he can so simply say, "Use the savings, and I will pay you back," but not think of how that will affect my accounts at the bank. I am really at the point where I feel I can't keep going with this battle of wills, and I pray every minute of every day that we will sign papers on Thursday.

I was thinking the other night before bed about life a few years ago. Hakan and I lived parallel lives, and I felt that I always had to erase the "evidence" of mine. I guess I should explain. Every time a friend came over for tea or lunch, I would clean up all those extra dishes and put them away before he came home. That way, he would never know and never get upset that I had friends and he didn't. I realize now that I was making myself invisible and not seeing that my life and friends had value. Even now, I feel like my life is invisible to him, like he doesn't really want to see who I am. My needs seem less important than his, which makes me feel a bit insignificant in his worldview. I am so tired of these walls that we have built around ourselves. It all comes down to trust. Doesn't it always? I don't trust him enough to tell him what I plan to do for work because I may be ridiculed, or it may affect the alimony. He may be afraid to trust me because then he might actually see who I am inside and realize how much he let go.

Now it is 6:45 p.m., and I have to be the bad guy and tell them they need to start getting ready to say goodbye so Mina can go to bed. I will be met with defiance from both ends. Does it matter that he was forty-five minutes late today? Does that mean he is entitled to get extra time if he was late? I don't think so, but this is what I am going to have to deal with. It gives me such a headache.

8:53 P.M.

There was a sigh and a whine when I went down to give a ten-minute "time for bed" warning, but all in all, it went smoothly.

After a cup of tea and some silly TV, I thought I would just try my hand at meditating for a few minutes and see how it went. While I was sitting there, I asked myself to show me something. It truly amazes me how the mind works sometimes. This is what I saw:

I saw myself as the ringmaster of a circus. Dressed in a sparkling long coat and top hat with a big, enormous smile on my face, I was directing the circus below me from the high wire. The "circus" was set up in three rings: the ring on the right held my family, the one on the left held Hakan's family, and in the center were Hakan and Mina enclosed in a wire sphere (the metaphorical bubble). From high above, I would crack my whip as the "animals" from each ring got pissy and moved toward the center ring, to create chaos in my bubble (the family unit)!

All I could hear in my head was his mother telling me to smile bigger and all the problems would go away. Little did everyone realize that I was up on the high wire, sitting on a chair that was, itself, balancing on a unicycle that was balancing on the wire. The only thing I had to keep me steady was a tiny cocktail umbrella. There was no way I could balance things and keep the stresses away from my family unit forever. I understand that now.

This brought me back to coffee yesterday with Laura. She told me that it is so helpful for her to talk to me about all of this because *no one* talks about this sort of thing. It is not exactly the conversation you bring up with random people at a dinner party. When someone asks, "How are you?" you automatically answer, "Things are great!" Inside you are screaming, "Things are not fine! I am in a marriage that is drowning. And you?" But you put on some more lipstick, plaster a bigger smile on your face, and refill your wine glass.

April 8, 2011

At the moment, I am wrapped up in Mina's ice cream cone snuggly, watching the snow fall, sitting in the dark, and trying to figure out how to write about our mediation session.

Today I am filled with extreme sadness that two people who had so much love in their hearts for each other had to sit in separate rooms with lawyers and talk through yet another person. There is a photo in my head of the two of us when we first met. He always had both arms around me, hugging me, like he couldn't be apart from me for a second. Now here we are as separate as can be—with physical walls and doors between us.

I realized today that Tuesday is our official tenth wedding anniversary. It seems foreign to me to say out loud that I have been married a decade.

When I started this process, I never thought I would still, technically, be married when the decade marker came up.

I feel strangely calm after the whole mediation session, mainly because I knew that the mediation was for him to understand the legality of certain things. Hakan wasn't hearing me or my lawyer on certain issues, and it needed to come from a former judge to sink in.

I liked the mediator, Lisa, right off the bat. She was fun and quirky. She had read all the documents my lawyer had sent over and thought it best to begin with Hakan. An hour later, she came back, fanning herself, and said, "Boy, did he have a lot to talk about!"

He is absolutely petrified that I will move back to Rhode Island with Mina, and that was the main reason he wanted to revisit custody. He believed, incorrectly, that if he had joint custody, he could prevent me from moving. Lisa educated him and set him straight. Does that settle that portion of our stipulation? No idea.

Moving onto school and the "final say" issue, he was convinced that Uintah (the public elementary school) was an alternative, private school. Lisa educated him again and clarified, again, that we live in the Uintah school district and that Uintah is a *public* school. She continued by explaining that test scores show that the high schools in our district are poor and that this was the main reason I was thinking of a private *high school*. "Oh" was his response. What pisses me off is that it was clearly articulated in our last stipulated response all the things I would *not* do, that Uintah was a public school, and that I was considering private high school due to the public schools' overall scores! Why did I need to spend another $350 to have that explained by a mediator? Can't Hakan and his lawyer read themselves?

Now, was that portion of the settlement solved? Don't know.

I guess that brings us to the trips to Turkey portion of our settlement. He came in very sure of the situation and adamant that Mina was not to have time on his dime with my family. After a few back-and-forth exchanges, my lawyer and Lisa agreed that a trip to Turkey should be off the table for this summer. It would be in Mina's best interests *not* to go this summer, not until things are straightened out. Now, all of a sudden, he is interested in how I wanted to plan a time-share over there.

Can we say that *this* portion of the settlement was solved? Nope, no idea.

Everything was completely overshadowed by his lawyer pushing for a specific time frame for when Mina would do overnights at Hakan's house. This kid is not comfortable going with him in a car yet, and you want me to give you a date for when she will be comfortable sleeping at his house? His lawyer wants it *done*, now, within three months. Are you kidding me?

In my opinion, his lawyer has been the biggest problem in this whole process. I found out that *he* was the one who told Hakan not to pay me the money over the past few months because I had the savings to survive on. He did nothing to correctly inform Hakan about the joint custody issues and moving out of state. He does not trust divorcing wives and seems to advise his clients not to trust their soon-to-be ex-wives either. He is more concerned about what is best for his client than about what is best for the child.

My lawyer and Lisa proposed a play therapist to help Mina and Hakan work out their issues and help them moved toward a stronger relationship. Hakan's lawyer does not like therapists because they are unreliable, and you cannot count on a speedy recommendation toward overnights from them. He wants to call in a child custody evaluator to quickly evaluate the situation and recommend overnights ASAP. What is more important: winning or having a better relationship with your daughter? If it takes eighteen months until the therapist thinks she is ready for overnights, why wouldn't you trust her judgment?

Hakan became so overloaded with all this "education" that after hour three, he walked out with his lawyer behind him. I was completely in shock when I saw them walk out. I was stunned.

I stayed and spoke with Lisa and my lawyer for another forty minutes. Lisa advised us to come up with a six-month transitional plan toward overnights. Also, my lawyer is going to file to get the unpaid $10,000 back under the heading of promised temporary relief and will file officially with the court system come Monday if she hasn't heard from Hakan's lawyer by then. Since his lawyer screwed up that whole payment agreement, my lawyer is going after the full sixty-five months beginning the day the divorce is decreed, not backdating it to January 1, 2011. She pulled out the claws yesterday, and I don't think it will be pretty for Hakan's lawyer. His lawyer has created a lot of problems when there weren't any and has been the biggest impediment of them all.

At this point, we are dealing with two egos: Hakan's and his lawyer's. Winning doesn't mean much if you rush things with your daughter and screw everything up.

April 18, 2011

Yes, I have been avoiding this journal. I have just been trying to make sense of a lot of wacky things that have been happening lately.

First, the universe took charge and sent me a book in the mail. It kind of freaked me out a bit, and I couldn't look at it for a week, and it just sat in the box. I finally finished it, and it reaffirmed so much in my life.

It all began with the book *Everyday Sacred*. I was at Oasis Cafe a few weeks ago and came across a few used copies as well as the author's first book, *Plain and Simple: A Woman's Journey to the Amish*. I put them all down and decided that I would find them used on Amazon at a better price, and I was right. After adding five *Everyday Sacred* books to my cart for Mina's teachers, I decided to add an extra one for the parents of one of Mina's school friends. They were going through a rough time with their eighteen-month-old. Done, order sent. Well, unbeknownst to me, the universe had other ideas. My gift to Mina's friend's family boomeranged back to me. By mistake, *Plain and Simple* got sent instead of *Everyday Sacred*. Instead of getting upset at the mistake, I took a closer look at the mistake and asked, "Why?" I got my answer: Elif, you need to take care of yourself and have this book. It is not time to give to Isabelle's family.

I have been going back to the basics in my life and enjoying the everyday-ness of things. Mina and I take time to do things and enjoy making bread or washing the floors together. Little did I know I was mimicking a very Amish way of life. Celebrate life in everything that you do, and you will feel the love in doing the ordinary. Stop rushing; be present; be one with who you are right now!

> It is the enjoyment of every step in the process of doing, everything . . . If accomplishing is the only goal, all that it takes to reach that goal is too slow, too fatiguing—an obstacle to what you want to achieve. If you want to rush to the accomplishment, it is an inevitable disappointment. Then you rush to something else. The disappointment is reaped over and over again. But if

every step is pleasant, then the accomplishment becomes even more, because it is nourished by what is going on. (85)

Where I refer to life as puzzle pieces, she refers to life as a nine-patch quilt. Basically, quilts, in essence, are made from scraps of old discarded material. A quilter takes these worn, torn scraps and creates beauty. You move the pieces around until the quilt's spirit comes through. There is no waste. All of our mistakes and hardships lie next to or near the wonder of our lives, making a glorious life quilt.

Second, it has been so nice to have a new/old friend, Laura, back in my life. Again, I feel like a force bigger than I sent her back here. We are to help each other through all this. It is so nice to have someone from home here. It's very comforting. She told me the other day that one of the main reasons she moved back to Utah instead of directly back to Connecticut was to hang out with her favorite professor's daughter. Over the two weeks since she has been back, we have really bonded as friends and old schoolmates.

Third, there is Zep, Anna's father. I think he is . . . kind of . . . flirting with me. I spend my weekends these days divided between time with Amy, Anna's mom, and Friday afternoons with Zep.

Last Friday, as I was driving in to pick up Mina from school, Zep called. "Hello, Mama Elif. Where are you? Are you going to the girls' art exhibit today?"

"Hello there! I am just pulling into the parking lot as we speak. Just so you know, it is completely full if you are looking for a parking space!" I said as I pulled into the last space.

"I am right behind you and would gladly move the roped-off spots for you if you need a space! I was wondering what you and Mina were doing after the show. I thought maybe we could take the girls for a picnic at Liberty Park. When I was at Smith's, I picked up some picnic stuff: some bread, roast turkey, marinated mozzarella and tomatoes, and of course, some jelly beans for the girls!"

I don't think my car was big enough to house the smile on my face. I had to step outside to finish the conversation and meet him by the school's entrance.

"I think that is a wonderful idea! What a lovely way to spend the afternoon!"

Not only was Zep at the exhibit, but Hakan was as well. The two dads paired off together and followed the girls around to see their exhibit.

Soon, the girls rushed up and bombarded me with questions: "Mama, what are we doing after class? Can we play together? Can we go somewhere? Can we, can we, please?"

Okay, what was I to say? "Um, we may be going to a park," I answered quietly.

I cannot get a vibe on this guy. Zep has a very unnerving way of looking at me, and I can't read him. There is definitely some sort of energy there, but I can't exactly put my finger on it. Thing is, I wouldn't mind if he *was* flirting. We have a really great time together. My head is in a tizzy—again. How do I find myself in these messes?

I have had a lot of gifts come my way lately as well. Linda had her dinner party and paid me more than I asked and gave me a lovely bottle of white wine. Daisy gave me her old composter and some gardening supplies. I got my Costco dividend in the mail. I got that book in the mail. And I think that is it.

Not much movement on the divorce—what else is new? My lawyer put together a six-month transitional timeline for Mina to do overnights with Hakan: month 1—get her comfortable going in the car with him; month 2—introduce her to his house; month 3—one visit needs to be at his house for at least six hours on a non-school day; month 4—all visits at his house; month 5—overnights every Friday night to noon Saturday; month 6—standard every other weekend. Phew!

There has been no reply. My lawyer has the paperwork filled out for temporary relief and will submit this week. There has been no mention of going or not going to Turkey. I can't plan anything for the summer—camp for Mina or a trip to Rhode Island—until things get settled. Again, life is on hold. I have such a headache from all of this.

April 25, 2011

Let us begin by pouring another glass of wine! I have been reading and dreaming again. I reread *The Alchemist* by Paulo Coelho, and it had so much more meaning this time around. Reading it, however, reminded me of how I came in contact with it to begin with. It seems like a story out of *The Alchemist* so many years later.

It was 1997, and I was still working in Boston. Friends had heard of this fabulous tea-leaf reader somewhere in the woods. We drew lots, and I drove. I remember a dark, rainy night and a car filled with starry-eyed twenty-something girls all looking for love. The woman took us in, gave us some towels to dry off from the thunderstorm, and made us a cup of tea, with tea leaves at the bottom. When we were finished drinking, she looked at the patterns and told us our fortunes. Specifically, she told me about a boy (isn't it always about a boy?) and gave me his initials, his birthday, and a crazy description of his occupation. This boy turned out to be in my History of the Middle East graduate studies class. His name was Brendan, and the exactness of the reader left me speechless. He had a tattered copy of *The Alchemist*, and there were notes and passages underlined everywhere. He told me that it was a living book and each person who read it added to it before they passed it on.

Reliving that experience as I began reading it again was powerful, and I knew I needed to pass on my new copy as well. I figured the book would tell me who needed to read it, and it did: Zep. My book suddenly took on a life of its own and sent *me* a message: Zep needed to read this book because he was now on his own journey. Coupled with this message, I got another image—a chocolate bar, not just any chocolate bar, but one I had seen at Tony Caputo's a while back. *Okay*, I said to myself, *let's go check out this chocolate bar*, feeling kind of silly at this point. This bar was made with coffee beans. It was created for those people who love lots of cocoa in their coffee. Immediately, I understood why he needed *this* bar. Back in February, when I first sat and had coffee at Anna's house with Zep, he had pulled out the container of cocoa and spooned in massive amounts of cocoa into his coffee.

"All right," I said to no one in particular, "I get the message," and I bought the damn chocolate bar. Amy had needed nice fancy soap to bring her back to herself, and Zep seemed to need good chocolate.

This all brings me to my dream from the other night. I guess I was feeling a bit weird about possibly giving this very spiritually based book to Zep, who is agnostic. In my dream, he had walked me to my car, and I handed him the book and chocolate. In response, he asked me if I was religious and believed in God. I simply answered that my religion was love. I now know that I am here to help others feel loved, appreciated, and validated, no matter who they are, without sacrificing myself in the process. I am a giving, loving soul, and I should not feel ashamed or hide that anymore.

I have taken the time to learn to be alone and listen. I value my quiet time after Mina goes to sleep to read, learn, and find out who I am again. As I have come in contact with various friends who are in various stages of divorce or separation, I have realized that I need to find the time to love myself before loving someone else. If another comes into my life, lovely. If not, I am okay with that too. I do not need a man in my life to complete me. I have been feeling a bit like an alien in the midst of so many moms these days, and I am okay with it. Yes, my child goes to bed at 6:30 p.m. and is up at 6:00 a.m. Yes, my child can be dramatic. If you need to rethink Mina's friendship with your child, so be it. I love that Mina and I can each read our own books, silently, side by side on the couch at 7:00 a.m. I love that we can collaboratively create something magical at 8:00 a.m. I love that we move through our mornings with such ease that there is always time to dance before leaving the house. We do not rush; we experience. We do not shovel our food to finish in time to get out the door; we savor. We do not aimlessly pass by the flowers in the garden; we take a few minutes and wake them up for the day as we move toward the car. Life has meaning, and the days are full.

Mina and I will be spending Wednesday afternoon with Zep's mom. She is in town visiting from Canada for a few weeks and I offered to take her for an outing with the girls while Zep was working. We haven't decided what to do yet, but we will have to eat. I am planning a fun picnic, and I decided, what the hell? I am going to get some nice cheeses and sliced meats at Tony Caputo's. You know, doing something nice does not always have to cost a lot! At first glance, it may seem excessive to go to an Italian deli and get specialty meats and cheeses for someone you don't even know. In the end, six slices of this meat cost maybe $.22, that one cost $.95, this cheese cost $1.20, and so on. You get the idea. With some homemade fresh bread and a salad, we will be eating like royalty! So many of us get boxed into what is "acceptable" and what may be considered "excessive." These preconceived ideas prevent us and hold us back from crossing that line.

C'mon! Cross the line! Jump over it! Do the cha-cha around it! Live a little! I dare you!

Of course, here I am saying that, but I am rethinking the gift of the book and chocolate to Zep. Too late now, actually, because I left it with

Anna at her day care today for him to pick up. I need to feel secure in my truth and be okay if someone else doesn't. It is about honoring what you feel inside to be the thing you need to do, regardless of another's opinions. Whatever Zep and Amy learn from their books is their business. My part in that cycle ended once I handed them the books I felt would be helpful for them.

My wine is done, and I need some rest.

May 7, 2011

Life becomes very interesting when you just let it flow and watch events unfold without forcing your will on the outcome. It has been so delightful to spend time with Zep's mom and my mom, really just lovely.

Zep ended up coming to the picnic at Red Butte Garden. I am so used to doing everything myself that it catches me off-guard when someone offers to help me. As I was unloading all the picnic paraphernalia, Zep just took the basket off my hands, saying, "I can help too, you know." We all set the fancy table together and enjoyed eating among the daffodils under the sunshine.

I was relieved to find out that Claire, Zep's mom, spoke very good English! We were able to talk about all sorts of things, such as gardening, sewing, and art, over the course of her stay.

Mom flew in that Friday, and I briefed her on all that was going on. We met Zep, the girls, and Claire at the dinosaur museum Saturday afternoon. What a nice day! Mom and Claire chatted up a storm. Zep and I played with the girls in the dinosaur sandbox, excavating a skeleton. Before heading home, we had some snacks in the cafe. Anna and I were having a lovely conversation about dinosaur popcorn, and it just kept getting crazier and crazier with all the ingredients. Mom said that it was getting a bit complex. Zep immediately piped up and said, "It's okay if it is complex." It was nice and surprising to have someone stick up for me.

I have no idea what, if anything, is going on between Zep and me, but whatever it is makes me happy. He texted me later, saying, "Your mother is sweet . . . Now I know how you will be in thirty years!" It has been a long time since someone has made me smile or giggle, and it feels nice.

Tomorrow is Mother's Day, and I had planned a simple day at home with Mina, gardening. Well, it looks like we have other plans: Zep texted yesterday inviting Mina and me to join them. It will be a fun day at the pool with a picnic afterward. I can't think of a nicer Mother's Day.

I finally received Hakan's stipulations, and we are definitely moving in the right direction. However, I feel that it was hastily put together, with many clerical errors that need immediate correction. For example, "petitioner" and "respondent" have been reversed in many areas. I don't want to get screwed because of absentmindedness. Also, it states that the back-pay is from January to March. Um, we are in May now, so that needs to be adjusted as well.

Regarding the trips to Turkey, they are playing with the length of time. If I choose to accompany him and Mina, and the trip is for five weeks, he will pay my airfare. If it is less than five weeks, I will pay my airfare. No, five weeks is too long.

I feel, at this point, Hakan needs a slap on the wrist about the lack of money flow in my direction. I am not feeling so cooperative about backdating the payments to January 1. I will easily get the money back if we go to court and pull out the e-mails showing that we had intended to apply for temporary relief back in December, but that he and I entered into a verbal agreement of monthly payments. I want the money owed dating back to January 1 as temporary relief repayment ($15,000) and the alimony starting when the divorce is decreed. Hakan needs to realize that there are consequences to poor choices.

I am willing to make a trade. I will agree to backdate the alimony to January 1 if he reduces the trip to Turkey to four weeks. Let's see if he will accept.

The verbiage about custody was revised, but it seems a bit ambiguous. If either party moves 150 miles or more away, we have to come together and revisit the custody issue. However, during litigation, both parties and child must remain in Utah until we resolve things. I have my lawyer going over the new verbiage and proofreading the whole document.

Hakan's lawyer was two weeks late e-mailing the documents to us, and Hakan wrote to apologize. He also felt that we were close to an agreement and that maybe we should meet face-to-face to finalize things. I sat on that e-mail for a few days, thinking. I felt that things could easily escalate unintentionally and ruin the respectful rapport we have developed over the past few months. I think it would be me who would get pissy this time. The money issue has really frustrated me. I have had to scrounge and be highly aware of my money because there has been none from him.

I haven't been able to buy my goji juice for my hip for five months because it is expensive, and I had to conserve money in order to buy *food!* I have had to sacrifice the possible health of my hip to put food on the table for our daughter. A case of goji juice is almost my food budget for a month. How can I justify buying the juice when I don't know how long this drama will take to resolve? I need to be able to put food on Mina's table. Has my hip been affected by the lack of juice? Yes. My hip has started clicking again when I move, and it hasn't done that since before I began using my juice, four years ago. That lack of juice and still sleeping on the floor have not been a good combination. I haven't bought a new mattress because, again, I need to conserve my savings. Mom is going to get me a new mattress for my birthday, so at least that has been resolved. I will pick one out this week, and they will pay for it.

Yeah, I am a bit pissy. I feel that if he and I met face-to-face, I might say something and screw up everything.

Oh, yes! One final note before I start my day: My mother-in-law wrote me this morning stating that she was thinking about coming out to help Hakan in his new house and asked if I needed anything from Turkey. If everything goes according to plan, she will fly out *Monday!* So much for thirty days' notice on visits! I actually feel really calm about the whole thing. It will be interesting to hear how he mentions it to me today when he comes.

9:02 P.M.

Hakan drove up today in his brand-new, fancy, turbo Subaru this afternoon, and it was really too much for me—the stark contrast between his new car and how I have been extra careful with money because he has chosen *not* to give us, me and Mina, any. The priority, it seemed to me, was not me or Mina, but a cool, fast car.

I left soon after he came in to go to the market for picnic supplies. I was so overwhelmed with emotions and frustration that I had a meltdown in the car in the Whole Foods parking lot. I cried and cried and banged on the steering wheel and got plain ol' mad at him, at myself, at just everything. That was just too much for me. I had had enough. I got myself in such a state that I had to open the car door to throw up on the pavement. It was total déjà vu for me because I had gotten this upset from something he did or said when Mina was six months old. I remember that time, Samantha was talking me down from hyperventilating. Right now, I don't remember what he said that upset me so much back then, but maybe I really don't want to remember. All I remember thinking and saying to Samantha was that I was *done* with him and the marriage. That was four years ago. Here I am again, a crying mess sitting in a parked car. I know I have made progress, but today, I am just so beyond done that I cannot even articulate it.

After calming down, I pulled myself together and remembered a deodorant commercial from a long time ago: never let them see you sweat. He *wanted* me to see the car; he *wanted* me to have some sort of reaction. Well, I am not going to play into it anymore. I went home, kept my cool, and decided to take my aggression out on evicting my dandelions.

MAY 10, 2011

It is 5:30 a.m., and I am sitting at the dining room table reflecting on so many things. Mother's Day was really nice, but it did not go completely according to plan. Zep called around 10:45 a bit upset. Amy was upset that we had planned all this without her. He was trying to get her to come along, but to no avail. He said that he really wanted to come to the pool and would try to work it out. They were not able to come, but Mina and I went anyway. We had a lovely time and spent over three hours at the pool. We had our picnic inside on one of the rocks in the lobby. How could I be upset that Zep couldn't come when he'd planned a wonderful day! The idea of the pool and bringing toys to play with and a picnic all worked out how he had envisioned it, just without him and the girls. It was the best Mother's Day that I have had because I stepped out of my normalcy and into a new experience.

Last night, I decided to reread Deepak Chopra's book *Spontaneous Fulfillment of Desire*, about coincidences. I finished it and put it down and had just begun to write a note of thanks to Zep for planning a wonderful day when (at the same instant—talk about coincidences!) Amy texted me stating that everyone was at her house and to pick Anna up for our Spiral Jetty trip from there. Hmm, I may be entering into a difficult conversation regarding Mother's Day and Zep.

I sat with this for a moment and made a decision. This ambiguity had been going on between Zep and me for a couple months, and now it was time to just say it out loud. I refuse to passively live my life anymore, so I wrote out a letter. What do I really have to lose by being honest? I have handled far worse rejection, so bring it on—seize the day!

The only paper I could find to write on was pink construction paper. Oh well, words read the same on any colored paper, right? Here is what I wrote:

Dear Zep,

As I was putting down the book by Deepak Chopra about coincidences, I decided to write you a thank you note (enclosed) for the way you planned out Mother's Day. Mina and I had a lovely time due to your forethought and fun ideas. When I put pen to paper, I got a text from Amy telling me to pick Anna up at her house instead.

I have a feeling that I may be entering into a very confrontational situation tomorrow morning.

I realized I had a choice to make at this junction. I was reminded of a quote, which, of course, I can't completely recall, but the general idea is this: The biggest regrets in life come from things not done or words left unsaid.

So, here I am, feeling very "high school" at the moment, writing you a note, in essence, saying, "I think you are cute." Corny, but true.

I have enjoyed your company over the past few weeks. You have helped me remember how to laugh again after so many years of tears. I thank you for that. I guess I may be overstepping my bounds or inappropriate in writing this, but I felt it needed to be said.

I understand that you and Amy have lots of unresolved issues, and my being around may create more anxiety and stress than you need.

After all of this, I am not sure how we all stand in each other's lives. If we all need to part ways, then I am extremely grateful for the lessons I learned through our friendship.

Can I be selfish and say that I would like things to continue? Yeah, I would.

One thing I have realized through my journey is to appreciate the happiness that comes my way and not to sacrifice myself in failed attempts at making someone else happy. We all have one life to live. By finding what makes us happy, we draw to us those who are positive in our fulfillment.

"Life is a journey, not a destination. There are no mistakes, just chances we've taken."

All we have is right now, and right now I hope you have a beautiful day

E.

Tuesday 5:30 a.m.

Okay, okay, okay, so I can't stop talking . . . I just have one last thing to say, okay?

Think about what you, Zep, want for yourself and the girls. If you sit quietly, the answer will come. I just want what's best for you and the girls.

So, that's the letter. Do I give it? Not give it? Well, all I know is that I felt so much better for writing it out and fell asleep instantly after purging it all on paper. Today, we are going on a road trip to see the Spiral Jetty with Laura and Margaret. Hakan's mom landed last night, and he had planned to bring her over today. But I told him that we already had plans that were made way before my two-day notice. He is a bit irritated, but he couldn't say anything. I have a feeling that I need to lay the foundation now about visits with his mom because I have an inkling that she may have gotten an open-ended ticket, which means she could be here for months.

I haven't heard from my lawyer, but I got her bill the other day. *Wow!* I have used up all the money in the retainer ($2,500), and now I owe her about $900 more. That mediation session really socked me for more than I thought. My parents have been really supportive and don't care how much this all costs as long as it is resolved appropriately.

I am not sure how this day will turn out, between face-to-face with Amy and Hakan's mom's visit. I don't want to wish the day away because

I have wanted to go see the Spiral Jetty for years. Instead of the "day by day" mantra, it will be minute by minute today. Time to go make some sandwiches for our road trip while Mina sleeps.

May 11, 2011

Yesterday was a good day. Everything went about as smoothly as it could go. Picking up Anna was easy; there was no tension. On the way to the highway, we went past Zep's house, and I put my note in his mailbox. Of course, for most of the ride up to and back from the Jetty, I couldn't stop thinking, *I can't believe I just did that! What was I thinking? I am such a dork!* But I had to trust my instincts from last night and leave it be.

The Spiral Jetty was such an amazing experience. I had always been told that it was difficult to drive there. When we made it to the Golden Spike National Park and asked which way the Jetty was, the patrol guy scrunched up his face and advised us not to go down that road because of the big rocks. Laura and I looked at each other and decided to go forth and conquer, take risks, and reach our destination. It is amazing what happens when you trust yourself: the road was perfectly fine, and the sun came out overhead while we were there (it had been pouring the whole way up). We and the girls walked the spiral as much as we could. Even though the water was getting pretty deep toward the center, preventing us from completing it, we could really appreciate the magnificence of this entity.

After dropping Anna off at day care, we returned home just before Hakan and his mom showed up. There was no tension with her either or any sense of a strained relationship. She came in, I made tea, and we resumed our normal roles in each other's lives.

Today, however, there was a little frustration on her part that Mina would not speak Turkish to her and that Mina was hesitant to go to the slide park around the corner with her. After a half hour of cajoling, I was able to get Mina to go across the street to the community garden and feed the chickens. Mina looked at me and said, "I will just go to the garden and come back. I am not comfortable going to the slide park alone with Babanne yet." Do whatever makes you comfortable.

It was a bit tiring for me to help them reacquaint themselves with each other. Mina has grown into a very determined little girl with a mind of her own and cannot be easily led to one activity or another. If she doesn't want to do it, she won't do it. The more you push, the more she will refuse. Welcome to age four!

His mother gets tense when I discipline Mina, which sends Mina off crying in her room. She visibly seems to think I am being mean or too harsh to Mina. Mina has been pushing her limits lately, and I will not have this house run by a four-year-old. At this point, she knows that having a tantrum or fit will not get her anything from me, and if she continues her fit, she must stay in her room until she has calmed down. It has been a difficult week with fits over baby doll diapers and Band-Aids for baby dolls. I am worn out and feel like crap. My glands have been swollen for two days, and I haven't been able to sleep more than four hours a night for the past few nights. These are the times that I wish there was another person here to make *me* chicken soup!

I did get an interesting response from Zep about my note: ". . . I sure like having you around and do not think it is necessary to break down bridges . . . ." But he has a lot to sort out on the home front, he said. Completely understandable. I told him that he was right, that time and communication were the key, and that we all needed to heal, but that I was opening a door to possibilities. His response: ";)"

All in all, I feel good that I did it.

May 15, 2011

When Mina and I finished up story-time last Friday, I really wanted to get another book for the weekend. All I wanted was a simple mystery or fiction that I could get lost in and not have to think about so much. I asked Jenny for suggestions, and they all seemed nice, but I was distracted and felt compelled to see what other Paulo Coelho books they had. It was as if the book was whispering to me across the room to come and read it. It was *The Zahir*. All right, I give in—I will buy you and read you, okay?

Wow! I read it all in one day and found it immensely profound, with so many insights into my own life. It was the first time in years that I had felt the urge to write notes and underline passages. I did not have a pen handy while I read it, so I kept turning the page corners, marking the important passages. I think I may have to make another appendix in the back of this book of all the passages for reference, but there is one that elucidates the concept most succinctly.

The Zahir was a fixation on everything that had been passed from generation to generation; it left no question unanswered; it took up all the space; in never allowed us to even to consider the possibility that things could change.

The all-powerful Zahir seemed to be born with every human being and to gain full strength in childhood, imposing rules that would thereafter always be respected:

People who are different are dangerous; they belong to another tribe; they want our lands and our women.

We must marry, have children, reproduce the species.

Love is only a small thing, enough for one person, and any suggestion that the heart might be larger than this is considered perverse.

When we marry, we are authorized to take possession of the other person, body and soul.

We must do jobs we detest because we are part of an organized society, and if everyone did what they wanted to do, the world would come to a standstill.

What other people think is more important than what we feel.

If you behave differently, you will be expelled from the tribe because you could infect others and destroy something that was extremely difficult to organize in the first place.

Our children must follow in our footsteps; after all, we are older and know about the world.

We must never make our parents sad, even if this means giving up everything that makes us happy.

We must play music quietly, talk quietly, weep in private, because I am the all-powerful Zahir, who lays down the rules and determines the distance between railway tracks, the meaning of success, the best way to love, the importance of rewards. (231-232)

After reading that passage, I felt like I had been fighting *this* my whole life until recently when I said "*Enough!*" I am not going to settle and see my life evaporate with everyone else's. This dogma is perpetuated over and over in every language and culture. I see it here, I see it in Turkey, and I am sure it exists to various degrees everywhere else. Why are we teaching our children this? Why is it *not* okay for us to live fully the life we are given?

This passage mirrors Hakan's aunt's life views completely. I feel like I have smashed that mirror and walked through, "infecting" others around me, and I am proud. Laura told me that seeing me speak my truth with Zep last week had inspired her to seek out her soul mate in Brazil. She had met Mr. Brazil through work while she was married but could never do anything about it. Even though she *knew* he was her soul mate, she couldn't act on anything due to marital constraints. She refused advances, sent back Valentine's Day roses, and so on. Feeling emboldened now, she wrote Mr. Brazil a long e-mail expressing everything she had kept in for so long. She too was tired of being afraid. Really, after all this, there is not much to lose, but so much to gain. The gain is much more than reciprocation; it is honoring yourself, who you are inside, and not hiding it away anymore.

May 18, 2011

How do I begin to explain the past few days? Hakan's mom is doing some work around Hakan's new apartment and asking to borrow some sewing and cooking supplies. Totally fine. It is just weird how normal it seems to be that he and I have our own places now. He finally invited Mina and me over to see his house on Monday afternoon. That would be fine, I thought, but I kind of need to know where you live. An address would be helpful.

Now, anyone who knows me knows that I have absolutely no sense of direction and need a bit more guidance than most people. I get it from my dad—he and I got lost in a library once when I was young and couldn't find our way out. We kept circling and circling the library for almost half an hour. Get the point?

So when I got just a street address in an e-mail without any further instructions, I knew I was in trouble. I went past it twice and had to turn around. Now where was I to park? How did one work this intercom thingy? I guess I am still expecting too much to think that someone I lived with for twelve years would know that I needed a bit more information that just a street address.

The whole thing just set my irritation button off and made the beginning of the visit that more uncomfortable.

Of course, I came prepared to make *him* feel a bit uncomfortable! Mina's tuition deposit of $450 is due June 1. The tuition is automatically charged to his AMEX card. Since we are splitting the tuition, I went to the bank and withdrew $225.00, put it into an envelope, and gave it to him. Yep, I pay what I owe *on time*! I could have sat and not paid anything, out of spite, because *he* hasn't paid anything. But it didn't feel right to me. I reminded myself that I was going to do what felt right for me so that I could look myself in the mirror. As I handed him the envelope of money, I told him that I wanted to pay him so that he would have the money to cover my portion of the charge. He was dumbfounded. He told me that I didn't need to pay it now, but I told him that I like to pay things when they are due. "Oh," he said. Yes, I just paid him enough money to cover one month of food for Mina and me. Sigh.

The visit went okay. Mina saw her bedroom, her bed, and her new toys. After putting together a little dollhouse, it was time for tea. I should have brought a book because they all played, and I was just there for Mina's comfort.

After three hours, it was time to get Mina home. I think seeing her bed and room at his house was a bit overwhelming for her. I think she really understood that there will be times when she will actually be *staying* there. It made putting her to sleep extremely difficult because she just wouldn't settle. She was afraid that if she fell asleep, I wouldn't be there anymore and would leave. After hour two, Mommy was losing her patience. I set a time when I would leave whether or not she was asleep. When that time came, I left. Boy, was she upset and screaming. I calmly walked to the fridge, got a beer, sat on the couch, and surfed the Internet on my iPad. I told her she was not to leave her bed, and for a while she listened. Then she came out to plead with me to go back with her. "This is Mommy time," I said, "and you will march yourself back into *your* bed, pull the covers up, and go to sleep." Well, she did it, and she even closed her canopy. Ah, silence!

Oh! I forgot to mention the check that came in the mail that day! After returning home from Hakan's, I found our tax return waiting in the mailbox: $3,200! I felt that I had somehow been "rewarded" for doing the right thing by giving Hakan the tuition deposit.

As I move through this process, I have been trying to offer growth opportunities to Hakan. I texted him, letting him know the check had arrived. If he was feeling a bit guilty about not paying, then he *could* suggest that I keep the whole check. No.

He came the next day to sign it, and I told him that I was going to go to the bank, have them divide it, and deposit half in my account and half in his. Again, he had another opportunity. He could have said to deposit it all in my account. But he didn't. Did I really think he would? No. Yet again, I gave him money. In the past six months, Hakan has paid Elif $0; Elif has paid Hakan $1,600.00. Sigh.

His mom is here, but that doesn't mean that her visit needs to take over my life. At the beginning of each week, I make a visit schedule. Take it or leave it. It is usually most generous, so he takes it. His mom will probably stay at my house for a couple of nights the beginning of next week.

On a positive note, the things I have been doing around the house to cut our bills have worked! By not using the dryer, I cut my electric bill $7 in one month. By turning off the heat when we are not home, I lowered the gas bill by about $5. I have planted more vegetables and will be able to cut out my Costco list (tomatoes, cucumbers, lettuce) when they all start to come in. For a few months, I will save about $25/month there. Baking bread saves $20/month. There are all sorts of ways to cut your budget if you really take a look around.

May 22, 2011

I have been a bit of a grump-a-loo lately, so I thought I would wait to write until I had come to my senses. I had a realization the other day, and it infuriated me. The issue of the trips to Turkey has gotten out of control. Because we are not going to Turkey this summer, we are now talking about only *two* trips—that's it—until Mina turns eight. At this point, with all this back and forth between lawyers, we have probably spent more money on lawyer fees than what my tickets would cost. Oh yes, my realization: this issue is *not* about actually paying for my tickets, but about control over the situation. It hit me the other day that he would be paying for my tickets with Delta Miles. It has *never* been about the money, but rather how much he could push and pull me to do it his way. Well, I have officially lost cooperative feelings and let the lawyer just cross out his whole proposition in his latest stipulation. It will be four weeks, that's it, using two weeks of his alone time. My lawyer was funny. She commented that it had all gotten out of hand, was too complicated, and needed to stop. *We are talking about just two trips to turkey! C'mon!* Argh! It was kind of satisfying to see her pen cross out huge sections of the stipulations.

We fixed their clerical "error" in the time-line of repayment: It said repayment was January–March. Um, we are now approaching June. She crossed out the vague "revisiting custody" issue. I told her that it seemed really vague to me and seemed like it left the door wide open for any interpretation. If she felt comfortable with the wording, then I would too. She crossed that section out too.

This frustration fed other annoyances. I got annoyed, again, that his mom had to come over and "fix" things for him. He can't get his child to go with him in his car, so his mom has to come over and fix his problem. How does anyone learn from their mistakes when mothers always fix everything? He *chose* not to be part of this family for years. Now he wants to just press the start button and have the father-daughter relationship that most families have. Last Wednesday, his mom and I were talking about Anna and her family. She asked me if Anna stayed with Zep, alone. Of course! But that relationship started out completely different! One cannot just apply the same visit schedule interchangeably with every father. It is not black and white.

Mina just amazes me more and more each day, and I am so proud of her. On Friday, she and Audrey, from across the street, played together at Audrey's house for almost two hours. It was the first time that Mina had felt comfortable going there on her own to play without me. I sat outside with Sonya, my next-door neighbor, having white wine and enjoying the brief bit of sun. It was a perfect summer afternoon. All the kids were running between houses, playing here, there, and everywhere. Later in the evening, Mina came and confessed that she'd had ice cream at Audrey's house even though I'd told her no. She knew it was wrong, and she was sorry. I dropped her, for the first time, at Hakan's apartment for the day. It was a day filled with toy stores, TV, and of course, his mother's meatballs. Every year, his mom makes it her mission to make Mina *love* her meatballs. It is as if she will not be complete as a grandmother until her granddaughter loves meatballs. It is her way of wielding control. Mina came home and told me she liked it, but it stung her tongue. I told her that was fine, but she can eat the meatballs at her father's house because red meat makes my stomach hurt. This began the conversation about what exactly is in the meatballs.

"Mama, was there meat in the meatballs?" Yes. "What kind? What animal was it? Was it alive? Did it have a head? Why can't you eat it?" Red meat; cow; yes; yes; the blood makes my tummy hurt. "I didn't like it, and don't want to eat bloody cow's meat."

I am trying to give her the ability to make her own choice for her own body. If she likes it, that's fine. I pointed out that she likes hotdogs, and those are a combination of cow's meat and pig's meat. I liked those hotdogs too! I am not against eating meat, but I am against the forcing of it onto another person like it is a quest.

At the moment, I am trying to figure out how to arrange this week with overnights and his mom, activities for Mina, and quiet time for Mama. I am just overwhelmed. This juggling act is too much, and I have to find a way to tactfully ask Hakan how long his mom is staying. Hopefully, we are halfway through. It will be two weeks on Tuesday since her arrival.

Time to get the day started. I need to expel this pent-up ickiness—I think I will throw myself into learning how to make bagels. That should keep my mind occupied!

May 30, 2011

My last entry seems so long ago! Over the past week, I have made bagels twice; my ex-mother-in-law stayed at my house for two nights; my response to Hakan's stipulations were sent out; I made yogurt cheese from freshly made yogurt; and I threw a bagel-baking brunch that was a smashing success. Phew! I am tired just looking back on it all.

The pervading feeling throughout the week was anxiousness. I was anxious about his mom staying with us and being alone with her. I didn't know what sort of conversations would come up and how I would handle them. I am always anxious when stipulations and responses are sent out. I was anxious about pulling off the bagel brunch. Last, I was anxious about seeing Zep at the brunch. Needless to say, nothing ever does come close to how your imagination builds it.

We were so busy while his mother stayed with us that Mina went to bed so late that I crashed with her. Hakan has actually been really nice this week and came to dinner on Tuesday night with his mom. His e-mails ended nicer than usual too: "I hope you can enjoy the sun today." And today he mentioned that he had noticed the kitty litter in the trunk for the past few days and asked if I would like him to bring it into the house because it is so heavy and not good for my hip. Um, okay? I half expected him to just bring the litter and leave it just inside on the floor, but he took it all the way down to the basement where the litter boxes are. These actions catch me off-guard, and all I can do is say thank you and think to myself, *Why now?*

Zep: it was good to see him yesterday. For me, it is always the little things that people do that mean the most. These things show they care if you just stop to notice. Even though it was just a small gathering for bagels, he took the time to shave, and he looked nice. Vanessa, Jaime, and little Ashlan from Mina's school also came, as well as Laura, Margaret, and Daisy. Baking bagels was quite the adventure, and we all enjoyed the nice spread, the company, and the conversation. When we were all quite done, Zep decided to help by stacking the dishes and clearing the table. I was so surprised that he did it on his own, just to help me out. He and I both quietly worked, side by side, in the kitchen: him scraping the dishes in the garbage and handing them to me to rinse and put in the dishwasher. It was such a comfortable silence as we moved around the kitchen.

Most everyone left by 3:00 p.m., but he and the girls (Anna and Bella) stayed until after 5:30 p.m. It seemed weirdly normal for him to be sitting in the recliner reading to both of the big girls while I made soup for Bella and fed her at the table. Is this what it is supposed to be like? Vanessa texted me later and said that he and I had seemed very comfortable with each other, like we had known each other for a long time.

Oh yes, and he brought me a bottle of wine: wine he had made and bottled himself. It was so thoughtful (and yummy). When he was explaining the bottling process, he said that he had given me one of the first bottled ones because the last few bottles had a bit more yeast at the bottom. I didn't realize until I went to open it that he actually had given me the very first bottle—it had the number 1 on the cork. I was touched. I saved the cork (and will save the bottle too after the contents have been thoroughly enjoyed).

Mina and I walked them to the car to say goodbye. Before he left, he bent down to talk to Mina. It was so sweet. "Mina, now you need to help Mama out with stuff around the house, like the cooking and cleaning and the picking up, because Mama gets tired. We don't want Mama Elif to get so tired, so can you do me a favor and help her?" While he was still kneeling in front of Mina, I unconsciously put my hand on his head as a thank you and then thought that maybe I was being too familiar.

JUNE 4, 2011

I have had a lot of time to myself this week, with Mina spending most of the day at Hakan's house with his mom. The quiet had me entertaining all sorts of thoughts, and in this quiet, I was able to find and place another long-lost piece of my life puzzle. A long time ago, before even meeting Hakan, I had my navel pierced. To me, it seemed like the tangible evidence that I used to be young, fun, confident, and carefree. When times were bad with Hakan over the years, it was my little reminder or tether back to who I was, inherently. I made it through pregnancy without having to remove it, but I *had* to remove it when I underwent an MRI for my hip. I cried. I just felt in my soul that I would somehow lose myself if I took it out. Everyone had told me that once you take out a navel ring, the surrounding skin closes up almost instantly. I accepted that and never tried to put the ring back in, until now! I was sitting, listening to old music, and said to myself, "Hmm . . . I wonder . . ."

I got up, found a simple earring, and was able to easily slip it through the old navel piercing. Feeling reconnected to yourself happens differently for each person. For me, it was this. It was as if I had found a dusty puzzle piece and was able to put it back into place. It was such a metaphor for life in general, for me anyway. To suddenly realize that the strength, power, and knowledge, or whatever it is, was in *me* all this time was profound. All the noise in my head from the stress, arguments, and such had prevented me from looking to myself for sustenance. I always could have put the ring back in if I'd felt that I had the confidence to do it. I felt that another part of my life had come full circle, and I celebrated. I went out and bought some new bling for my button!

Reconnecting with yourself is like having coffee with an old friend. Last night, the new-old me enjoyed herself with friends, wine, and jazz on Caputo's patio. Maybe we are all not clubbing until 3:00 a.m., but with things shifted a little for the kids, we had a lovely time drinking Spanish wine, eating lovely cheeses, and enjoying beautiful weather with the girls dancing under the stars to a smooth saxophone.

June 6, 2011

I couldn't sleep last night—another night of thoughts swirling around every which way. Gaia came over for lunch, and it was so nice to see her after so many months. It is always good and grounding to get her perspective on things. She asked about all the boys who are making my head nutty and heart fluttery. Coming from a relationship that was devoid of so much emotion, it is easy to get carried away by even the simplest gesture. This is not to say that something will not work out with either Zep or K, but these warm gestures and affections are at least showing me that these things exist, and maybe each of these men is a stepping stone to the person who will embody all the attributes that will completely sweep me off my feet.

Once I fell asleep, I dreamed a lot and came to a few conclusions. I woke up exhausted, as always, from such marathon dreaming. It was almost as if I were changing dream channels. First came a dream visit from Zep's sister. It was a Wednesday, and there was a knock on the door. Now, since I have never met his sister, I could only sense that it was her in the dream. It was an awkward meeting because we had never been formally introduced before the dream. She asked if Anna was with us because she wanted to say goodbye to her before leaving and to meet me. I was a bit confused because school was out, and Anna wasn't at our house on Wednesdays anymore. Also, I thought that she had returned to Montreal a while ago. In essence, I got the feeling that she was very protective of her brother and was upset that he was hurting over the divorce. She said that she didn't know how things would develop or if things would develop between Zep and me, but that she wanted to make sure he wasn't hurt again. I told her that only time would tell what will happen and that we all needed to heal our old hurts first, but I had no intention of hurting him. She seemed satisfied and went on her way.

Click! Changing channels, to Dream 2:

I was on a quest to find the right bagel recipe and had resorted to old recipe books. The one I was searching through in the dream was a seventeenth-century French bagel-baking cookbook. It was highly ornate and big. There were frilly pictures of French nobility in their finest attire eating bagels—lots of gilding and pink shimmery colors. There were recipes that called for cocoa to be added to the batter, and one used water chestnuts somehow. I couldn't really understand all the recipes, so Zep was helping me translate them from French to English.

Click! Changing channels, again, to Dream 3:

Before I get into the dream, I should preface it by saying that K popped back into my world last week. He sent a lovely "I miss you; how are you?" e-mail, and it sent me spinning again. I had kind of weaned myself off of him a few months ago. His e-mail came at a time when I had started thinking about him again. I had been talking about my idea for a Sea Maiden/Man in the Moon book with Ashlan's dad, Jamie. He is going to illustrate it for me. I went back and reread the story and started thinking about K all over again. His e-mail kind of sent me into an emotional tailspin because I felt that I had willed him back into my life again by thinking so much about him. How can two people so far apart seem so connected at times? We wrote back and forth, and I told him that I wasn't going to Turkey this year and that he should look into coming here—ha-ha. He responded with a smiling emoticon.

Well, in last night's dream, he figured out a way to come. Somehow, my friends and I were on a cruise. He disguised himself as a chef and cooked up the night's pasta. When he came into the dining room, he said that a taste tester had been chosen at random and called out my name. I have to say, I was only half-listening to the chef talk and didn't realize who it was until K was there, standing before me with a plate of rotini pasta, smiling at me. I simply said, "You came."

He said that pretending to be a chef was the only way he could sneak away to come see me. We were able to steal a few moments alone together. There came a time when we were each called away. He told me that we needed to meet one more time before he had to go away. At that point, I woke up.

All these dreams mixed up with semi-sleeping daydreams of Zep made me wake up and realize something. I got up around 2:00 a.m., sat at the table munching on a piece of Mina's rainbow-swirled Italian semolina bread, and had another epiphany. Why am I utilizing so much of my energy worrying about whether they like me or what will happen? I have a lot to offer someone, and if these guys can't realize it, then it is their loss. Over all, my personal report card averages "C's." Confused? Well, let me list them: I am *cute, caring, creative, confident,* and *cognizant* of others; I can *cook*; and I am *capable* with an electric drill and other tools—I am a good *catch*!

June 13, 2011

Since I switched off the boy-related channel surfing that was keeping me up at night, I have slept so much better, and my brain feels clearer. With that clarity, I was able to articulate my frustrations with Hakan regarding his mother and her extending her trip by nine days. Yes, two days before her scheduled departure, she changed her ticket. I had already made plans for this week, thinking she was not going to be here, and I do not feel that I need to bend and change things last-minute. So, as Mina would say, "You get what you get, and you don't throw a fit." They will see Mina when my schedule allows this week. In my opinion, if you feel like you need to hide something or not tell someone about an action until it is completed, then it is a red flag for discussion. It tells me that you knew that the other person may be upset but chose to go ahead with your own plans, regardless.

I wrote to Hakan and told him that there needs to be at least thirty days' advance notice of visits so that the grandparents' visits do not overlap and that I wish I had heard about his mother's trip from him and with more than two days' notice. After much back and forth, he concurred: he should have given me more notice and will do so in the future.

Hoping there had been some sort of movement on the divorce front, I wrote to my lawyer for an update. She responded, "So sorry, sweetie. I haven't heard anything from their side, and I haven't had a chance to file that motion for temporary relief."

Great, just great. It was supposed to have been drafted over a week ago and sent in. Can't it be faxed or e-mailed these days? Really. Laura's lawyer hasn't gotten her stuff filed either. I guess it is just a painfully slow process where time seems to move at a snails pace.

FOUR

BREATHE, RELEASE, AND LET GO

*"Breathe deeply and gently through every cell of the body,
laugh happily, and release the head of all worries and
anxieties; and finally breathe in the blessing
of love and hope."*

—*Pundit Acharya*

June 16, 2011

Happy early birthday to me: I signed divorce papers this week! Monday morning, I wrote to my lawyer and asked how to get this divorced wrapped up. Within minutes, she sent over Hakan's revised stipulations. He had acquiesced to everything we had asked for. The tone of his lawyer's letter was much softer this time. I think we were all ready to be done. The only thing that Hakan wouldn't budge on was the custody. However, they added some extra wording that made it more comfortable for me to accept.

I sent the revised stipulations to everyone to proofread and double-check because they just seemed too good to be true. My lawyer was in meetings all day and didn't get a chance to review them, but I felt okay going and signing on Tuesday after dropping Mina at Hakan's. Once I was there, though, she was able to take five minutes and sit with me while I signed. She would review the papers and send them over to Hakan's lawyer. Since his lawyer had drawn up the papers, Hakan would be the one filing officially with the court, and Hakan would be paying those fees.

It is so anticlimactic. Laura asked me if I was sad. Honestly, I didn't really feel anything. I had already moved through so many emotions over the past year and especially the past six months. I guess you could say it was more of a visual release than an emotional one. Signing the papers, visually for me, was quietly closing the last door and walking away. Full closure will come when I receive the reimbursement check. I actually sat down and calculated how much it should be. Child support and alimony combined come to about $3,300/month over six months, or $19,800. All the scrimping and saving to conserve money has really been an asset because I have been able to save an extra $2,000 over the past six months. I have learned how to do more for myself instead of letting others do it or taking the easy road. If you had told me that I would be up on a ladder cleaning out my gutters that were caked with three inches of compacted dirt, I would have told you that you were nuts. Well, after seeing poppies blooming from my gutter, I knew I needed to do something. I told myself that I needed to try first. If I physically couldn't extract the dirt, then I would call Bob, my handyman. It rained so much the other day and softened the dirt. I was able to weed my gutter and wrench handfuls of icky dirt out of it. It was really disgusting, but I did it, saved myself some money, and felt proud of myself for following through with it. I have felt a bit overwhelmed at times with how much I need to do around the house, but I take baby steps and try to accomplish one house project a day. Today's project: fixing the side door by removing the doorknob and unjamming it from the door frame. Last week's hurricane winds blew the door open, slammed it shut, and jammed it. Today, I will be victorious (hopefully!) and get it open again with my handy-dandy screwdriver!

It has been so great to have Laura here. We have been brought together to help each other through this process. I have really felt cared for by so many friends lately, and it is such a comfort. On Monday, Daisy brought over homemade raspberry rhubarb pie, and Karen sent me a lovely poem, "One Day," by Patricia Jabbeh Wesley.

I am truly grateful for everything that I have had to go through because it has pushed me to really get to the bare-bones of who I am, what I want, and who I want in my life. I wouldn't change a thing.

JUNE 18, 2011

I got the word yesterday from my lawyer that the divorce has been officially decreed! Hakan signed the papers and submitted the papers. Now I wonder when and how I will get the back payments. Laura and I were cracking each other up last night over a bottle of red wine as we imitated Cuba Gooding Jr.'s "Show me the money!" scene from the movie *Jerry Maguire*. She told me that I should post the video clip with the news of the divorce decree. She said that it would totally go viral on Facebook in a matter of minutes. We were on the floor laughing so hard!

When we were leaving Caputo's after their Friday night jazz music concert was done, Tallulah, the owner Ted's daughter, asked Mina what she was doing over the weekend. Mina said that she was going to spend some time at her father's apartment. Tallulah asked why he had a separate apartment, and I told her the story of the avocado pizza family. It was interesting because she totally got the point immediately. She understood and said, "It's sad." Mina concurred. It is sad because as Mina spends more time with Hakan and they get to know each other, she is feeling the loss. She has been working it all out while she sleeps. Sometimes, she thrashes around in her bed like she is really angry with someone. Then, the following night, she is sleeping and totally inconsolable and scared that Mommy has left her in a scary place. She cries and calls for me, not realizing that I have totally enfolded her in my arms and am cradling her head. Finally, exhausted, she falls back asleep.

At the moment, I am watching *Eat Pray Love* (again) and reflecting on last night at Caputo's. Laura and I sat and drank an entire bottle of lovely Spanish wine. Over the course of the night, I noticed this beautiful man staring at me. Laura calls him "Mr. White-teeth" because of his perfect smile. It reminds me of a gum commercial from when I was young in which the salesman's teeth sparkled at the end. The fact that this beautiful man was sitting and staring at *me* was so alien for me. Over the years, the words I have used to describe myself have been "wife," "climber," "friend," "mother." Now maybe I can add "beautiful."

I asked Laura over our third glass of wine, what do you *say* to the other person at the finality of a marriage? Congratulations? No. I'm sorry? No. Is there a Hallmark card for this? Probably not. Thanks for the memories? Um . . . not really. Does it just go unsaid as we step over it to the other side?

When he came to pick up Mina this morning, I was setting up for a yard sale. While cleaning the basement, I had come across more of his stuff and put it in a bag. It just feels so weird to be handing him a bag with eight things of deodorant and a Costco-size bottle of mouthwash.

Interestingly enough, I think we may actually come out of this as friends. He is reaching out in his own way with the little things he adds at the end of the e-mails about Mina's pickup times. Today, he wrote and said they were going to try to get seats at Eggs in the City tomorrow for Father's Day. Then he added that he hoped my yard sale had gone well.

We have all grown in so many ways through this process, and I think—hope—that we will come out as a happier family apart than we were together.

Each time I watch this movie, something else hits me. I just had to hit the pause button to get it right:

Liz is in India, sitting at a picnic table with Richard from Texas, drinking a Thumbs Up cola. Liz is talking about David and how much she still cares about him, and then Richard says to her (and, it feels, to me), "I know you feel awful, but your life's changing and that's not a bad thing . . . You know, if you could clear out all that space in your mind that you are using to obsess over a guy and a failed marriage, you would have a vacuum with a doorway. And do you know what the universe would do with that doorway? *Voom!* It would rush in and fill you with more love than you have ever dreamed of!"

Since Gaia is in India now, maybe she can bring me back a Thumbs Up bottle as a reminder of that moment.

June 23, 2011

> Try not to resist the changes that come your way. Instead, let life live through you. And do not worry that your life is turning upside down. How do you know that the side you are used to is better than the one to come?
>
> —*The Forty Rules of Love*

If you can take a moment to step outside yourself, you might see the organic, free-flowing nature of your life. It is a living organism within you as well as outside you. I have come to realize and accept that there are certain things that need to come into your life as well as out. It is the ebb and flow that is most interesting.

I received a book from Hakan's mom for my birthday this year. It is the first time she has ever given me a book. I had given her the *same* book, in Turkish, last year for her birthday (April 2010). It was called *The Forty Rules of Love* by Elif Shafak, her favorite author. My mom then brought and left the English version at Christmastime. She told me that I would enjoy it, but I wasn't ready then—I re-gifted the book to Sofia's mom. Well, again, the universe had other plans for me and brought the book back into my hands this Tuesday, at the right time. Since I had gifted this book twice and received it twice, I thought I should sit down and read it.

Wow! Yeah, that about sums it up. The twenty-first-century character Ella is a stay-at-home mom, approaching forty, who is living in a loveless marriage. Having taken a part-time job as a literary editor, she is sent a book, *Sweet Blasphemy*, about the thirteenth-century poet Rumi and his friendship with Shams of Tabriz. Sufism is the main foundation of this book, and through it and the book, Ella changes.

There were so many parallels to my life with regard to my personal home front, my connections with K and Zep, and the concept of living in the now.

Ella and the author begin a correspondence and become fast friends. With my birthday yesterday, this passage hit me like a ton of bricks: "Birthdays have always made me happy, but this morning I woke up with heaviness in my chest, asking the questions too large for someone who hadn't even had her morning coffee yet. I kept wondering, is the way I've lived my life the way I want to continue from now on?" (114).

Their correspondence becomes more frequent, and soon she is giddy with anticipation of the next exchange. My god! I feel like I am reliving last December when K popped into my life! "Soon exchanging e-mails with Aziz made Ella feel that she was somehow breaking away from her staid and tranquil life. From a woman with lots of dull grays and browns on her life's canvas, she was turning into a woman with a secret color—a bright red. And she loved it" (143).

I found Zep in a chapter by Rumi: "Bountiful is your life, full and complete. Or so you think, until someone comes along and makes you realize what you have been missing all this time. Like a mirror that reflects what is absent rather than present, he shows you the void in your soul—the void you have resisted seeing. That person can be a lover, a friend, or a spiritual master" (193).

The book came back to me at the right time. It gave words to feelings and experiences that seemed so hard to articulate.

Speaking of Zep, I have actually seen him a few times this week: once when I brought over cookies from Mina for Father's Day and yesterday (coincidentally, on my birthday). It was nice to actually sit and chat with him as two adults and have adult conversation on Sunday with no kids around. He is currently reading *Eat, Pray, Love*, and it was really interesting to hear his perspective. I can see how books like this may romanticize divorce and its aftermath. Talking with Zep made me more aware that the last few books I have read contained a wife in an unhappy marriage who chose to leave: *Eat, Pray, Love*; *The Zahir*; and now *The Forty Rules of Love*. Do books like these empower women to better their lives in a positive way, or do they, at times, glorify the process or outcome? Do they give false hope for future happiness if you leave your husband? Is there not enough emphasis on what brought the women to their own breaking point? I don't know. I think that each of these books can be read on multiple levels. How deep you want to go is up to the individual reading it.

Personally, I felt a kinship with these women; I felt not so alone. Why is it the woman who usually gets up and leaves? The men may be there physically taking up space, but they are gone emotionally and spiritually for a long time before that. Zep asked me if Mina and I were lonely. The absence of Hakan's physicality can be felt sometimes, but he left me *emotionally* a long time ago, soon after Mina was born.

It was really lovely the way my birthday unfolded itself to me. Anna was going to come to Mina's dance class but got sick in the morning. Later, Amy texted and asked if I could watch Anna from 12:00 to 1:00 p.m. Zep would be able to leave work around that time and take over after that.

We ended up spending the rest of the day at Zep's, and it was a lot of fun. He inflated the little pool for the girls, and they splashed around until they learned how to use the Super Soakers! Let's just say, by the end of the afternoon, the munchkins were chasing me around the yard, and I was soaked. I escaped them by climbing a tree in the middle of the yard. Zep came out and started laughing at me up in the tree. I told him that I was part cat, and instinct had taken over!

His garden is quite lovely, and he has so many roses that I wondered, aloud, if there was enough to make rose jam one day. Hours later, when we were leaving, he asked if I wanted to take some roses home with me. Of course, my mind went back to the earlier conversation about the jam, and I said I didn't think there were enough good roses left for a batch of jam. He clarified and said, "Would you like some roses for your personal enjoyment in the home?" Oh! Sure. So he picked a few roses, snipped off the thorns, and added them to the bunch of radishes he had picked for me earlier.

It was really one of the best birthdays I have had in years and no one even knew it was my birthday. The day just opened itself up naturally to a lot of unexpected fun.

July 6, 2011

It will be a month this week since we signed the papers and the divorce was decreed, and still no money. My lawyer has sent out a reminder letter to Hakan's lawyer stating that the money was due at signing. It is just so confusing to me, this whole repayment issue. The other day, Hakan handed me a check for half of the dance camp ($44) so easily. Daisy and I spent the morning at Starbucks pondering all of this. If someone owed another person a lot of money, how could he be so nonchalant about giving such a small check for the class? Wouldn't he be uncomfortable, knowing that he owed so much more? Does he somehow think that he has *paid* the money? Has he handed over to his lawyer all the necessary information or an actual check for his lawyer to send? Has his lawyer somehow screwed this up? Even if he has, let's say, left a repayment check to cover January to June 9, there is still the issue of actual, decreed, regular payments that have been missed too. The papers were signed June 9. That means he has missed the second payment in June and the first payment of July thus far. I really just don't get it. He is very agreeable, cooperative, and friendly, with no animosity or antagonism. Does he not *realize* he could really get in big trouble now that everything is signed and official? Legally, nonpayment is considered a felony in Utah. He could get jail time or his wages taken away. Hasn't this been explained to him by his lawyer? I hope this gets worked out soon because the savings account is slowly dwindling.

Now that we are entering July, I can look back at June and realize that I escaped my reality by playing a lot: Caputo's on Friday nights, a mermaid party, and spending time with Zep and Anna.

Whether they are here playing with us after one of our parties or we are there splashing in the pool, it has been such a fun, playful time that makes me forget all the other less pleasant realities. On Sunday, we spent the whole day at their house playing in their new above ground pool. It was a lovely family-like day. We played in the pool. He made corn on the cob and pretended to swallow the cob whole to the delight of the girls. Then we all gathered around the table and played Princess Monopoly before going back into the pool again.

I am really taking the time to enjoy these moments and not get too preoccupied with what could be or future stuff. The present is now, and I really enjoy those moments with them. Do I think he is interested? Yes. Is he conflicted with all that is going on in his life and his divorce? Yes. At the moment, I am enjoying his friendship and enjoying each day as it comes. I like that I can be who I am—silly, crazy, whatever—and it's okay. I don't feel like I have to hide who I am or be judged for being "too" talkative, friendly, or playful. I feel accepted.

July 9, 2011

In case you were wondering, it takes a little over three hours to shred ten years of bank statements, credit card bills, medical receipts, and so on, and it all fits nicely in a big blue IKEA bag. Today, I began my paper begging-bowl project. I needed to transform the hurt, resentment, and frustration into something beautiful. I needed something tangible. I needed to create something beautiful that could be a metaphor for all that I have gone through. It was a hard day. So many memories came flooding back as I sat and shredded. I let go and cried—cried for him, cried for me, cried for Mina, and cried for what could have been. I didn't ask for this. I didn't ask to be divorced and alone. I remembered how much we had loved each other and how much I had loved him.

> He was my North, my South, my East and West,
> My working week and my Sunday rest,
> My noon, my midnight, my talk, my song;
> I thought that love would last forever: I was wrong.

> —W. H. Auden

I knew I needed time with this project, so I told Hakan to take Mina to dinner at Mazza today. She didn't need to see me as an emotional wreck. I cried and screamed while I stirred my flour paste on the stove. I released and let go as I worked with the shredded paper and paste. I made sixteen bowls today. The first bowls (the ones I made when I was so upset) are definitely not attractive at all. It is as if all the hurt emotions became embedded in them. As I moved through the process, they got better, and I *felt* better. To me, they are my healing bowls and will be given out to all my friends who have helped me on my journey. In Japanese, the word for begging bowl is *oryoki*. It means "just enough." Each person has just enough in her life or bowl, metaphorically speaking. For whatever is put into your bowl, good and bad, you should say thank you because it is what you need at that moment to grow into a better you.

Today, I placed another piece of my puzzle. Today, I added another descriptive to who I am: artist. It has been a long time since I felt like that. Little by little, pieces of me, thought lost, are reemerging and saying, "Hello again! What took you so long?"

July 14, 2011

I made myself a cup of vanilla rooibos tea, put on Enya, and am taking in the full meaning of the day.

It is finally over. Hakan gave me two checks today, one for the child support ($6,909.00) and one for alimony ($16,100.00), for a total of $23,009. If I hadn't had help from friends and family, I would have been exactly at $0 right now because when this started in December, all I had left was $23,000 in savings. I don't know what I had expected to feel once I got the checks, but I felt anger. I didn't let it show, but I was angry. I also got an enormous headache. Can someone feel numb, sad, and angry all at the same time? That kind of sums it all up. I needed to clear my head, so I cleaned the house. I cleaned like I had when he first moved out: floors, walls, cupboards, closets, anything and everything. I washed everything I could and hung two loads of laundry out to dry in the sun.

Now, as Mina plays downstairs with a friend, I need to let the music and the tea calm me down as I release everything from the past year. If someone were to ask me how I feel after all of this, I would say "taller." I feel proud of everything I have gone through and overcome. It has allowed me to grow up and realize how strong I really am. Maybe all of my ideas for making money did not pan out as I had hoped, but they helped me move forward. Having the opportunity to read as much as I did, apply the ideas to my life, and see the positive changes helped me the most. I needed to get to know myself again, and I was able to do that only when I took the time for myself to be quiet and listen to what I needed—not what others needed, but what I needed for *me*. I have moved from a place of fear and anxiety to a place of peacefulness. I really, truly am not afraid of the next day and what it will bring. Good or bad, I will welcome it.

APPENDIX

BOOKS THAT HELPED

Bender, Sue. *Everyday Sacred: A Woman's Journey Home*. New York: Harper Collins, 1995.

Bender, Sue. *Plain and Simple: A Woman's Journey to the Amish*. New York: HarperOne, 1991.

Byrne, Rhonda. *The Power*. New York: Atria Books, 2010.

Coelho, Paulo. *The Zahir: A Novel of Obsession*. New York: Harper Perennial, 2006.

Coelho, Paulo. *The Alchemist*. 2nd ed. New York: Harper Collins, 2006.

Loeb, Paul Rogat. *Soul of a Citizen: Living with Conviction in Challenging Times*. New York: St. Martin's Press, 2010.

Lindbergh, Anne Morrow. *A Gift from the Sea*. 50th anniversary ed. New York: Pantheon, 1991.

McGhee, Christina. *Parenting Apart: How Separated and Divorced Parents Can Raise Happy and Secure Kids*. New York: Berkley Books, 2010.

Rubin, Gretchen. *The Happiness Project*. New York: Harper Collins, 2009.

Rubin, Margery. *What Your Divorce Lawyer May Not Tell You: The 125 Questions Every Woman Should Ask*. New York: Fireside Books, 2009.

Shafak, Elif. *The Forty Rules of Love: A Novel of Rumi*. New York: Penguin, 2011.

Printed in Great Britain
by Amazon.co.uk, Ltd.,
Marston Gate.